W9-BQY-760

DATE DUE

MAR - 9 2004		
JAN - 6 2006		

Grading and Reporting Student Progress in an Age of Standards

Grading and Reporting Student Progress in an Age of Standards

Elise Trumbull and Beverly Farr, Editors

Credits

Every effort has been made to contact copyright holders for permission to reproduce borrowed material where necessary. We apologize for any oversights and would be happy to rectify them in future printings.

Memo to principals regarding converting rubric scores to letter grades used by permission of Linda L. Elman, Ph. D., Central Kitsap School District, Silverdale, Washington

Excerpts from *Improving Classroom Assessment: A Toolkit for Professional Developers,* Regional Educational Laboratories, 1998, Available from: MWREC, 101 SW Main, Suite 500, Portland, OR 97204

Christopher-Gordon Publishers, Inc.
1502 Providence Highway, Suite #12
Norwood, MA 02062
(800) 934-8322

Printed in the United States of America

10 9 8 7 6 5 4 3 2 1   05 04 03 02 01 00

Library of Congress Catalog Card Number: 99-66212
ISBN: 1-929024-05-3

Contents

Foreword

If schools are to be effective—that is, if instruction is to result in maximum student learning—then educators must communicate effectively about student achievement. Important decision makers need access to dependable information about student achievement in order to do their jobs. Without it, how can they diagnose student needs, allocate resources, pace instruction, evaluate the effectiveness of instructional interventions, or provide feedback to students? If we are to communicate effectively, we must first articulate clear achievement expectations and then transform those targets into accurate assessments. Only then can we deliver usable results into the hands of their intended users.

This book offers a comprehensive analysis of the challenges of communicating effectively about student achievement. Each successive chapter takes the reader more deeply into the complexity of meeting those challenges, adding urgency to the need to do a good job.

This book will not put you at ease. It is clear that the editors and chapter authors do not intend to make readers feel comfortable about their communication task, whether they communicate through report card grades, portfolios, conferences, or test scores. Rather, the editors and authors have done an excellent job of forcing the reader to confront the discomfort that accompanies the many roadblocks to effective communication. The result is a detailed and accurate portrait of the problem. It is indeed a problem, and the work associated with solving it remains with the reader.

This is as it should be. We live in a pluralistic society in which various segments of our diverse communities hold vastly different opinions about sound educational practice. Practitioners need to consider the information needs and desires of all assessment users. When it comes to communicating about student achievement, we have options at our disposal. Our collective professional responsibilities are to understand all of the options, reflect carefully and make smart choices, evaluate the effectiveness of our communication, and adjust to better practices as we move forward. This book can help the reader to understand how to do these things.

When we confront the challenge of implementing sound grading practices, for example, we must make many crucial decisions. First, we must decide the purpose of grades. Will they serve to motivate, or to communicate? What if those two purposes come into conflict with one another—which wins out? For example, what if we choose to factor the students' level of effort into their report card grades and the result is miscommunication about some students' real level of academic attainment? Or what if honest communication about low achievement is demoralizing for the unsuccessful student, causing that student to give up in hopelessness? Is that an acceptable result of communication? There are no easy answers to these questions, but they must be answered if schools are to be truly effective.

Second, after articulating the purpose of grades, we must decide what it is that we wish to communicate through grades. Do we wish to share information about achievement, intelligence, effort, attitude, compliance with the rules, or some combination of these? What happens when we pack all of these together in one grade and the message receiver is unable to sort out the contribution of our various ingredients and thus is unable to discern what the resulting grade really means? Can effective communication result? Those who resolve these issues successfully can achieve effective communication, and this can contribute to student success. But unsound answers lead to miscommunication, and students suffer the consequences.

Our questions don't stop here. When we gather information about student achievement for report card grading purposes, we must decide what specific data sources to tap. Shall performance on homework count? Is that likely to be dependable information? Might this source misrepresent real achievement—might it be biased? How shall we know? What should we do about it? Should performance during class discussions be factored in? What are the arguments for and against this? What aspects of achievement are reflected in traditional paper-and-pencil tests, performance assessments, and once-a-year standardized tests? Again, we have choices, and wisdom lies in making smart choices. This book can help the reader to understand these complexities.

In addition to all of these choices, when it comes to determining the final grade, we must decide the following:

- How to assess student performance
- How much evidence of achievement to gather
- When to gather it and how to store it
- What evidence to count and what to disregard because it may be inaccurate
- What achievement levels to reference in assigning grades
- How to summarize achievement information for transformation into a grade

We must learn to anticipate what can go wrong with the standard setting process, the assessment process, and the process of transforming evidence into effective communication. Make sound decisions, and students prosper. Make bad decisions, and we place students directly in harm's way.

This volume frames all of these challenges. It offers a refreshing combination of conceptual discussion mixed with practical reality. Both are important. The editors and contributors adopt a consistent context for their presentations: the emerging importance of standards-based education. From that common foundation, they strive to connect their own ideas with points covered by the other contributors. As a result, the divergent pieces fit together.

For example, in chapter 3, John Carr frames two wonderfully clear portraits of vastly different world views of students and learning that teachers might bring to the grading process. He implies that these divergent philosophical perspectives can give rise to bias in communication. In chapter 6, Elise Trumbull provides a far-reaching treatment of sources of bias that can creep into assessment and grading. She brings Carr's important implications into the sunlight for all to see. In chapter 7, Henriette Langdon and Elise Trumbull demonstrate how issues of bias can impact students who bring special needs to the classroom. They reveal the genuine human impact of assessment bias in that manner. In this way, this book offers an uncommonly complete treatment of issues related to assessment and grading in the context of special education.

However, the conversation is not limited to grades and grading. In chapter 4, Kathleen Busick extends the scope of the presentation to include communication through rating scales, portfolios, and various conference formats. In chapter 5, Louise Bay Waters recounts one school district's journey to a comprehensive, instructionally relevant assessment and communication system. In chapter 8, Tanja Bisesi and others open the scope of the presentation on effective communication to include student-involved conferences and standardized test scores. Thus, few stones are left unturned. Chapter 9 reminds readers of the scope of the issues and their interrelationships and offers concrete suggestions for how districts can proceed to evaluate and improve their grading systems.

I am convinced that readers who take this book seriously and carefully study the issues it frames will improve both their understanding of the challenges of effective communication and their ability to meet those challenges.

—Rick Stiggins
Assessment Training Institute
Portland, Oregon

Preface

Variations on the following conversation went on, it seems, for more than a year.

Elise: I'd really like us to attack the issue of grades for our next book. Interested?

Beverly: I'd like to collaborate on another book, but I'm not at all sure about grades. I don't feel like I know enough about it, and it's hard for me to get excited about it.

Elise: There's a lot I don't know, either, but I want to write this book in order to learn as much as possible so that I can provide better help to teachers and principals. We've both been doing work to help people develop standards-based assessments and accountability systems, but when it comes to translating scores into grades, people are doing all sorts of things that clearly violate measurement principles: converting rubric scores into letter grades without consideration for what each represents, for example. How can teachers explain to parents (and students, for that matter) that they base instruction and assessment on a set of content standards and then give grades that incorporate attendance and attitude? It seems so important to clarify these issues.

Beverly: I'd like to write another book with you, but I'm not at all sure about grades. . . .

Beverly eventually came around and even got excited about the topic, but what we both came to realize through this continuing dialogue was that Elise's desire and Beverly's reluctance stemmed from the fact that grading seemed to be such an intractable problem. We had both had personally unsatisfying experiences trying to grade students fairly. If we took the problem on, we wanted to be able to offer our readers some real solutions.

Elise's Grading Experiences

When I taught special education students in the 1970s and 1980s, I was spared the trauma of having to assign them actual grades. The elementary school system in which I taught used a system of narrative reporting, and special education students were evaluated by the objectives on their individual education plans (IEPs). Reports were written in terms of the progress that a student had made toward his or her own goals that had been gauged as realistic. There were rarely any terrible surprises. There was no awful summative symbol that branded anyone a failure, and we were able to communicate successes quite well through the language of the report. Whew! A narrow escape!

I didn't get off the hook so easily when I taught upper division psychology students at a state university. Letter grades were the norm, and the pressure was on. These students were required to take my course in psycholinguistics, and if they didn't get at least a B, it was bad news for them. To this day I don't know what happened to the few dangling students to whom I gave an "Incomplete" rather than a low grade. I was a visiting lecturer, and so I didn't really have to face any long-term consequences of unwise or unfair grading practices (such as a nasty letter in my tenure file from an irate student who didn't agree with my criteria for assigning her a grade!). I am struck in retrospect by the discrepancy between how well prepared I was to organize curriculum and design "authentic" assessments and how miserably prepared I was for the grading game. It is one thing to give meaningful project assignments and construct essay questions that get to the heart of a course. It is another thing to decide how to determine the level of difficulty of each question and fairly weight each assessment in an overall grading scheme. Beyond those problems, how is a teacher to devise a system that motivates without unnecessarily punishing those who may need the most support? My college students who spoke and wrote English as a second language were certainly penalized to some extent by having to write so much. Should their language differences be accounted for in some way? I'm sure that any teacher who has had to assign grades has grislier tales to tell.

Beverly's Grading Experiences

In all the teaching situations that I had found myself in over the years—and I truly loved teaching—the thing I absolutely loathed was giving grades to my students. I felt unprepared and that the grades I assigned were somehow unsubstantiated. I felt as though the grades interfered with the bond I had established with each of my students. I devised systems that came as close to being defensible as I could make them. Even so, students occasionally (not often, but enough to worsen the discomfort) questioned the grade I gave them, and I searched for ways to explain how I had arrived at the decision. I taught 6th grade, I taught 10th grade, and I taught graduate courses. My experiences with grades and the feelings associated with giving them were the same for the most part. Some of my 10th graders in an urban high school in Chicago were reading at 3rd- and 4th-grade levels. When they tried hard, finished all the assignments I asked them to do, produced a commendable project, and moved up in their reading ability by more than one grade level, what grade was I to assign? Should they be compared to their peers in the other English sections who were reading *Beowulf* and *The Canterbury Tales*? Were they to be given Ds because they couldn't possibly be shown to be on a par with the other students in 10th-grade English?

My brother, a professor of Reading Education at Indiana University and co-author of chapter 8, ran an experiment one year in which he told his students that he was going to grade them on a pass-fail basis. I remember him telling me that he saw no decline in the quality of students' work, but, in fact, he thought they had worked harder. His experiment was eventually rejected, however, by an educational bureaucracy that has a hard time accommodating such change.

When my first-grade daughter (whose mother, father, and uncle were all involved in Reading Education) got a B in reading. I was a little surprised, since I knew that she was already reading quite a bit, certainly every night with us at home. After I finally got up the nerve—intimidated, as many of us are, by the educators with the grading pens—to ask why she received this grade—the teacher told me that she didn't read very loud, and she didn't like to finish her phonics worksheets—shortcomings that I'm sure were deserving of a B!

This same daughter attended her first year of college at a school that was proud of its long-standing tradition of not giving grades but instead giving written narratives on each student in each course. When she showed me some of these reports and in one case counted up the number of times the word *average* showed up, she asked, "So, do you think that's about a B?" At other times, she would assess the superlatives that were used and ask me to support her judgment that this clearly seemed to be an A. I don't fault the use of narratives, but the use of grades is so entrenched in our educational lives that we find it difficult to think in other ways. This is the challenge that we face in moving to standards-based practices. We have to think in new ways and accept the fact that report cards may look quite different.

What Can We Do?

As we continued to think about these concerns, we searched for colleagues who had similar thoughts and questions about grading practices and wanted to share either what they had learned or what they were doing to move toward innovative systems. We identified a set of issues that we thought should be addressed and outlined a series of chapters that we thought would provide the help that educators would need to step out of the grading trenches and onto higher ground.

We wanted to look back at the history of grading practices, to examine our reasons for giving grades to students, and to identify the technical issues associated with grading practices. In addition, we wanted to have a principal tell the story of developing a new standards-based accountability system in her school and provide some guidelines for school staffs that were ready to move in similar directions. Finally, we wanted to be sure to address some issues that are close to our hearts: avoiding bias and ensuring fairness when assessing diverse groups of students. None of these issues turned out to be either immediately clear or without complications as we worked on them. In some cases, we became quite embroiled with our contributors in discussions about different approaches to grading practices and the design of a standards-based system. In the end, however, we believe that we have succeeded in providing essential information that will help educators to considerably improve grading practices. At the very least, our readers will have a good grasp of what is entailed in reforming grading practices and some concrete ideas for how to go about doing so. We should qualify our judgment of success by saying we believe that this book represents the best information and insights currently available. The knowledge base upon which educators can build new systems is growing every day. It is, indeed, a unique time in the history of American education because—although periods of school reform are not uncommon, and educational experiments have come and gone—the changes with which educators are now dealing are among the most fundamental ever proposed.

Acknowledgments

In the early planning stages of this book, we recognized that if it were to do justice to all of the important issues in grading, we would have to persuade experts in several areas to contribute to it. We were extremely fortunate to succeed in getting John Carr, Kathleen Busick, Louise Bay Waters, Henriette Langdon, Tanja Bisesi, Roger Farr, Beth Greene, and Elizabeth Haydel as partners in this endeavor. They have met the challenge of writing thoughtful work in the face of overly demanding jobs—something that is true of every one of them. Interacting with them has expanded our own knowledge base immeasurably and has made us believe that the book will be a valuable resource to the education community.

The authors of our Foreword and Afterword, Rick Stiggins and Ursula Casanova, were expressly chosen for their ability to get to the heart of the matter: the importance of ensuring fair, equitable, and informative grading practices that do not harm students. We appreciate their insights and their ability to communicate them so clearly.

We have both learned a great deal from our colleagues on the numerous projects with which we have worked in our respective organizations, WestEd and the American Institutes for Research. It would be impossible to thank them individually here, but we want to extend our gratitude to all of them collectively.

Finally, we thank our anonymous reviewers, who offered excellent constructive criticism (and some encouragement), along with friends and family members who made helpful suggestions that improved the "reader friendliness" of various chapters. Chief among this last group was Jerry Salzman, Elise's husband.

Introduction

In an age when educators at state and local levels are building accountability systems based on content and performance standards, grading practices have remained largely untouched. Practices that can be tracked back to the late 1800s are still the most common in our schools. School and district staffs as well as parents are beginning to wake up to the contradictions between standards-based scoring and traditional grading practices. This book shows how to align grading and reporting practices with the goals of standards-based education.

The book offers concrete guidance on how to do the following:

- Evaluate current grading and reporting practices in light of school and district goals and philosophy
- Ensure that grading and reporting systems are technically sound and equitable
- Plan a course of action to implement a grading and reporting system that meets school and district needs and communicates well to parents

The book presents an extensive repertoire of examples from current practice. These can be used to equal advantage by teacher educators in measurement courses, district staff responsible for evaluation and testing, and teachers who want to take the lead in bringing grading and reporting into line with the principles of standards-based education.

Grading Practices: An Overview of the Issues

Beverly P. Farr

1

Adrift in the tides of change, teachers need assistance to ensure that they are not swept out to sea in the process! Classrooms are moving from a "testing culture"—where teachers are the sole authority, students work alone, and learning is done for the test—to an "assessment culture"—where teachers and learners collaborate about learning, assessment takes many forms for multiple audiences, and distinctions between learning and assessment are blurred. The challenge remains for teachers—with the support of their district, their professional organizations, and the educational measurement community—to devise grading systems that adequately reflect this shift.

—Marcia Seeley
"The Mismatch Between Assessment and Grading"

The Shifting Sands of Assessment and Grading Practices

In the last decade, we have seen a marked shift in perspective and practices related to assessment in American classrooms. Efforts to redesign how we assess students are seen in large-scale testing and in investigations of alternative assessment formats. Assessment reform has, in many cases, become the driving force behind efforts to improve American schools. The following innovative practices (Cizek, Fitzgerald, & Rachor, 1995–96) are widely evident:

- Local and state educators develop new accountability systems based on local or national content and performance standards.
- Teachers gather more varied information to determine whether students have met standards.

1

- Students collect portfolios of work to demonstrate what they know and are able to do.
- Districts and states rethink retention and promotion policies and the measures used to make such decisions.
- Test publishers incorporate a wider variety of assessment formats in their products.

"Dualing" Paradigms

Such an alteration in perspective is often referred to as a "paradigm shift," but the problem in this case is that grading and reporting practices have not generally made the same shift, and thus schools have been operating with dual, competing paradigms within their accountability systems. The following statement by Cizek et al. captures the situation well: "Sadly, as the range and quality of information about educational performance available to students, teachers, parents, administrators, and the American public have improved dramatically, teachers' grading practices remain unchanged" (p. 161).

While it is often difficult for educators to unseat practices that have been well entrenched for many years, the progress that has been made in current assessment reform has laid the groundwork for a new consideration of grading practices, which many schools and districts are doing. School and district educators have become aware that the goal of building a coherent accountability system cannot be accomplished if one of the primary methods for reporting the results of student learning is not aligned with the other parts of the system. As a result, teachers and administrators are now reconsidering their beliefs about grading, and they are learning more about standards-based approaches to grading practices. The close involvement of teachers in the development of policies and practices associated with assessment and reporting is in itself of great potential benefit to the design of effective approaches to using accurate assessment data in the classroom. There are high stakes associated with grading practices—they are used to determine if students will move to the next grade, graduate, go to college, or receive special honors and scholarships. Given these stakes, it seems obvious that we must do the work that is required to ensure the implementation of grading practices that are valid, reliable, fair, and meaningful. To accomplish this goal, the following conditions must be met:

1. Within a school or district, there must be clear policies, a coherent philosophical basis, and consistent criteria for making judgments about student performance.
2. All stakeholder groups must be involved in the development of policies and procedures.
3. Teachers, administrators, students, and parents must share a clear understanding about standards and grading methods.

To compile this book, Elise Trumbull and I identified topics that we thought were critical to an understanding of grading practices in American schools and how we can move to "standards-based" practices that are aligned with school and district accountability reform efforts. To address these topics, we invited a group of educators with knowledge of psychometrics, school policies and practices, and reporting systems to write about their experiences in these areas. These educators have also been (or currently are) very involved with schools (districts and state departments of education), so they have a deep understanding of how schools operate and of the changes necessary to ensure effective school reform. Chapters 2–4 and 8 focus on theoretical issues involved in grading practices: purposes for grading, technical methodology, and reporting. Chapters 6 and 7 focus on issues of bias and fairness and the assignment of grades to specific groups of students. Chapters 5 and 9 provide examples of individual schools' or districts' models for a standards-based system and some guidance for moving toward such a system.

Looking Back: How Have Grading Practices Changed?

As any historian will note, it is often valuable to plot our course forward by examining where we have been. Grading practices in schools are an aspect of educational history that have been almost impervious to change, but they are familiar to us all. Throughout our lifetimes, it seems that conversations about school have often included questions or comments about grades: "So you're in college now. Are you getting good grades?" "I never got good grades in school." "Mrs. Whitley was really a hard grader." "My parents gave me a new stereo when I got all As my junior year." Or "Wad-ja-get?", a question that will sound familiar to most readers and was captured in a 1971 publication, *Wad-ja-get? The Grading Game in American Education*.

When we think about the large part that grades have played in our schooling, it seems unthinkable that so little attention has been paid to establishing systems that are soundly based on good measurement principles. One might also find it inexplicable that teachers have been so ill prepared to apply such measurement principles in their classrooms. Grading practices as we know them in American schools can be traced back to the late 1800s and exhibit a rather inglorious history, considering how significant they are in our educational memories. Studies by Starch and Elliott (1912, 1913) produced a discouraging picture that more recent reviews of research (Brookhart, 1994; Hoge & Coladarci, 1989) reveal has not changed much (Cizek et al., 1995–96). Starch and Elliott (1912) stated the following:

> The reliability of the school's estimate of the accomplishment and progress of pupils is of large practical importance. For, after all, the marks or grades attached to a pupil's work are the tangible measure of the result of his attainments, and constitute the chief basis for the determination of essential administrative problems of the school, such as transfer, promotion, retardation, elimination, and admission to higher institutions; to say nothing of the problem of the influence of these marks or grades upon the moral attitude of the pupil toward the school, education, and even life. The recent studies of grades have emphati-

cally directed our attention to the wide variation and the utter absence of standards in the assignment of values. (p. 442)

The research reviews document a confounding of constructs in the determination of composite scores that results in grades without defensible meaning. This situation can be most clearly explained by teachers' lack of exposure to assessment principles and practices. It is often not a requirement and is given scant attention in teacher preparation programs.[1] Yet there is a strong consensus among educational experts that knowledge about assessment for teachers is fundamental to effective teaching and that such knowledge is also key to educational reform (Stiggins, 1988, 1991). The following excerpt could be taken from any current report on school reform in a school or district that has set up task groups for planning:

The Committee on Grading was called upon to study grading procedures. At first, the task of investigating the literature seemed to be a rather hopeless one. What a mass and a mess it was! Could order be brought out of such chaos? Could points of agreement among American educators concerning the perplexing grading problem actually be discovered? It was with considerable misgiving and trepidation that the work was finally begun.

In fact, this was written by Middleton in 1933! Yet even today, as school and district educators embark on journeys they hope will take them toward "the perfect school," issues of assessment, evaluation, checking, grading, and reporting continue to perplex and confound us all. While we have been experiencing a sea change in approaches to assessment and accountability, we are also experiencing a severe misalignment of these new approaches to traditional grading practices. It is much like traveling around the world today by using maps drawn in the late 1800s. Thus, while assessment reform has become a centerpiece of efforts to improve American education, a student's performance is still usually reported as a grade.

Thomas Guskey describes the history of grading practices in Figure 1-1. An interesting aspect of the history of grading practices is the shift from the early use (late 1800s) of narrative reports (progress evaluations) to the use of single numerical (or letter) grades based on some quantification of learning, most often a percentage. This shift from the use of narratives to a more reductionist approach is attributed to significant increases in the student population. Much like current debates about time-consuming measurement approaches such as portfolios and performance tasks, the use of narrative reports was attacked at the time on the basis of a lack of cost-effectiveness and the amount of time required. Even so, some schools and colleges today have taken stalwart positions on the positive effects of using narrative reports, although they have sometimes made compromises to accommodate traditional systems in other institutions that interface with their own. For example, some schools that use portfolios or rubric-based grading systems encounter problems of translation when students move, for example, from a high school to a college or from one school district to another.

---

[1] Wolmut (1994), for example, reported that only 11 of the 50 states require teachers to have competence in assessment as a precondition for being licensed as a teacher.

Figure 1-1. *A Look Back at Grading Practices*

Although student assessment has been a part of teaching and learning for centuries, grading is a relatively recent phenomenon. The ancient Greeks used assessments as formative, not evaluative, tools. Students demonstrated, usually orally, what they had learned, giving teachers a clear indication of which topics required more work or instruction.

In the United States, grading and reporting were virtually unknown before 1850. Back then, most schools grouped students of all ages and backgrounds together with one teacher. Few students went beyond the elementary education offered in these one-room schoolhouses. As the country grew—and as legislators passed compulsory attendance laws—the number and diversity of students increased. Schools began to group students in grades according to their age, and to try new ideas about curriculum and teaching methods. Here's a brief timeline of significant dates in the history of grading:

Late 1800s: Schools begin to issue progress evaluations. Teachers simply write down the skills that students have mastered; once students complete the requirements for one level, they can move to the next level.

Early 1900s: The number of public high schools in the United States increases dramatically. While elementary teachers continue using written descriptions to document student learning, high school teachers introduce percentages as a way to certify students' accomplishments in specific subject areas. Few educators question the gradual shift to percentage grading, which seems a natural by-product of the increased demands on high school teachers.

1912: Starch and Elliott publish a study that challenges percentage grades as reliable measures of student achievement. They base their findings on grades assigned to two papers written for a first-year English class in high school. Of the 142 teachers grading on a 0 to 100 scale, 15 percent give one paper a failing mark; 12 percent give the same paper a score of 90 or more. The other paper receives scores ranging from 50 to 97. Neatness, spelling, and punctuation influenced the scoring of many teachers, while others considered how well the paper communicated its message.

1913: Responding to critics—who argue that good writing is, by nature, a highly subjective judgment—Starch and Elliott repeat their study but use geometry papers. Even greater variations occur, with scores on one paper ranging from 28 to 95. Some teachers deducted points only for wrong answers, but others took neatness, form, and spelling into account.

1918: Teachers turn to grading scales with fewer and larger categories. One three-point scale, for example, uses the categories of Excellent, Average, and Poor. Another has five categories (Excellent, Good, Average, Poor, and Failing) with the corresponding letters of A, B, C, D, and F (Johnson 1918, Rugg 1918).

1930s: Grading on the curve becomes increasingly popular as educators seek to minimize the subjective nature of scoring. This method rank orders students according to some measure of their performance or proficiency. The top percentage receives an A, the next percentage receives a B, and so on (Corey 1930). Some advocates (Davis 1930) even specify the precise percentage of students to be assigned each grade, such as 6-22-44-22-6.

Grading on the curve seems fair and equitable, given research suggesting that students' scores on tests of innate intelligence approximate a normal probability curve (Middleton 1933).

As the debate over grading and reporting intensifies, a number of schools abolish formal grades altogether (Chapman and Ashbaugh 1925) and return to using verbal descriptions of student achievement. Others advocate pass-fail systems that distinguish only between acceptable and failing work (Good 1937). Still others advocate a "mastery approach": Once students have mastered a skill or content, they move to other areas of study (Heck 1938, Hill 1935).

1958: Ellis Page investigates how student learning is affected by grades and teachers' comments. In a now classic study, 74 secondary school teachers administer a test, and assign a numerical score and letter grade of A, B, C, D, or F to each student's paper. Next, teachers randomly divide the tests into three groups. Papers in the first group receive only the numerical score and letter grade. The second group, in addition to score and grade, receive these standard comments: *A—Excellent! B—Good work. Keep at it. C—Perhaps to do still better? D—Let's bring this up. F—Let's raise this grade!* For the third group, teachers mark the score and letter grade, and write individualized comments.

Page evaluates the effects of the comments by considering students' scores on the next test they take. Results show that students in the second group achieved significantly higher scores than those who received only a score and a grade. The students who received individualized comments did even better. Page concludes that grades can have a beneficial effect on student learning, but only when accompanied by specific or individualized comments from the teacher.

—Thomas R. Guskey
Source: H. Kirschenbaum, S.B. Simon, and R.W. Napier (1971), *Wad-ja-get? The Grading Game in American Education* (New York: Hart).

One would hope that the dramatic changes in assessment techniques that have occurred could result in a more widespread use of narratives or other means of reporting progress, but such has not yet been the case. There has been an increase, however, in the number of teachers and administrators developing standards-based grading practices (see chapters 4, 5, and 9). While many of these efforts are still in pilot stages, there is evidence that they are more reliable than traditional practices and provide a much richer context for presenting a picture of student performance and progress. These systems also have the advantage that teachers have been more closely involved in their development, and students are better informed about the standards and criteria against which their academic performances are being judged. With the element of increased student awareness, one can hope that the significant negative effects (often unintended) of grading practices can be reduced.

Purposes of Grading: What Are Your Intentions?

An important starting point for the development of a grading system is the consideration of the purpose(s) of grading students. The wide variation in traditional grading practices is due in part to the lack of clarification of purpose, although most educators will tell you that the purpose is "obvious." It is evident that grades often reflect conflicting views of the purposes of schooling. For those who see the purpose as helping students to master certain knowledge and skills, the status of a student's achievement against an explicit standard is important. For those who see the purpose as developmental, grades describe the effort and progress the students are making. Finally, for those who see the job of schools as providing multiple programs that respond to individual student differences, grades differentiate performance among members of classes, grades, or age groups (Austin & McCann, 1992). The important point is that one method doesn't serve all purposes well. (In chapter 2, Elise Trumbull provides in-depth information about the purposes of grades, a few of which I discuss briefly here.)

In addition to differences in philosophy, it has been noted in the literature that the purpose of grading is different for teachers at different grade levels. Teachers of the lower grades often report that they do it only because it is required, not because it is important to them. Guskey states, "Teachers don't need grades or reporting forms to teach well. Further, students don't need them to learn" (Frisbie & Waltman, 1992). Secondary teachers, however, indicate that grades are necessary for informing students, other teachers, and colleges about performance.

From research conducted on the purposes of grades, Ornstein (1994) made some important observations about student perspectives on grades. He noted that young students (below fourth grade) "have little understanding of the meaning of grades," and that it increases with age. He suggests that it is not until eighth or ninth grade that students understand "complex schemes such as a grading curve, grade point average, and weighted grading" (pp. 55, 56). This observation underscores the importance of considering student perspective and understanding when we establish grading policies and practices. It is a very important consideration in devising innovative (and sounder) approaches to grading. Students need to understand the various purposes of grading and the criteria used to arrive at particular scores or grades. With a better understanding of teacher expectations (the criteria), students are better equipped to evaluate their own learning. In this regard, Daro (1994) offers a simple account of the experience of his two daughters, which is illustrated in Figure 1-2. I have used this set of passages in my own work with school staffs who are redesigning their accountability systems. They generate rich discussion about the use of standards, student perspectives, and purposes of grading. It helps to accent the issues surrounding grading practices and the need for reform by reconsidering the purpose(s) of giving grades.

Figure 1-2. *Daro's Daughters*

Daughter 1's Story

Daughter 1 came home from school in tears. She swore she no longer cared about math, and she showed me why. She had gotten her math test back. The grade was bad. Again.

Daughter 1 was determined and had studied hard for this test. I know. I studied hard with her. So did her friends. She has a talent for trying hard, and that has paid off for her in many arenas. But not in math. Before my eyes, in front of my heart, I saw her deciding not to try hard in math anymore. I could see her realizing that it did not pay off. I could see our school teaching my daughter to give up, to quit. The message was: Hard work does *not* pay.

But hard work *should* pay. A student who worked hard in a good program should succeed. And worse, my daughter was not being held to any standard. She was being told merely to put in her time taking the test, and no matter how badly she did, she would be done! Once the bell rang, class was dismissed and the test was done. The time clock drove the performance. But the real world doesn't work like that. In business, if you have a deadline, you stay at work until you've done it right—until you've met the standard.

Daughter 2's Story

One day Daughter 2 came home from school. She was angry. Furious. I asked her, father-like, what was the matter.

"Mrs. Jones is a brat," she said. "She wouldn't grade my paper. I have to do it over. She said she expects better of me and not to insult her with a lick and a promise. How does she know I can do better? If it is good enough for me, why can't she just give me my grade? Why do I have to do it over?"

I asked whether she had been shown what to do.

"She showed me what Janice, Barbara, and Rachel did to get As. She showed me a story she liked that I wrote before Christmas. She showed me parts where I didn't try hard. . . . How does she know?"

I knew she hadn't worked hard. I was a witness. Over the next few days, my daughter attacked the paper, revising and crafting like never before, complaining about Mrs. Jones the whole time. She did a great job, got a good grade and delivered quality work for Mrs. Jones after that. Since then, she has had the confidence that she could do good work anytime she set her mind to do it. And she often has. Mrs. Jones held my daughter to a high standard of performance. My daughter had to deliver the work. Sitting there with the ability to do it was not enough. Until Mrs. Jones's class, my daughter could get by just fine by being clever enough to get good test scores. She was not learning to write or think. Worse, no one was telling her that she wasn't learning. Finally, someone was holding her to a standard that was high, and she knew what to do to attain it.

Technical Issues and a Few Solutions

Technical issues have swirled around traditional grading practices, but without much attention being paid to them despite the high stakes that are often associated with grades. Teachers have had considerable autonomy and significant power in assigning grades to their students, and only infrequently have they had to defend or change a grade when questions or protests were raised. While technical issues range from a lack of a coherent philosophical basis to a lack of validity and reliability, several are highlighted here that can be remedied by moving to a standards-based system. In chapter 3, John Carr discusses technical issues more fully (e.g., problems with different grading practices, such as "grading on a curve") and provides some suggestions for determining which approach is best for the individual teacher. He also considers differences in philosophical orientation (e.g., comparison of "YAC" and "MAC" teachers).

Policies and Procedures: What Counts?

A common thread through the research on grading practices has to do with teacher preparation and guidance for grading practices. A number of studies have surveyed teachers to find out how they develop their practices, how they decide what counts, and what technical means they use. Cizek et al. (1995–96) noted, "Despite the fact that nearly every school district has some kind of grading policy, only about one half of the teachers in this study said that they knew their district had a policy, and few of these teachers were able to supply any details about their district's policies" (p. 173). They also noted that there was a significant lack of professional collaboration on matters of assessment.

In short, teachers have essentially been "on their own" when it comes to grading practices. Teachers have, in many ways, taken grading as their domain, often reflecting their own individual philosophies or ignorance of measurement issues, ignoring (or failing to investigate) district policies. This is not to indict teachers. With little preparation or guidance offered to them, teachers have taken an important aspect of teaching in hand and developed practices and systems that may not always have felt satisfying to them but have met the requirement. It is not difficult to see, then, how such wide variability in grading practices has unfolded and remained largely undisturbed for many years. (See chapter 5 for an example of a school district that has adopted a coherent policy and procedures for grading.)

Let Me Count the Ways: Variability in Grading Practices

Apart from the inherent subjectivity of grading practices, a primary factor contributing to the great variability in (and unreliability of) grading practices is the wide array of factors that teachers have traditionally taken into account when assigning grades. This has included student achievement (measured in all sorts of ways), learning ability, attitude, motivation and effort, interest, and even personality. In general, educators who are now taking a closer look at grading practices recommend that achievement or the acquisition of knowledge and skills be the "sole ingredient in determining grades" (Stiggins, Frisbie, & Griswold, 1989).

Learning ability and attitude, for example, are complex student characteristics that certainly influence student learning, but they are difficult for teachers to define and assess dependably. While level of effort and "seriousness of purpose" is highly valued in our culture, it, too, is difficult to assess in a reliable manner, and furthermore, it can be manipulated by students. If feedback is to be provided on level of effort, it should be done separately from the grade. Both interest and personality are clearly also difficult to define and measure. If we remove all these other factors, however, we must then consider what will "count" and how it should be "added up." If we only take student achievement into account, how should it be measured and against what criteria?

One Alone Is Not Enough: The Problem of "Naked Scores"

Discussing the benefits of narrative-based grading systems, Grant Wiggins (1994) states that they play down "naked scores and crude comparisons" (p. 28). Using a single grade to capture a student's learning over the course of some arbitrary grading period raises serious questions about the validity and value of such information. A single grade can hide much more than it reveals. Wiggins' notion that a single grade is a "naked score" reflects the problem of information being presented without any context or reference to a well-founded set of criteria. Such grades or scores are often used to make comparisons that must be accompanied by a multitude of questions: "On what basis?" "Compared to what or whom?" "Over the entire period or for a selected part of that period?" "What does it represent?" "What predictions can be made based on that grade?" "How does it compare to expectations?" "What body of work does it represent?" The use of a single grade to reflect achievement, progress, and growth leads to the difficulty of grading fairly.

Teachers today experience numerous tensions regarding their instructional and grading practices. On the one hand, they are encouraged—even required—to provide opportunities for students to engage in complex thinking, problem solving, and performance-based activities and to assess them using measures that tap a broad range of abilities and knowledge. Yet all of this information is often still recorded as a single grade. In describing this mismatch, Seeley (1994) rightfully asks, "How can grades adequately reflect student progress to date, and still encourage students to persevere?" (p. 4).

For many years it has been common for educators to invoke the spirit and words of Edward Thorndike (1918), an educational scholar who wrote insightfully about such matters and is often referred to as one of the fathers of educational measurement. In matters related to grading practices, his words remind us again that these issues are hardly new. Eighty-one years ago, he wrote that scores should "redirect [the incentive of rivalry] into tendencies to go higher on an objective scale of absolute achievement, to surpass one's own past performance" (p. 288). His comments reflect his efforts to change a grading system because of its "relativity and indefiniteness, the fact that a given mark did not mean any defined amount of knowledge or power or skill." His comments also lend support to the development of a standards-based system.

Two Plus Two: Does That Make Four?

One of the most niggling of technical issues at the heart of grading practices is how to combine pieces of information—numerical, observational, anecdotal, or narrative—and arrive at a "judgment" that is valid, fair, credible, and constructive. This has been a primary source of variation in grading practices as well as a source of error in the measurement. In chapters 3 and 4, John Carr and Kathleen Busick touch on these issues, suggesting possibilities for combinations in a standards-based system. In chapter 5, Louise Bay Waters describes the extensive work done with her school and in her district to devise a system that allows teachers to combine information in more defensible ways.

Decisions about grades usually devolve into comparisons—most often crude comparisons. In many cases, they are comparisons against "norms" that may reside only in the teacher's mind. "Compared to last year's students . . . to other students in the class, school, state, nation, world . . . this is the grade I think this student deserves" exemplifies the thinking that might go on. Merely comparing performers can be misleading at best and hurtfully unfair at worst (Wiggins, 1998). Scores can be thought of as pure performance data, and they are worth analyzing and reporting. A letter grade represents a translation of that pure score into a personalized judgment based on expectations (Wiggins, 1994). Therein lies the rub. How are these things to be translated in ways that are consistent among teachers and reliable?

Additional technical problems related to combining and translating strategies are inherent in methods such as grading on a curve, averaging, and translating from one type of scale to another. For example, when scores or grades on a disparate group of performances are averaged, it supports the notion that every performance is of equal value, even when the dimensions of performance are complex and diverse. Using weighting mechanisms doesn't always address the problems associated with such averaging procedures. Averaging over time does not make sense, either, since one should not include earlier grades to get a picture of how a student is *currently* doing. Nor is the use of personalized narratives alone enough to address the dilemmas of reliable grading practices. What is needed is a reporting system that yields a more accurate and rich profile of the student's accomplishments. Wiggins also points out that while in architecture the aphorism has been "form follows function," in schools the opposite is often true. In grading practices, this means that the form of the report card and what is counted often determines what and how teaching takes place. It also determines how students engage in learning.

Of Baseball Cards and Panty Hose:
Using Context and Combining Scores

A challenge associated with the use of approaches to assessment that incorporate rich and diverse performance measures is to find technically sound ways to combine those measures into defensible grades. For the most part, teachers over the years have used multiple elements and combined them in some way (usually devised by the teacher) to arrive at a single grade to represent a student's accomplishment in learning. Today teachers are even more strongly encouraged to use more than one measure to assess student learning. Legislation governing large federally supported programs require that students who are served in those programs be assessed using "multiple measures." The directive is to arrive at some indication of whether the student is "proficient," "below proficient," or "advanced."[2] This means that teachers are required to use a variety of measures *and* to arrive at a single indicator of how well a student is doing. They are given precious little guidance, however, on how to combine the measures that may use different scales in ways that are meaningful and reliable.

There are times when real-life examples give us keen insights into new ways to think about old problems, serving as metaphors to help us understand something that is abstract. Wiggins (1994) uses the following example of a baseball card to explain recommended grading practices.

> For each baseball player, we see a brief description of the previous year's performance in data highlighting the many subdimensions of performance: hits, runs, home runs, runs batted in, walks, strikeouts. Subjectivity and judgments about potential or expectations are minimized: These are the raw scores, without explicit meaning.
>
> We can derive much meaning from the numbers, though. Did the ballplayers play 140 or more games (hence, they were starters)? Were their averages high, compared to other players? We also see the longitudinal trends, since the data are reported for all past years.
>
> This example clarifies why the parent needs those normative comparisons and teacher judgments cast in letter grades, despite all the data, to place the child's performance in context. It also makes clear why a single letter grade is so unhelpful. Who would feel confident giving a single grade to each ballplayer, given 12 data categories? Such a reduction to a single grade is arbitrary—even if computed "objectively"—whether in baseball or school.
>
> Why would it be arbitrary in baseball? Because runs, hits, and strikeouts are *independent* of one another with no clear or agreed-upon "weight" relative to other data. Some hitters strike out often, but they also hit many home runs and drive in many runs; others hit only singles, but score lots of runs since they are frequently on base. Some pitchers win many games but have a high earned run average (runs allowed per nine innings); others have the opposite numbers. (p. 34)

Wiggins makes clear that there is no simple or valid formula for combining all the data. Averaging all available scores to arrive at a single grade obscures the fact that one is giving equal weight to all the elements. This is even more inappropriate in schools where the dimensions of performance are more complex and diverse.

Another example was described to me recently by Dale Carlson of the California Department of Education, who devised some models for combining mul-

---

[2] This guidance is provided in the Improving America's Schools Act of 1994, which includes these provisions under the section of the law related to Title I programs.

tiple measures using the example of the sizing chart commonly found on the back of panty hose packages. This is illustrated in Figure 1-3. These charts present an approach to combining several indicators to arrive at the appropriate designation of panty hose size. Essentially, it involves laying scales on top of one another so that the distributions can be seen (and made sense of) in an integrated fashion.

Figure 1-3. *Simulated Panty Hose Chart*

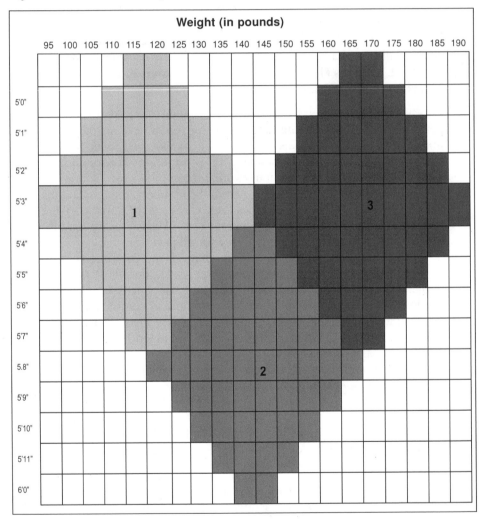

The application of the "panty hose method" of taking more than one piece of data into account can be seen in the chart presented in Figure 1-4.

It may seem that the use of such models for explicating a complex technical issue means that these issues cannot be taken seriously, but this is far from true. Educators and measurement specialists agree that the use of multiple measures, including ones that allow students to demonstrate complex skills and deep under-

Figure 1-4. *NRT Scores*

A compensatory model using three measures with different levels to determine combinations of assessments that meet grade level standards (MGLS) (California Department of Education, 1998)

Grades	Writing Scores	1-29	30-39	40-49	50-59	60-69	70+
A	6		MGLS	MGLS	MGLS	MGLS	MGLS
	5		MGLS	MGLS	MGLS	MGLS	MGLS
	4		MGLS	MGLS	MGLS	MGLS	MGLS
	3			MGLS	MGLS	MGLS	MGLS
	2						
	1						
B	6		MGLS	MGLS	MGLS	MGLS	MGLS
	5		MGLS	MGLS	MGLS	MGLS	MGLS
	4			MGLS	MGLS	MGLS	MGLS
	3				MGLS	MGLS	MGLS
	2						
	1						
C	6		MGLS	MGLS	MGLS	MGLS	MGLS
	5			MGLS	MGLS	MGLS	MGLS
	4				MGLS	MGLS	MGLS
	3					MGLS	MGLS
	2						
	1						
D	6						
	5						
	4						
	3						
	2						
	1						
F	6						
	5						
	4						
	3						
	2						
	1						

standing, is critical to the accurate assessment of students' learning. They also agree that providing context is essential to understanding scores and grades. If simple real-life examples shed light on complex technical issues, then clearly they are useful and help to ensure that everyone involved in the education of children will take these issues seriously. The use of grades *is* a serious issue; both the stakes and the potential for negative effects on children are extraordinarily high. This leads to yet another significant issue in grading practices.

Effects of Grading Practices: Was This What You Had in Mind?

Over the years students have frequently asked teachers questions about teacher expectations and the relationship between classroom instruction and grades. "Are we going to be tested on this?" "Does this count for a grade?" "Why are we going over this if it's not going to be on the test?" "What were you looking for on that paper?" "What do I have to do to get an A?" Yet despite their relentless questions on this matter, students have largely remained in the dark with regard to teacher expectations or grading criteria. This has presented a significant dilemma for them (and for the teachers). While "making the grade" has been a high-stakes proposition for them, they have often been shooting at a target that was unclear or confused by " a lot of noise in the system."

The teachers' desire to feel that they have succeeded in teaching is often quashed by students' poor performance, despite the fact that their teaching may actually have been effective although the measures were flawed. Teachers receive little training in the development of assessment devices, in aligning those tools with specific learning outcomes, or in evaluating students' performances. The weaknesses in preservice and inservice preparation of teachers in classroom assessment are generally acknowledged. But as Cizek et al. (1995–96) point out, "Despite the fact that they lacked training in assessment, most teachers in this study reported that they develop their own tests, quizzes, and examinations" (p. 173).

We know that grading practices are inherently subjective—a fact that constitutes not a denunciation of education but a truth that needs to be told. In chapter 6, Elise Trumbull presents compelling information about the issue of bias in grading practices, and in chapter 7 she and Henriette Langdon explore issues of grading related to special needs students. The fact that assigning grades includes some element of subjectivity is not necessarily bad when teachers really know their students and understand the various dimensions of students' work and what needs to be accomplished to demonstrate learning. It is not difficult, however, for subjectivity to slide over into bias, and this is one aspect of grading practices that can have severe, negative consequences. Students' behavior often influences a teacher's judgment about their academic performance. A student with behavior problems has little chance of receiving a high grade from a teacher who is blinded to strong classroom performance by an irritating pattern of behavior. Researchers have documented a more pronounced effect in judgments of boys (Bennett, Gottesman, Rock, & Cerullo, 1993) and have even identified "infractions" as minor as messy handwriting as significant factors in the determination of grades (Sweedler-Brown 1992).

A significant body of disturbing evidence also points to bias when teachers make negative judgments (represented as grades) about children from different cultures, children who speak languages other than English, and children whose dress and demeanor reflect a background of poverty. As with other aspects of a children's educational experience, these negative reactions often result from a teacher's lack of knowledge about different ways of learning, knowing, and demonstrating skills and knowledge. Whatever the reason, a child who is struggling to assimilate to the culture of the school and who encounters more challenges in doing so because of his or her language, culture, or background suffers enormously from what is often a relentless barrage of poor grades in school.

While educators would undoubtedly agree that motivation to learn should be intrinsic, they have to acknowledge that many students see high grades as recognition for success. On the other hand, when teachers use grades (or students perceive grades) as a "weapon," the consequences of receiving low grades are obvious. No studies support the use of low grades as punishment. Gusky (1994) quotes some colleagues in noting the following:

> Instead of prompting greater effort, low grades usually cause students to withdraw from learning. To protect their self-image, many students regard the low grade as irrelevant and meaningless. Other students may blame themselves for the low mark, but feel helpless to improve. (p. 19)

Thus the students ask teachers, "Is this what you had in mind?" If we do not consider the serious negative impact that low grades can have on student motivation, attitude, and self-image, and we do not work to find a way to change that fact, then we will continue to write off thousands of students who didn't understand what the teacher "had in mind." If, on the other hand, we can give students clear information about what is expected and what constitutes good work as well as clear guidance about how to improve, then a student who *does* receive a low grade will at least have a frame of reference for understanding his or her performance. If, as stated in the Improving America's Schools Act of 1994, our goal as educators is to help *all* students reach high standards, we will certainly find it more attainable if we can all look at those standards together and figure out the best ways to help children reach them.

Reporting Achievement Results: What Does It All Mean?

Report cards have always been intended as a means of communicating information about how well children are doing in school. They have carried this data to students, parents and other family members, administrators, and often other teachers. Other reports have resulted from standardized tests. Depending on the particular test, this information is usually of some (but less) interest to students and parents and of more interest to administrators and especially school board members, other community members, and state and federal education officials.

While standardized tests are often maligned—if not by members of the community who were once subjected to them, then by teachers who have to administer them—the biggest problem with them has been their misuse and misinterpretation. Thus, when we think about grading and reporting practices, we need to be mindful of the differences in reporting mechanisms—how one relates to the others, which ones are of greater interest to which audiences, and how they can contribute to a confusing picture of how students are doing in school. In chapter 8, Tanja Bisesi, Roger Farr, Beth Greene, and Elizabeth Haydel describe a real-life development project that highlights the problems of reporting grades or standardized test scores with little contextual information and little consideration of how the parts of an accountability system fit together.

The real test of grading practices in American schools happens when report cards go home. Very few of us have escaped our parents' scrutiny of those report cards, and parents were (and are) most often left to limited possible interpretations: "You did worse (or better) than last semester/quarter/year." "You do better than your brother/father/grandmother did in school." Sometimes information has been provided that lets parents know that students are or are not "good citizens," "big for their age," "quiet in class," "too social," "inattentive and given to daydreams." What do parents infer from such comments, and how do they integrate that with a student's grades? If a student does less well than a parent hoped, and the comment "too social" is included on a report card, the parent will naturally conclude that the child's sociability is the cause of the lower grades. An alternative explanation might be that this student learns best from his or her peers or in a group and, deprived of such opportunities, does less well. Similarly, what does a parent conclude when a child's report card grades are consistently high, but he or she is reported to be in the 65th percentile on a standardized test report?

Generally speaking, it has been difficult for parents (and students) to "make meaning" from the information provided either on a report card or a test report, largely because the information is provided in a kind of code and is not given with reference to standards. Context is everything. The parent cannot review all of a student's work. It is the teacher's job to make it meaningful to parents (and to students), to interpret the "code" and present documentation that helps to provide the necessary context for understanding how students are progressing with respect to a particular standard of performance or instructional goal.

The "performance-based" terminology that is showing up with greater frequency on student report cards is no less a code than any that has been used in the past. Parents and others from the community do not readily understand terms such as "rubric," "continuum," "content standard," or what a "3" means as a proficiency level. The facts, judgments, and prescriptions that are included in a report on a student must be user-friendly, or easy to interpret. Wiggins (1994) captures the need to make report cards meaningful when he states that there is value in

> reporting both level of performance and judgment about the result in terms of appropriate expectations. Implicit in this argument is the need to think of the report card as a mere cover page or "executive summary," supported by documentation to justify and amplify the meaning of the grades given. (p. 36)

An additional issue in reporting is the frequency. While students often have some idea of how their grades are "running" through the course of a grading period, quarter, or semester, sometimes they don't, and parents usually don't. Thus, when a grade shows up on a report at the end of the period, it can be quite a surprise, and it provides no opportunity for a student to address problem areas or for parents to support their children's learning. I recently heard about a school district in the state of Washington that has established an Intranet Web site on which both students and parents can check students' grades throughout the grading period. Students can check regularly to see how they are doing and to find out about missing assignments. Using the student's I.D. code (assuming the student provides it), parents can also monitor on an ongoing basis. Early reports indicate that the Web site is used by the majority of students in the school and that they are following up on the information provided—checking on missing assignments, discussing particular grades with teachers, talking to parents about their progress (see Figure 1-5).

Figure 1-5. *Intranet WebSite*

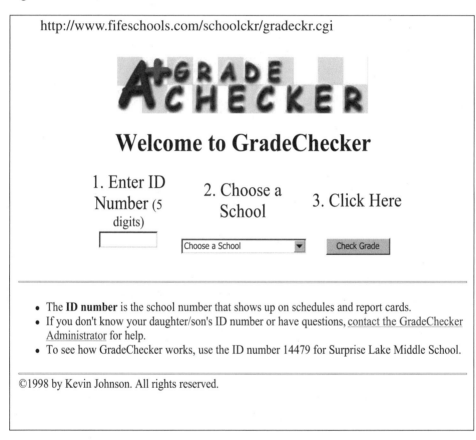

http://www.fifeschools.com/schoolckr/gradeckr.cgi

Welcome to GradeChecker

1. Enter ID Number (5 digits)   2. Choose a School   3. Click Here

| | Choose a School ▾ | Check Grade |

- The **ID number** is the school number that shows up on schedules and report cards.
- If you don't know your daughter/son's ID number or have questions, contact the GradeChecker Administrator for help.
- To see how GradeChecker works, use the ID number 14479 for Surprise Lake Middle School.

Putting It All Together and Taking It on the Road

In chapter 9, John Carr and I provide what amounts to a gentle nudge in the "right direction"—that is, the development of a standards-based report card. Along with chapter 5, in which Louise Bay Waters describes the system her school devised that is now being used in the entire district, this should provide the reader with enough material to move in the direction of a better reporting system. The goal should be to establish a system that is more valid, consistent, and fair to students, and one that gives you, as an educator, a greater confidence that when you assign grades your judgment is sound. From teaching 6th and 10th grades as well as undergraduate and graduate college levels, I know that I was never confident that my grading system was completely valid or equitable. Giving grades was always the worst part of teaching for me.

In all of the chapters of this book, you will find good suggestions about how to use standards-based grading as an approach that helps to remedy some of the traditional ills of grading practices. As I have the advantage of "first position," I'm going to avail myself of the opportunity to make a few initial suggestions. I have been working for quite a number of years now on the development of assessments and accountability systems from various perspectives. I have done everything from writing standardized test items and performance assessments to helping schools develop standards and report card systems. I have welcomed the "paradigm shift" that has occurred in the use of assessments and the more healthy and exciting approaches to classroom-based assessment. In all of this, what I have appreciated most is seeing the gap narrow between school-based educators and the so-called assessment experts. As teachers and administrators have participated in the scoring of performance tasks, on committees developing content and performance standards, and in "accountability dialogues" that are becoming fashionable, they have developed a much greater understanding of the usefulness of quality data about their students' learning.

Teacher Knows Best: The Importance of Teacher Involvement

Teachers are the ones who must take children's learning most seriously. Teachers have the best firsthand (often intuitive) knowledge about how children learn, what motivates them, how they show what they know, and what information they need to keep learning. The problem is that teachers have often been "left" in their classrooms while experts or measurement specialists or testing companies decide what and how they should teach, how and when to test and assess, what the scores mean, and even what to tell parents about how the students are doing. If the press for assessment reform does nothing else, it will accomplish a great deal if the great gulf is bridged between practitioners on the front lines and assessment experts in the back offices. Teachers, administrators, experts, parents, and students must work closely together to develop accountability systems that make sense, promote learning, and support the possibility of success for all students.

Teachers should be involved in the development of standards and local assessments by participating in discussions about what it means to develop standards-based accountability systems. They should receive a great deal of professional development and guidance in selecting assessments that match instruction and are aligned to standards. They should be given the information that they need to understand how to translate scores and combine measures in order to accurately assess students' learning and give grades that satisfy their criteria for performance levels and that students feel they have earned.

A Few to "Grow On"

Here are just a few more suggestions I'd like to share for you to think about as you work toward the establishment of new grading practices in your school or district:

- Distinguish between standards-referenced and norm-referenced achievement. If scores from a norm-referenced test are included in a report, these must be differentiated from the student's performance against a set of credible content standards.
- Provide information about the level of performance and a judgment about the result in terms of expectations.
- Couch reports about the quality of a student's work in a description of the level of difficulty of the work.
- Explain the grading system to students. For younger students, explain it verbally and use concrete examples. For all students, frequently provide exemplars of student work that reveal what constitutes quality work.
- Base grades on a variety of sources. The more sources of information that are used and weighted appropriately, the more valid is the grade (Ornstein, 1994). Gather enough evidence to allow the teacher to accurately judge a student's accomplishments (Stiggins et al., 1989).
- Do *not* use a normal curve distribution as the basis for determining a grade distribution. Most classrooms contain far too few students for it to be appropriate, nor is it appropriate for standards-based systems. The reference should be to learning criteria.
- Above all, view the reporting of information about a student's learning as a lesson for everyone concerned. Use it as a regular opportunity to discuss what a child is achieving and to plan ways to support more learning and to help a child reach his or her unlimited potential.

Summary

This chapter has provided an overview of the issues associated with current grading and reporting practices. Starting with a discussion of the problem of competing paradigms—the mismatch of traditional grading practices with the move toward standards-based systems—the key issues discussed in the remaining chapters of this book have been highlighted. A brief history of grading practices is followed by a short section on purposes. There are many technical issues that must be addressed to establish grading and reporting practices that are compatible with other components of a standards-based system. The first step is often for a school or district to establish a coherent policy to guide teacher practices in assigning grades. The guidelines must define what counts in grading, how to combine scores, and how to assign grades using standards as criteria. This chapter has also provided information about reporting and suggestions for moving toward a standards-based system.

References

Austin, S., & McCann, R. (1992). *Assessment in the classroom*. New York: McGraw-Hill.

Bennett, R. E., Gottesman, R. L., Rock, D. A., & Cerullo, F. (1993). Influence of behavior perceptions and gender on teachers' judgments of students. *Journal of Educational Psychology, 85*, 347–356.

Brookhart, S. M. (1994). Teachers' grading practices: Meaning and values. *Journal of Educational Measurement, 30* (2), 123–142.

Cizek, G. J., Fitzgerald, S. M., & Rachor, R. E. (1995–96). Teachers' assessment practices: Preparation, isolation, and the kitchen sink. *Educational Assessment 3* (2), 159–177.

Daro, P. (1994). *Common standards: A common-sense approach*. Pittsburgh, PA: National Center on Education and the Economy.

Frary, R. B., Cross, L. H., & Weber, L. J. (1993, Fall). Testing and grading practices and opinions of secondary teachers of academic subjects: Implications for instruction in measurement. *Educational Measurement: Issues and Practices, 12* (3), 23–30.

Frisbie, D. A., & Waltman, K. K. (1992). Developing a personal grading plan. *Educational Measurement: Issues and Practice, 11* (13), 35–42.

Guskey, T. R. (1994). Making the grade: What benefits students? *Educational Leadership, 52* (2), 14–21.

Guskey, T. R. (1996). Introduction. In *Communicating student learning* (ASCD Yearbook). Alexandria, VA: Association for Supervision and Curriculum Development.

Hoge, R. D., & Coladarci, T. (1989). Teacher based judgments of academic achievement: A review of literature. *Review of Educational Research, 59*, 297–313.

Middleton, W. (1933). Some general trends in grading procedure. *Education 54*, (1), 5–10.

Ornstein, A. C. (1994). Grading practices and policies: An overview and some suggestions. *NASSP Bulletin, 78* (559), 55–64.

Seeley, M. M. (1994). The mismatch between assessment and grading. *Educational Leadership, 52* (2), 4–6.

Sperling, D. H. (1994). Assessment and reporting. *Educational Leadership, 52* (2), 7–13.

Starch, D., & Elliott, E. C. (1912). Reliability of the grading of high school work in English. *School Review, 20*, 442–451.

Starch, D., & Elliott, E. C. (1913). Reliability of the grading of high school work in mathematics. *School Review, 21*, 254–259.

Stiggins, R. (1988, January). Revitalizing classroom assessment: The highest instructional priority. *Phi Delta Kappan*, 363–368.

Stiggins, R. (1991). *A practical guide for developing sound grading practices*. Portland, OR: Northwest Regional Educational Laboratory.

Stiggins, R. (1997). *Student-centered classroom assessment* (2nd ed.). Upper Saddle River, NJ: Prentice-Hall.

Stiggins, R., Frisbie, D. A., & Griswold, P. A. (1989). Inside high school grading practices: Building a research agenda. *Educational Measurement: Issues and Practice, 8* (2), 5–14.

Sweedler-Brown, C. O. (1992). The effect of training on the appearance bias of holistic essay graders. *Journal of Research and Development in Education, 26* (1), 24–29.

Wiggins, G. (1994). Toward better report cards. *Educational Leadership, 52* (2), 28–37.

Wiggins, G. (1998). *Educative assessment: Designing assessments to inform and improve student performance.* San Francisco: Jossey-Bass.

Wolmut, P. (1994). *Assessment competencies for teachers: What do licensing laws demand?* Paper presented at Classroom Assessment: Key to Unlocking Student Achievement Conference, Portland, OR.

Why Do We Grade— and Should We?

Elise Trumbull

2

> *Being "graded" is a basic part of the experience of growing up in America. From the time the American child receives his first gold star for brushing his teeth until he grasps his final sheepskin, he is graded—he is evaluated and compared, sorted and classified, passed and failed, promoted and held back. . . . Yet the familiarity of grading has perhaps dulled our sensitivity to its full educational meaning.*
>
> —R. Hiner
> "The Cultural Function of Grading"

In this chapter, I discuss the usual purposes for grading and raise questions that probe beneath the surface of the traditional justifications for many of these purposes. In the process, I hope to stimulate thinking about not only the pragmatic purposes of grading but also the philosophies and cultural beliefs underlying the practice of grading. I try to answer the questions "What is the educational *meaning* of grading?" and "What are the personal and systemwide costs and benefits of grading?" The answers to these questions are not simple, and they depend to some degree on how grading is done. As Hiner (1973) observes, grading is not just a pedagogical or psychometric practice, but a cultural ritual. Behind this ritual are (often) hidden beliefs.

A common metaphor—so familiar that we hardly think of it as a metaphor—is that of grading as the social and cultural "currency" of the school "economy" (Brookhart, 1993; Himer, 1973). We speak of students' "earning" grades. In effect, they are rewards, "earned" on the basis of certain rules, such as attaining a certain number of points or participating in classroom discussion. Teachers consistently use words like *perform, work,* and *earn,* demonstrating a belief that the grade is the pay or reward a student receives for his or her performance (Brookhart, 1993). The grade as payment earned is simply one piece of a larger economic metaphor of schooling that portrays the teacher as boss and the student as worker. It is a metaphor whose usefulness has been questioned by many (Kohn, 1994; Marshall, 1988, 1990; Sessions, 1995).

Neil Postman, in his sometimes humorous, sometimes alarming book *Technopoly* (1993), suggests that a grade is a type of technology. Using a numerical or letter symbol to judge someone's behavior or intellect is really quite peculiar in a sense. He credits William Farish, a tutor at Cambridge University, with giving the first numerical grades in 1792. In a provocative statement, Postman says:

> And yet his [Farish's] idea that a quantitative value should be assigned to human thoughts was a major step toward constructing a mathematical concept of reality. If a number can be given to the quality of a thought, then a number can be given to the qualities of mercy, love, hate, beauty, creativity, intelligence, even sanity itself. When Galileo said that the language of nature is written in mathematics, he did not mean to include human feeling or accomplishment or insight. But most of us are now inclined to make these inclusions. (p. 13)

What food for thought!

Grading systems reflect a fundamental tension in American values: treating people as equals, on the one hand, and recognizing individual achievement, on the other (Hiner, 1973). To understand tensions like this that contribute to the debate over grading practices, it is helpful to recognize how such culture-based values and metaphors related to them are operating. Then we can understand why teachers are conflicted about grading purely on the basis of achievement. All students do not have equal opportunities to learn or equal aptitudes for learning, so teachers question whether it's fair to grade them all according to the same criteria.

The Purposes of Grading

The three main purposes of grading have been summarized as *giving feedback*, *motivating*, and *sorting* (Kohn, 1994). These three can be broken down into several separate but related purposes. Table 2-1 summarizes categories and subcategories of purposes, which are then discussed below. Assumptions about the purposes of grading are not always explicit. In fact, teachers, administrators, parents, and students may implicitly understand grading to address very different purposes. As will be argued elsewhere in this book, grading systems should be aligned with the stated purposes. Not all systems fit all purposes, and some purposes may conflict with each other (e.g., sorting may conflict with giving feedback to support student learning). In addition, all who are affected by grading systems have a right to understand why they are designed as they are, what purposes they are intended to serve, and what grades can be taken to mean about a student's achievement or learning profile.

Giving Feedback

Informing Parents

Parents as well as the students themselves deserve to know how students are faring in school. Without grades or some equivalent indicators of student performance,

Table 2-1. *Purposes of Grading*

Giving Feedback	Motivating	Sorting
• Inform parents • Account to community • Recognize good work • Identify unacceptable work • Promote student self-evaluation • Identify instructional gaps (feedback for teacher)	• Encourage students to improve or keep working (promote student learning) • Reward students who are doing well	• Make placement or grouping decisions • Certify competence, permit graduation, advance student to next grade • Predict future achievement

how are parents to know how students are doing? Some form of reporting student progress is clearly required. However, parents may not be getting the sort of information they expect from grades. They may believe that grades reflect achievement alone even though teachers are actually factoring in student effort and attitude as part of the grade (Pilcher, 1994). "To be meaningful, however, grades must be interpreted by all members of a school community in the same way" (Seeley, 1994, p.5).

Accounting to the Community

Schools may insist that teachers grade children because that is what the public expects. Doing away with grades would, in most communities, cause a major brouhaha. Community members would most likely feel that information was being withheld from them and they no longer had a basis on which to judge their children's success in school. This kind of response would be ironic in light of the serious limitations of most grading systems in terms of the actual information they convey. Other forms of standardized (though not necessarily traditional, norm-referenced) assessment at this point are more reliable indicators than grades (e.g., Brookhart, 1993; Hoge & Coladarci, 1989).

Bishop (1992) also argues for grades on the grounds of accountability. He favors externally graded competency assessments keyed to the secondary school curriculum, using absolute standards to define competency. His focus is really on ensuring a reliable system for making judgments about student (and presumably program) success. To Bishop's way of thinking, if the public were able to trust assessments and grades, they would be more willing to vote for higher taxes to support schools.

Recognizing Good Work

Busick (personal communication, July 12, 1998) has mentioned a purpose of grading that often goes unmentioned—to recognize good work (see also Regional Educational Laboratories, 1998). When an example of good work is held out to other students as a model, it demonstrates performance criteria. Grading may then serve the goals of letting students know what to strive for *and* motivating good students to persevere. Alternatively, grades can be used to identify an unacceptable performance.

Promoting Student Self-Evaluation

Another purpose of grades is to provide information to the students themselves for self-evaluation (and hence, presumably, for setting goals). Elbow (1986), among others, believes that the evaluation of student learning—measuring student performance and commenting on it—should eventually result in the student's ability to evaluate his or her own performance. The portfolio assessment process, often used to this end, promotes student self-evaluation skills. An essential part of the portfolio process is student reflection on performance and the use of evaluation data to set new goals. Elbow comments, "We see here that the agenda for grading reflects what seems to be the agenda in many cognitive activities: the organism must learn to make internal and autonomous an activity that originates as interaction with something outside itself" (p. 167).

However, translating teacher commentary, scores, and grades into learning goals is an inscrutable process for many students. A grade of A, B, or C on the top of a paper communicates nothing about what is good or bad about the paper. The quality of the information and how it is delivered matters. Many students will not know how to move from cursory feedback to appropriate goal setting. Initially they need teacher support to engage in the process successfully. Elbow argues that over time the appropriate use of portfolios reduces the need for grading because teachers can gradually transfer evaluation to the student. This would please educators from certain philosophical perspectives, who believe that grades and evaluation "amount to wrongful and coercive impositions on the child's intellectual autonomy" (Curren, 1995, p. 427).

Identifying Instructional Gaps and Assessing Teaching Effectiveness

Besides being a source of information for diagnosis of individual student needs, grades also provide a means to evaluate the success of a program itself. If too many students fail a course, something may well be wrong with the curriculum, instruction, or assessment (or all three). In such cases, the teacher then may be encouraged (or decide on his or her own) to make changes in the program that result in better student learning. Alternatively, particularly at the college level, "too many"[1] students' receiving high grades may imply that the program is not holding standards high enough. Pressure may be put on the instructor to raise standards, even though it is also possible that good instruction and good student performance have led to a high-end distribution of grades. Thus, grades can partially determine both who enters a program and what a program looks like in the long run.

---

[1] It is not easy to ascertain exactly what constitutes "too many" As, particularly when standards are not explicit or constant across courses of the same level and type. However, it is widely believed that grade inflation is a serious problem in postsecondary education.

Motivating

A commonly cited purpose of grades is to provide students with incentives to learn. It is argued that students will be motivated to attain good grades and avoid low grades along with their negative outcomes. There are arguments about whether grades are necessary to motivate student achievement, and some research suggests that undue emphasis on grades motivates something else—cheating (Anderman, Griesinger, & Westerfield, 1998).

Individual characteristics of students, such as age and grade level, can influence the effects of grades on motivation and on undesirable side effects like cheating (Newstead, Franklyn-Stokes, & Armstead, 1996). Several studies found that college students could be categorized as "grade-oriented" or "learning-oriented" (Janzow & Eison, 1990; Milton, Pollio, & Eison, 1986). These categories parallel those of extrinsic and intrinsic motivation, with "grade-oriented" being interpreted as an undesirable personal characteristic (Lowman, 1990; Milton et al., 1986).

Characteristics of the instructional approach can also influence student motivation and related behaviors. A mastery approach, in which learning for its own sake or mastering the task at hand is emphasized, supports the development of intrinsic motivation and puts less of a focus on extrinsic incentives like grades. If students see the primary goal of academic tasks as getting a good grade or demonstrating their ability (as opposed to learning for its own sake), they may see cheating as one way to achieve those goals (Anderman et al., 1998). I will delve further into the pros and cons of relying on grades as motivators later on in this chapter. What is obvious from even a brief examination of the research on grading and motivation is that there is not a simple and direct relationship between the two.

Sorting

Making Placement or Grouping Decisions

Grades may also be used to identify students for certain educational paths or programs, to certify that they have attained certain skills, or to group them within a classroom. Of course, grades are routinely used to make decisions about a student's readiness to pass on to the next grade level or to receive intensive remediation. Graduation depends on the attainment of passing grades. In college, qualifying for a particular major or career path may depend on maintaining a certain grade average above passing.

Predicting Future Achievement

In theory, grades can be used by parents, students, and others to analyze students' strengths and weaknesses and their promise of future success or failure. Prospective teachers and employers can likewise use grades as an index of a student's capacity, anticipating future performance on the basis of past achievement. However, this is a risky use of grades. There is not a consistent relationship between grades and later school or job success, although students, parents, and teachers believe that grades predict future achievement to some degree (Milton et al., 1986). Since there is often little quality control over grades (i.e., one teacher may grade "hard" while another grades "easy"), one might question why anyone would invest faith in them. In addition, the grade point average (GPA) is a suspect measure in that it combines grades from different disciplines and courses and reflects variation in teachers' grading methods and standards.

Some studies have shown that the high school GPA is a moderate predictor of college success—better than the Scholastic Achievement Test (SAT) or the American College Test (ACT) alone (Cowen & Fiori, 1991; Eldridge & Kim, 1996; Myers & Pyles, 1992; Noble, 1991; Nordstrom, 1989). Myers & Pyles, for example, examined the predictive validity of a composite score of high school GPA and ACT scores and found that for 420 college freshmen, this score accounted for 32% of the variance in freshman year GPA. Most of these studies looked at college grades as the index of success. Kanarek (1989), however, looked at graduation as a measure of success. Her study of five-year graduation rates revealed that both the SAT and high school rank (not equivalent to GPA but related to it) were poor predictors of graduation.

Despite a fairly consistent positive relationship between high school GPA and college grades, however, the predictive power of high school grades is only moderate at best. And although GPA is often factored into admissions decisions to counteract the lower predictive validity of standardized tests, particularly for minority candidates, this by no means solves the problem (Cole & Moss, 1989; Myers & Pyles, 1992; Rodriguez, 1996; Sue & Abe, 1988). The complexity of the relationships among grades, achievement motivation and other affective factors, ethnic identity, primary language, opportunity to learn, and subject area makes it almost impossible to make definitive statements about why grades seem to be predictive at some times and not at others. Rodriguez found that high school grades and rank and college admissions test scores were better predictors for Whites than for Mexican Americans, whereas academic self-concept and major field had important influences on Mexican Americans' achievement. Sue and Abe found that high school GPA was moderately predictive of university freshman grades for both Asian Americans and Whites. However, GPA tended to underpredict the achievement of those Asian Americans who said that English was not their best language and overpredict the achievement of those who said English was their best language.

GPA and other traditional measures are less successful as sole predictors of the achievement of high-risk students as well. Goolsby, Dwinell, Higbee, and Bretscher (1987) studied a sample of freshmen at a southern university who had been admitted conditionally because they did not meet admission requirements. The final grades of these students in a developmental algebra course *were* related to high school GPA and the SAT quantitative score. However, a combined measure that reflected student level of confidence and mathematics anxiety was also a significant predictor of course grade. Larose & Roy (1991) evaluated the role of prior academic performance and nonacademic attributes in the success of 173 high-risk college students. They found that personal characteristics such as fear of failure and examination anxiety were more reliable predictors than "academic potential." Similarly, Cowen & Fiori (1991) found that while the SAT and high school GPA had some combined predictive ability for freshman achievement, they were much less predictive of the achievement of more slowly progressing students. These few examples suggest how difficult it is to generalize about the value of grades as predictors of later school success.

A related purpose of grading is "certification or assurance that a student has mastered specific content or achieved a certain level of accomplishment" (Ornstein (1994, p. 56). In the context of an actual certification process, where grades are clearly based on explicit performance criteria, they may indeed serve as a more reliable predictor of future performance. For example, in a high school health course that is part of the preparation for a career as a nurse assistant, a student may have to demonstrate actual mastery of techniques for taking vital signs or administering first aid. A grade based on proficiency with the exact criterion skills that will be called upon in a future job is likely to be a more reliable index of success in that job than a grade that is based on performances less related to later job requirements.

Grading and Assessment: Getting in Sync

We have had a virtual revolution in assessment practices in the past decade. Yet, by all accounts, grading practices are only slowly evolving. Sometimes grading systems that are already in place actually subvert the good intentions of reformed assessment systems. For example, a state or district may adopt performance assessments that reveal more than the traditional multiple-choice assessments about students' learning, and it may employ scoring systems that rate students on several different aspects of performance. If writing is evaluated according to subdomains like "content/ideas," "cohesion/structure," and "mechanics," then to reduce scores on these three scales to a single grade is to obscure important performance differences. These distinctions may be useful for students, parents, and teachers in the process of setting goals for improvement.

If good assessment helps to reveal students' capabilities, it is undesirable to use grading systems that *obscure* students' true capabilities or give a reductionist representation of them. If good assessment encourages students to reflect on and evaluate their own progress and learning, then grading systems that provide no meaningful information for such reflection should be avoided. If good assessment emphasizes what is important, then grading systems should employ a thoughtful weighting process, so that less important aspects of learning are not given undue weight (see chapters 3 and 4).

It could be argued that grading is not necessary, that it is perfectly feasible to assess students, give them and their parents feedback on their progress, and target plans for instruction and learning without ever assigning a grade (Guskey, 1996). In this view, grades are simply an inadequate shorthand for describing a student's level of achievement vis-à-vis expectations. Kohn (1994) has taken this position. He suggests that "What grades offer is spurious precision, a subjective rating masquerading as an objective assessment" (p. 38). Most educators would acknowledge that there is considerable truth to Kohn's criticism. At the same time, it is unlikely that school districts will be involved in the wholesale elimination of grading systems. Instead, they may now find themselves in the position of trying to bring grading systems in line with standards-based curriculum, instruction, and assessment. In an ideal world, they would also be seeking ways to make grading systems equitable and "instructionally valid" (Newmann, 1991)—leading to improved instruction. Let us, then, look at the longstanding criticisms of grading practices with a view to reforming them rather than rejecting them entirely.

The Issue of Grades as Motivators

Perhaps the most controversial purpose of grading is that of motivating student achievement. It is widely assumed that grades are motivators for learning. This assumption is worth examining thoroughly, because it drives a lot of practice. Many teachers and parents believe that a grade is a motivator for good performance, and there is some research evidence to suggest that this is true. When teachers grade students on the basis of effort and performance, grades *can* be motivating (Brookhart, 1993; Natriello & Dornbusch, 1984). There may be differences by age group, however. Compared to the Brookhart study, which involved K–12 students, a study by Goulden and Griffin (1995) suggested that college students and their professors might give less weight to the role of grades as motivators. Only 6% of student responses and 10% of professor responses to the statement, "Grades are like ____" resulted in answers such as "rewards," "punishments," "carrots," or "sticks." Much more often these respondents mentioned that grades served to measure, sort, or communicate a judgment about student performance.

Students may also be motivated by expectations of other kinds of rewards contingent on their grades, such as money, parental approval, or social privileges. Down the line grades may, of course, contribute to college or graduate school admission—a fact that might motivate some students. However, grades can motivate undesired behaviors unrelated to learning, such as cheating (Anderman et al., 1998) or cause some students to focus on their grade point average almost to the exclusion of any concern for what they are actually learning (Becker, Greer, & Hughes, 1968; Milton et al., 1986; Placier, 1995).

Grading practices by teachers and use of grades by parents to control students' behaviors may encourage students to "learn for the purpose of receiving rewards or avoiding punishment" (Pilcher, 1994, p. 86). Some students—even naturally good students—might resist what they perceive to be a manipulative game, and grading may have the opposite of its desired effect. Such students may balk at completing assignments or studying for tests. In short, when grades are used to control or coerce students, they can have negative effects (Deci & Ryan, 1985; Pilcher, 1994). Pilcher asks, "Are grading practices and the interpretation and use of grades producing detrimental effects on student learning?" (p.87). The Pilcher study suggests that in their current and recommended states, grades are more harmful than beneficial to student learning because "Using grades to control student behaviors does not teach students to value learning."

Critics say that students do not need grades to motivate them to learn. If the curriculum is interesting and the instruction is good, the experience of learning should be motivating in itself (Kirschenbaum, Napier, & Simon, 1971; Kohn, 1994). For those students for whom grades are not the least bit motivating, who are just biding their time until they can get out of school, we might want to examine the possibilities for other sources of motivation. We could try to align curriculum with students' interests (as suggested above), make the targets of learning much clearer so that students would know when they were succeeding, and explicitly teach them to judge their own success (Stiggins, 1997).

Intrinsic and Extrinsic Motivation

Researchers have long been interested in the relationship between intrinsic motivation (the inclination to engage in an activity for its own sake) and extrinsic motivation (the desire to escape a punishment or get a reward). Some research suggests that reliance on an extrinsic motivator actually reduces engagement in learning (Deci & Ryan, 1985; Kohn, 1993; Lepper, 1981; Lepper, Greene, & Nisbett, 1973). In one study, children who were told that they would be graded on solving anagrams chose simpler ones and seemed to take less satisfaction in completing them than those who were not being graded (Harter, 1978). It is as if the reward got in the way.

The research on the value of extrinsic rewards, of which grades are only one example, is equivocal. Educators who believe that extrinsic rewards foster learning can find support for their position, as can educators who believe that extrinsic rewards decrease intrinsic motivation to learn. Cameron and Pierce (1994), in a meta-analysis of 96 experimental studies, concluded that "overall reward does not decrease intrinsic motivation. . . . [F]indings show that verbal praise produces an increase in intrinsic motivation. The only negative effect appears when expected tangible rewards are given to individuals simply for doing a task" (p. 363). Written positive feedback from an instructor is also, apparently, not damaging to intrinsic motivation. Natriello and McDill (1986) noted, "When the teacher takes the time to write encouraging and constructive comments on homework or other student papers, it has positive measurable effects on achievement" (cited in Ornstein, 1994, p. 57). Kohn (1996) notes, "Purely informational feedback about one's performance would not be *expected* to reduce subsequent intrinsic motivation . . ." (p. 1), nor would legitimate verbal praise for a job well done. Such verbal praise and positive feedback seem to operate differently from other kinds of extrinsic rewards or reinforcers: "When they are given and later removed, people continue to show intrinsic interest in their work" (Cameron & Pierce, 1994, p. 397).

Negative Effects of Extrinsic Rewards and Grades

Numerous studies have shown that extrinsic rewards decrease intrinsic motivation (as measured by performance, willingness to spend free time on a task, and/or attitude toward the task). The strongest conclusion that Cameron and Pierce were able to make based on their meta-analysis was that extrinsic reward *does not necessarily decrease* intrinsic motivation. While none of the experimental studies used grades as a reward, and only about half involved children or adolescents, some inferences may be drawn from them. It appears that extrinsic rewards can have a damaging effect when offered without respect to whether specific performance criteria are met. Reaping an external reward for just putting in one's time on a task may lower intrinsic motivation to engage in that task. Rewards should probably be made contingent on the *successful* completion of a task (Cameron & Pierce, 1994). In this context, a reward is a piece of information about one's competence. Teachers who reward children simply for completing a task, regardless of *how* it is completed, may want to reconsider the wisdom of that approach.

Of course, it is only high grades that can be considered a reward. Poor grades most often merely add insult to injury for many students who have difficulty learning. Moreover, fear of a low grade may have the undesired effect of causing some students to avoid difficult coursework at the high school or college level. In anticipation of future benefits of good grades for college admission or employment, they may select teachers or courses that will virtually ensure high grades for themselves. Another dampening effect on motivation relates to good students: Grades may actually lower the achievement ceiling for high-performing students who get As easily and might not see the point of challenging themselves further (Brookhart, 1991; Kohn, 1994; see also Waters, chapter 5).

Motivation is a function of many factors, including interest in a task or content area, past success or failure with similar tasks, support available to take on a task that is perceived as difficult, perceived value of the task, instructional emphasis on learning versus public performance, and one's mood or level of energy. Conclusions about how grades may motivate individual students in any particular circumstance must be made on the basis of information about all of these factors.

Confusing the Grade With the Person

One invidious consequence of grading is the confusion of the label with the person. It is not uncommon to hear a teacher say, "He's a C student." A secondary effect of such labeling is that it suggests a permanence to the condition. Even a student who habitually receives Cs on his or her tests and assignments should not be eternally consigned to the ranks of mediocrity. Every teacher and every parent knows of a child who (perhaps without the benefit of increased adult expectations) somehow discovered that he or she could excel in some academic area late in the school career.

Moving Beyond Extrinsic Rewards

It is worthwhile to consider to what degree grades might motivate students to persevere in school. If grades do indeed move some students away from engagement in learning rather than toward it, that is a very serious negative outcome. If schools want to promote "lifelong learning" (as so many mission statements proclaim), they cannot afford to perpetuate practices that actually discourage learning. Related research on "flow" sheds light on the importance of intrinsic motivation to learning and points out how great the loss is to individuals when they are not able to tap intrinsic motivation to achieve optimal learning experiences. *Flow* has been described as "a state in which people are so involved in an activity that nothing else seems to matter" (Csikszentmihalyi, 1991, p. 4)—the state people get in when they are having an optimal learning experience. Flow is experienced by students when they get so involved in solving a problem that time seems to stand still, or when their capabilities just meet the challenge of an experience. An essential part of achieving flow, especially in any sustained way, is the ability to free oneself from society's rewards and find rewards in the events of each moment. People in flow describe their goal as perfecting their own skills and competing against themselves rather than something outside. Feedback about how well they are doing is critical. "There is nothing wrong with helping students to internalize and work toward meeting high standards, but that is most likely to happen when 'they experience success and failure not as reward and punishment but as information'" (Kohn, 1994, p. 39, citing Bruner, 1961, p. 26)—that is, as immediately useful feedback.

All of this reflection on what creates motivation to learn or perform, on flow, and on optimal learning experiences is relevant to our discussion of grading practices. If these kinds of experiences depend on one's ability to take risks and move beyond external rewards to a more autonomous relationship to learning and developing, then practices that perpetuate a dependence on extrinsic motivation should be kept to a minimum.

Grading this reform, like most other reforms, is easier to implement from the beginning, with younger students. If grades are abolished, students who are accustomed to relying on them may not automatically begin to draw upon intrinsic motivation. In a humorous and provocative article titled "Zen and the Art of Grade Motivation," high school English teacher Liz Mandrell (1997) recounts her own experiment in dispensing with grades. After six weeks without grading, during which she observed steadily decreasing student productivity, she concluded, "Somewhere in a parallel universe I'm sure grades are abolished, but here on Planet Earth, I will continue to award grades." It may also be that for her English course to succeed in gradeless form, Mandrell would have had to revise her approach to curriculum, instruction, and assessment. Grading is just one piece of the puzzle.

Ethical Considerations in Grading

Ethical issues and "consequential validity" issues in grading need to be considered as well. A grade labels a student, and decisions are made on the basis of grades. If a grade is not reliable—that is, if it is not based on clear criteria and justified by adequate evidence regarding performance—then it is not ethical to have that grade influence a student's life outcomes. Teachers or others who are judging the student for the purposes of placement or future opportunities may draw false conclusions. A summative label—that is, an end-of-course grade—seems to be more potentially damaging than a profile or narrative keyed to a set of standards showing how a student "stacks up" against different sets of expectations. Numerous recent journal articles call into question current grading practices and suggest that they may be more harmful than helpful, partly on ethical grounds (Cizek, 1996; Elbow, 1996; Friedman, 1996; Krumboltz & Yeh, 1996).

Elbow (1986) and Wiggins (1996) believe that when multiple grades are used, instead of a single summative grade that collapses judgments across many domains (e.g., effort, attitude, progress, achievement), there is less risk of unfair and simplistic characterizations of students. "Using a *single* grade with no clear and stable meaning to summarize all aspects of performance *is* a problem" (Wiggins, 1994, p. 29). Wiggins calls single grades a "disincentive." However, they are not only a disincentive to participation or performance. One may well ask whether it is ethical to use an indefensible and unstable measure of student learning, given the potential for ongoing detrimental effects on students' lives.

One practice that has come into question is the ranking of students by GPA. To put it simply, ranking has no sensible place in a standards-based system. One absurd consequence of ranking is that students with minutely different GPAs are differentiated from each other (e.g., for the purpose of determining eligibility for some honor) when in effect their achievement has been virtually equivalent. Small, meaningless differences are magnified. Furthermore, the assigned ranks are suspect because of the lack of measurement soundness in most grading systems. Competitive grading, in which students are graded relative to each other (grading "on the curve") and not against an absolute standard, is the most destructive grading approach. Many believe that this kind of grading subverts the purpose of evaluating students to promote learning (Kohn, 1994; Krumboltz & Yeh, 1996; Wiggins, 1996) and can, in effect, turn teachers into students' opponents (Krumboltz & Yeh, 1996).

Subjectivity of Grading

No matter what method is used to grade, a great deal of subjectivity is involved. Elbow (1986) complains that "the present system . . . gives official sanction to whatever category [grading component or criterion] blows across the fancy of every teacher, without the slightest need to make it conscious or articulate, much less justify it" (p. 175). Teacher-made tests do not always adequately reflect the curriculum that has been taught, nor are they always constructed to weight the most important concepts or skills most heavily in scoring (Ornstein, 1994). The same problems prevail now as were highlighted nearly 90 years ago in the conclusion of a study of 11 high school English teachers' grading practices. Starch and Elliott (1912) observed that "it may be easily reasoned that the promotion or retardation of a pupil depends to a considerable extent upon the subjective estimate of his teacher" (p. 454). Their research showed a wide variation in how teachers graded the same papers, with the poorest papers having the greatest variability in grading.

Another problem is that even when behavior and effort are judged according to a separate scale from achievement, teachers' judgments of achievement may still be colored by students' behavior (Bennett, Gottesman, Rock, & Cerullo, 1993). Research results bolster the claim that teachers' judgments must be supplemented with other, objective evidence of academic performance when important decisions are going to be made. Another implication is that teachers need to be made more aware of this pitfall. Otherwise, the purpose of getting good information for decision making is defeated.

Even when there is agreement on the dimensions on which to grade students, teachers may apply different criteria for what counts as a good performance. Looking at the same piece of writing, some may judge a student to have "communicated ideas persuasively," while others may decide that the student has not met their performance criteria. Perhaps even more often, teachers use different standards entirely: One counts effort, while another doesn't; one counts neatness and format—or even spelling—while another thinks that those aspects of a performance are irrelevant. As Elbow (1986) warns, the meaning of grades is further complicated by the fact that the same teacher is likely to weight certain components more heavily, depending on the location of the student on the grade continuum. For example, teachers who incorporate effort in their evaluations often weight it more heavily for low-performing students.

Philosophical Alignment

Schools need to examine their reasons for grading before choosing a method, if they are going to grade. Such a decision-making process requires identifying beliefs about teaching and learning to ensure that grading practices are aligned with professed philosophies and ultimate educational objectives. As Stiggins, Frisbie, & Griswold (1989) say, "A teacher's judgment about the grading approach to be used should be dictated by the broader educational values (particularly the theory of teaching) that he or she holds" (p. 11). All of us who are in a position to make such choices need to be willing to question fundamental assumptions about how and why we grade. We may want to go beyond merely shoring up existing systems. We may well ask *why* we are evaluating students versus *how* (Kohn, 1994). We may want to ask the question "Should we grade?" And if the answer is yes, "What systems are compatible with our philosophy and the outcomes we want to drive?"

Tensions in Grading Practices

The tensions in grading are numerous (see Figure 2-1), and we have alluded to some of them. One is the tension between the desire for simple reporting systems and the need for more complex depictions of students. Sometimes this tension is resolved by using a single grade symbol; at other times multiple scales and narratives are used to convey a more thorough picture of student learning. Another tension lies between the belief that a grade should represent only achievement and the belief that it should represent growth and other factors as well; in a sense, the

Figure 2-1. *Tensions in Grading*

←	→
single symbol/indicator (keep it simple)	multiple scales, narratives (reflect complexity of performance)
judge achievement (recognize individual achievement)	judge achievement plus growth, effort, etc. (promote equality)
grade student against self (recognize progress)	grade student against benchmarks (compare to absolute standards)
grade selectively (allow for development before judging)	grade as much as possible (maximize data)
teacher as judge (uphold standards)	teacher as advocate (support students)

tension between equality and equity is part of this one (see chapter 7). A tension that we have scarcely touched on is between the need for adequate data to make a judgment about a student and the desire to keep grading to a minimum. Not every student performance has to be graded, especially those that are elicited while students are acquiring a skill (Stiggins, 1997; Stiggins et al., 1989).

The Tension in Teachers' Roles

Now we turn to a more personal tension, one that teachers face as they try to be both *judges of* and *advocates for* their students. On the one hand, they must maintain standards (explicit or not) related to the subject matter and the skills they teach. On the other hand, they need to nurture and protect students as they attempt to master the curriculum. Elbow (1986) frames the two poles as an obligation to knowledge and society (which has an interest in having educated citizens) and an obligation to students:

> Our loyalty to students asks us to be their allies and hosts as we instruct and share: to invite all students to enter in and join us as members of a learning community—even if they have difficulty. . . . Our commitment to knowledge and society asks us to be guardians or bouncers: we must discriminate, evaluate, test, grade, certify. (p. 143)

Bishop (1992) notes that in a court of law, a judge must disqualify him- or herself if a friend comes before the court. Yet teachers are friends to their students (or can be) and, in the tension of being judge and advocate, may lower standards or expectations or hide a "student's failure with charitable phrases" (p. 17). At other times, teachers "choose to hold students to high standards but sacrifice close supportive relationships with them."

Somehow teachers need to find a middle ground between these two roles that does not compromise either one. They must encourage and accept while holding students to high standards. Good teachers manage this apparent paradox, although some may tend to be more obviously student advocates (perceived as "soft" teachers), and others may tend toward emphasizing loyalty to subject matter and standards (perceived as "hard" teachers). Perhaps it is this tension that results in teachers' failure to follow the dictates of their measurement courses and focus on achievement data alone (Brookhart, 1991; Pilcher, 1994; Stiggins et al., 1989). Instead we see teachers giving students credit for their effort, making allowances for variations in perceived student ability, and providing opportunities to gain extra credit to pull up low grades. However, in a standards-based accountability system, achievement alone should be the basis of grades. If behavior or effort is to be rated, it should be reported separately.

A study of classroom pupil evaluation involving student teachers and their cooperating teachers found, "Neither cooperating teachers nor student teachers articulated clear criteria for the evaluation of pupil progress. Instead, a pervasive and unresolved conflict was evident between evaluation on the basis of performance and evaluation on the basis of effort" (Barnes, 1985, p. 48). Teachers were uncomfortable giving bad grades; they didn't want to make students feel bad. Teachers often seemed to struggle to balance "district demands for grading with pupil needs for affirmation and guidance." Barnes observes that the same discomfort, difficulties, and dilemmas associated with student evaluation have previously been documented with regard to adult (teacher) evaluation.

Teachers can be saved to some degree from what Elbow (1986) calls these "conflicting mentalities" (p. 151) by having the assessment process conducted or complemented by outside evaluators. This is the case in some European systems and in numerous certification and licensing processes in the United States. Another solution is to have teachers alternate between roles, making it clear when they are taking on each one. External assessment (e.g., outside review boards, commissions, and exhibition panels) can help teachers to take on the role of mentor or coach rather than that of judge. In a sense, a standards-based approach to grading can support a similar relationship. When the grounds for judgment are made explicit and external, rather than implicit and personal (in the teacher's mind and heart), the teacher can coach students toward desired performance levels. The capriciousness is taken out of the process, and students can begin to take over the responsibility for judging themselves against these known standards. This point of view is supported by Barnes (1985). In this study, teachers who did not experience the same conflicts in grading were associated with a mastery learning approach in which student progress was assessed against very specific goals and criteria. Barnes observes that student awareness of the system seemed to eliminate some of the tension surrounding grading.

If Grading Is a Given, What Can We Do to Improve It?

Explicit Standards and Criteria

Teachers can make grading and the whole evaluation process fairer, more reliable, and less stressful by getting criteria out in the open, in terms of what students are expected to know and be able to do as well as what a good performance looks like. Standards should be in writing for the benefit of students, parents, and teachers alike. Furthermore, students can be shown examples of papers or other products that represent different levels of performance, and teachers can explain why they assigned the grades they did. When learning targets are clear, students themselves can participate actively in the assessment process (Stiggins, 1997).

Selective Grading

A grade does not have to be assigned to every piece of work. This is not to say that a teacher should suspend assessing students regularly on the basis of standards. Teachers can put substantive commentary on assignments rather than grades. If students are concerned about their grades, a teacher can let them know where they stand by giving them the probable course grade they would get if graded on that day (Kohn, 1994). If students have not mastered something but are still honing a skill, a teacher can wait to grade them. When assignments are part of formative assessment (as distinct from summative assessment, at the end of a learning period), they should not be part of grades (Stiggins et al., 1989). Teachers might want to give students practice tests as a way of letting students gauge for themselves what they still need to learn. This approach is in line with a separation between formative and summative evaluation. Formative evaluation (giving feedback without grading, in this instance) can help students to concentrate on learning (Reedy, 1995).

When teachers give an ungraded exam or offer commentary on a paper without grading it, they are taking on the role of ally to students and at the same time pointing them to standards (Elbow, 1986). Elbow likens the use of the practice test to the teacher's taking the role of coach. It is a chance to "role-play the enemy in a supportive setting," he says (p. 156).

Multiple Graders

A recommendation for increasing the reliability of grades is to have more than one teacher grade any important assessment or performance, particularly if it contributes heavily to decisions about program placement, graduation, or grade promotion. This "moderation" process is used frequently in other countries and has been very successful in ensuring the reliability of formal assessments, such as those used for accountability purposes. It is not always possible to arrange for multiple graders, however, so a substitute for the moderation process is for teachers to monitor their own thinking and judgments more consciously while grading. It has been shown that when teachers engage in such self-monitoring, they make more accurate and reliable judgments (Elbow, 1986).

Multiple Measures

When the term "multiple measures" is used, it can refer either to the use of more than one assessment of the same kind (e.g., two writing samples) or to more than one type of assessment to examine the same kind of knowledge or skill.[2] Using multiple measures in both senses of the term increases the likelihood of a fair judgment of student learning. Multiple measures are particularly important for judging the learning of English language learners (see chapters 6 and 7).

Noncompetitive Grading

It is difficult to find a grading theorist who believes that teachers should force grades to conform to a "normal curve" distribution. Most think that the "normal curve" should be a symbol of teaching failure. It is argued that this kind of grading can easily lead to poor teaching, because it virtually requires that some students do poorly and "encourages methods of evaluation that misdirect and inhibit student learning" (Krumboltz & Yeh, 1996, p. 324). Most writers on this topic believe that the number of good grades should not be artificially limited so that one student's success makes another's less likely. The philosophical and measurement arguments against this practice are taken up in chapter 3.

---

[2] The term has also been used to refer to separate measures of language and achievement in the case of English language learners, where the two are easily confounded.

Attention to Quality of Curriculum and Instruction

Quality of curriculum and instruction deserves more attention than any assessment or grading system. When students have interesting things to learn, they do not need their motivation boosted artificially by outside rewards such as grades. "Improvement is not something we require of students so much as something that follows when we provide them with engaging tasks and a supportive environment" (Kohn, 1994, p. 40). Kohn takes a learner-centered stance toward education. He views education less as an investment in future workers than as a way to stimulate students' natural inclination to explore the unfamiliar, to construct meaning, and to develop various kinds of competence. One might even dare to hope for flow and optimal learning in this context.

Emphasis on Developing Self-Assessment Skills

An ultimate goal of good assessment (and grading) is for students to become more proficient at judging their own work—something that could result in less grading by teachers. Teachers have devised numerous strategies to encourage students to develop such skill in judgment. One is to have younger students translate standards and scoring rubrics into their own language, so that they have a clearer idea of what they are aiming for. Another is to have students review assessment items they missed or scored poorly on, explaining why they chose a wrong answer (multiple choice) or responded (on an open-ended item) as they did (Placier, 1995). Teachers can gain insights into students' thinking and then use those insights to facilitate students' own analyses of their learning. Somehow students need to become partners in the enterprise and not just objects of it.

As idealistic as it may sound to hold out the expectation that students become judges of their own learning, it is the logical extension of the expectation that students become self-directed, autonomous, lifelong learners. Before they get to this point, however, they need the guidance of experts (teachers) who can help them to understand recognized standards within various disciplines. Perhaps later they can contribute to refining those standards or adding new ones themselves.

Summary

Schools and teachers have many purposes for grading, most of which fall within the three major domains of *giving feedback*, *motivating*, and *sorting*. However, many of the assumptions that teachers hold about grading remain tacit and unexamined. Grading practices should be evaluated in light of the philosophy of learning that a school or district espouses and the goals it has for students. For instance, if a district has embraced standards-based education, it will find that sorting and ranking students according to grades is in conflict with the assumptions of that approach.

Other conflicts may be identified. For example, honest feedback about a student's poor performance may be more demoralizing than motivating. Motivation is one of the most complex issues in the beliefs and practices surrounding grading and has to be addressed thoughtfully—most crucially with regard to how to motivate less successful students.

Open, informed discussion about grading practices is necessary if teachers are to deal with the traditional tensions inherent in grading. Among these are the tensions between:

- Use of a single summative grade or of multiple indicators
- Grading for achievement or achievement plus growth and effort
- Grading a student against objective standards versus his or her own progress
- Collecting a large amount of data versus collecting selective smaller amounts
- The teacher's being judge and advocate in relation to the student

A clear, theoretical, and research-grounded philosophy of teaching and learning will help to resolve these tensions.

For districts that have taken a standards-based approach to education and want to bring their grading practices in line with that approach, the following general practices are recommended:

- Selective grading
- Multiple graders (on at least some occasions)
- Multiple measures
- Noncompetitive grading
- Attention to high-quality curriculum and instruction (and assessment)
- Emphasis on students' acquiring self-assessment skills

References

Anderman, E. M., Griesinger, M. S., & Westerfield, G. (1998). Motivation and cheating during early adolescence. *Journal of Educational Psychology, 90* (1), 84–93.

Barnes, S. (1985). A study of classroom pupil evaluation: The missing link in teacher education. *Journal of Teacher Education, 36* (4), 46–49.

Becker, H., Greer, B., & Hughes, E. (1968). *Making the grade: The academic side of college life.* New York:Wiley.

Bennett, R. E., Gottesman, R. L., Rock, D. A., & Cerullo, F. (1993). Influence of behavior perceptions and gender on teachers' judgments of students' academic skill. *Journal of Educational Psychology, 85,* 347–356.

Bishop, J. H. (1992). Why U.S. students need incentives to learn. *Educational Leadership, 49* (6), 15–18.

Brookhart, S. (1991). Letter: Grading practices and validity. *Educational Measurement: Issues and Practice, 10* (1), 35–36.

Brookhart, S. (1993). Teachers' grading practices: Meaning and values. *Journal of Educational Measurement 30* (2), 123–142.

Bruner, J. S. (1961). The act of discovery. *Harvard Educational Review 31,* 21–32.

Cameron, J., & Pierce, W. D. (1994). Reinforcement, reward, and intrinsic motivation: A meta-analysis. *Review of Educational Research, 64* (3), 363–423.

Cizek, G. L. (1996). Grades: The final frontier in assessment reform. *NASSP Bulletin, 80* (584), 103.

Cole, N. S., & Moss, P. A. (1989). Bias in test use. In R. L. Linn (Ed.), *Educational measurement* (3rd ed., pp. 201–219). New York: American Council on Education, Macmillan.

Cowen, S., & Fiori, S. J. (1991, November). *Appropriateness of the SAT in selecting students for admission to California State University, Hayward.* Paper presented at the annual meeting of the California Educational Research Association, San Diego.

Csikszentmihalyi, M. (1991). *Flow: The psychology of optimal experience.* New York: HarperPerennial.

Curren, R. R. (1995). Coercion and the ethics of grading and testing. *Educational Theory, 45* (4), 25–41.

Deci, E. L., & Ryan, R. M. (1985). *Intrinsic motivation and self-determination in human behavior.* New York: Plenum.

Elbow, P. (1986). *Embracing contraries: Explorations in learning and teaching.* New York: Oxford University Press.

Elbow, P. (1996). Grading student writing: Making it simpler, fairer, clearer. *New Directions for Teaching and Learning, 69*, 127–140.

Eldridge, H., & Kim, J. K. (1996). *Latent structure of academic performance among college students.* (Report No. TM026346). (ERIC Document Reproduction Service No. ED 406 421).

Friedman, S. J. (1996, September/October). Who needs to know that Andy got a D? *The Clearing House, 70* (1), 10–12.

Goolsby, C. B., Dwinell, P. L., Higbee, J. L., & Bretscher, A. S. (1987, April). *Factors affecting mathematics achievement in high risk college students.* Paper presented at the annual meeting of the American Educational Research Association, Washington, DC.

Goulden, N. R., & Griffin, C. J. G. (1995). The meaning of grades based on faculty and student metaphors. *Communication Education, 44* (2), 110–125.

Guskey, T. (1996). Introduction. In *Communicating student learning* (ASCD Yearbook, pp.1–5). Alexandria, VA: Association for Supervision and Curriculum Development.

Harter, S. (1978). Pleasure derived from challenge and the effects of receiving grades on children's difficulty level choices. *Child Development, 49*, 788–799.

Hiner, R. (1973). The cultural function of grading. *Clearing House, 47 (6)*, 356–361.

Hoge, R. D., & Coladarci, T. (1989). Teacher-based judgments of academic achievement: A review of literature. *Review of Educational Research, 59*, 297–313.

Janzow, F., & Eison, J. (1990). Grades: Their influence on students and faculty. In M. D. Svinicki (Ed.), *New directions for teaching and learning: Vol. 42. The changing face of college teaching* (pp. 93–102). San Francisco: Jossey-Bass.

Kanarek, E. A. (1989, April/May). *Exploring the murky world of admissions predictions.* Paper presented at the annual forum of the Association for Institutional Research, Baltimore.

Kirschenbaum, H. R., Napier, W., & Simon, S. B. (1971). *Wad-ja-get?: The grading game in American education.* New York: Hart.

Kohn, A. (1993). *Punished by rewards*. Boston: Houghton Mifflin.

Kohn, A. (1994). Grading: The issue is not how but why. *Educational Leadership, 52* (2), 38–41.

Kohn, A. (1996). By all available means: Cameron and Pierce's defense of extrinsic motivators. *Review of Educational Research 66* (1), 1–4.

Krumboltz, J. D., & Yeh, C. J. (1996, December). Competitive grading sabotages good teaching. *Phi Delta Kappan, 8* (4), 324–326.

Larose, S., & Roy, R. (1991). The role of prior academic performance and nonacademic attributes in the prediction of the success of high-risk college students. *Journal of College Student Development, 32* (2), 171–177.

Lepper, M. R. (1981). Intrinsic and extrinsic motivation in children: Detrimental effects of superfluous social controls. In W. A. Collins (Ed.), *Minnesota symposium on child psychology* (Vol. 14, pp. 155–214). Hillsdale, NJ: Erlbaum.

Lepper, M. R., Greene, D., & Nisbett, R. E. (1973). Undermining children's intrinsic interest with external rewards: A test of the "overjustification" hypothesis. *Journal of Personality and Social Psychology, 28,* 129–137.

Lowman, J. (1990). Promoting motivation and learning. *College Teaching, 38* (4), 136–139.

Mandrell, L. (1997, January). Zen and the art of grade motivation. *English Journal, 86* (1), 28–30.

Marshall, H. H. (1988). Work or learning: Implications of classroom metaphors. *Educational Researcher, 17,* 9–16.

Marshall, H. H. (1990). Beyond the workplace metaphor: The classroom as a learning setting. *Theory Into Practice, 29,* 94–101.

Milton, O., Pollio, H. R., & Eison, J. A. (1986). *Making sense of college grades*. San Francisco: Jossey-Bass.

Myers, R. S., & Pyles, M. R. (1992, November). *Relationships among high school grades, ACT test scores, and college grades*. Paper presented at the annual meeting of the Mid-South Educational Research Association, Knoxville, TN.

Natriello, G., & Dornbusch, S. M. (1984). *Teacher evaluation standards and student effort*. New York: Longman.

Natriello, G., & McDill, E. L. (1986). Performance standards, student effort on homework, and academic achievement. *Sociology of Education, 59* (1), 18–31.

Newmann, F. M. (1991, February). Linking restructuring to authentic student achievement, *Phi Delta Kappan, 72* (6), 458–463.

Newstead, S. E., Franklin-Stokes, A., & Armstead, P. (1996). Individual differences in student cheating. *Journal of Educational Psychology, 88,* 229–241.

Noble, J. P. (1991). *Predicting college grades from ACT assessment scores and high school course work and grade information* (American College Testing Research Report Series). Iowa City, IA: American College Testing Program.

Nordstrom, B. H. (1990, April). *Predicting performance in freshman chemistry*. Paper presented at the national meeting of the American Chemical Society, Boston.

Ornstein, A. C. (1994). Grading practices and policies: An overview and some suggestions. *NASSP Bulletin, 78* (559), 55–64.

Pilcher, J. K. (1994). The value-driven meaning of grades. *Educational Assessment, 2* (1), 69–88.

Placier, M. (1995). "But I have to have an A": Probing the cultural meanings and ethical dilemmas of grades in teacher education. *Teacher Education Quarterly, 22* (3), 45–63.

Postman, N. (1993). *Technopoly: The surrender of culture to technology.* New York: Vintage Books.

Reedy, R. (1995). Formative and summative assessment: A possible alternative to the grading-reporting dilemma. *NASSP Bulletin, 79* (573), 47–51.

Regional Educational Laboratories. (1998). *Improving classroom assessments: A toolkit for professional developers.* Portland, OR: Northwest Regional Educational Laboratory.

Rodriguez, N. (1996). Predicting the academic success of Mexican American and White college students. *Hispanic Journal of Behavioral Sciences, 18* (3), 329–342.

Seeley, M. M. (1994). The mismatch between assessment and grading. *Educational Leadership, 52* (2), 4–6.

Sessions, R. (1995, November). *Education is a gift, not a commodity.* Paper presented at the national conference of the Community Colleges Humanities Association, Washington, DC.

Starch, D., & Elliott, E. C. (1912). Reliability of the grading of high-school work in English. *School Review, 20,* 442–457.

Stiggins, R. (1997). *Student-centered classroom assessment* (2nd ed.). Upper Saddle River, NJ: Prentice-Hall.

Stiggins, R., Frisbie, D. A., & Griswold, P. A. (1989). Inside high school grading practices: Building a research agenda. *Educational Measurement: Issues and Practice, 8* (2), 5–14.

Sue, S., & Abe, J. (1988). *Predictors of academic achievement among Asian American and White students.* (Report No. UD026640). (ERIC Document Reproduction Service No. ED 303 555)

Wiggins, G. (1996). Honesty and fairness: Toward better grading and reporting. In T. R. Guskey (Ed.), *Communicating student learning.* (ASCD Yearbook, pp. 141–177), Alexandria, VA: Association for Supervision and Curriculum Development.

Wiggins, G. (1994). Toward better report cards. *Educational Leadership.* 52 (2), 28–37.

Young, J. W. (1990). *A general linear model approach to adjusting the cumulative GPA.* (Report No. TM014553). (ERIC Reproduction Service No. ED316581).

Technical Issues of Grading Methods

John Carr

3

Any error in any calculation will always be in the direction of most harm.

—Murphy's Law

This chapter explores the technical adequacy of grading methods and offers some alternatives. Five grading methods will be discussed as if a teacher uses only one method, but actual grading practices may reflect a combination of two or more methods. After reading this chapter, a teacher may decide that the best grading system should be based on one particular method or a combination of methods. A goal of this chapter is to help teachers understand their options, the implications of each, and the development of a good grading plan. A teacher should choose the right method(s) for the right reasons. A good grading plan accurately represents what students know and can do, supports best instructional practices, clearly delineates expectations to students, and truly informs parents.

Philosophy Behind the Grading System

Before we discuss the different methods for grading students, it is important to look at why different teachers choose different test scoring and report card grading systems. Let us start with the premise that one's grading system reflects one's philosophical approach to teaching and to life in general. Consciously or not, a teacher's beliefs and perceptions about life in general influence his or her teaching approach, expectations about student learning, and how he or she goes about grading students. For example, a teacher who believes that "it is a dog-eat-dog world" will be more likely to grade on a curve than a teacher who believes that life is about cooperation and that all students can achieve the standards.

Professional development on the topic of grading does not usually confront teachers directly about their worldviews or their basic philosophy of education. However, when grading policy and practices are addressed, such values will underlie any resistance to change. A person's beliefs and values must be taken into account and questioned when creating or changing the mechanics and criteria for grading in a school district.

A report card grade (and a test score) can reflect how well a student achieved in comparison to other students or to a performance standard. A performance standard refers to a common (districtwide) expectation about grade-level performance or achievement. Relative grades compare students to each other; absolute grades compare students to a standard. Some teachers may apply a mixture of relative and absolute judgments in their grading system, but the two types of grades will be treated separately for clarity in this discussion and because mixing types of grades is not recommended.

What philosophical approach lies beneath a teacher's choice to use a relative or absolute grading system? Consider the proposition that there are two types of teachers, the YAC and the MAC teachers, whose outlooks on life influence how they teach, how they grade, and what the grades reflect (see Table 3-1). The YAC and MAC teachers are at the two ends of a continuum; most real teachers fall somewhere in between the extremes. The YAC teacher believes that grades reflect solely on *You*, the student; grades should reflect the range of innate *Ability*; and relative grades rightly promote *Competition* among students, where only a few can get an A. The MAC teacher believes that grades reflect on *Me*, my teaching as well as your learning; grades should reflect actual *Achievement*; and absolute grades have the potential to promote *Collaboration* among students when all students have the opportunity to achieve an A.

Table 3-1. *The YAC Versus MAC Teacher*

YAC Teacher	MAC Teacher
• **Y**ou: Grades reflect on you, the student.	• **M**e: Grades reflect on me, the teacher, as well as you, the student. The teacher can have the most influence on student achievement.
• **A**bility: Innate ability to learn is the reason that some students succeed and some fail. It is my job to give them what they need to know; some will get it and some will not.	• **A**chievement: All students can achieve grade-level standards when their learning needs are met. It is my job to find ways to reach and teach all students.
• **C**ompetition: The world is competitive, so students must experience competition early and learn to survive.	• **C**ollaboration: Successful companies and schools value teamwork. Competition dooms many to failure; cooperation can enhance learning for many students, especially the traditional "low achievers."

The YAC Teacher's Philosophy

The YAC teacher's philosophy is that life is competitive, a "survival of the fittest." This outlook influences the teacher's belief that relative grading motivates students to try their best and compete for grades. This teacher says, "Competition is good for kids. It prepares them for the real world out there and toughens them up. It worked for me—I survived." This teacher assigns As to one or a few students because they are "at the top of the class," and so on down to the lowest students, benevolently stopping at Cs or going down to Fs. The YAC teacher favors grading on a curve (method 1, below), which is based on relative ranking, not actual mastery of course content.

YAC teachers do not believe that all students can succeed—that is, achieve at grade-level expectations. They believe that there is only so much intelligence or ability to go around, and the smarter you are, the more you will learn. Their underlying belief is that humans have a range of ability, and where a student falls within that range virtually determines that student's performance at the end of the year. Because people have a range of innate ability, some students will naturally be "high achievers," while others will naturally be "low achievers." The YAC teacher expects to see a range of student achievement—in fact, a bell-shaped distribution. The YAC teacher's philosophical approach leads to assigning a distribution of grades at the end of the year, with most students receiving a C and the numbers tapering off towards As and Fs.

If asked why some students received failing grades, the YAC teacher will blame the student: "Well, he's not very bright." "She doesn't care about learning, she just sits there quietly every day." "His home life is such a mess and he's in a gang, I think." Failure in school is wholly the fault of the student or others, but never the teacher.

The YAC teacher tends to see the teaching role as dispensing knowledge to students. There is one best way to teach, and students need to conform to that way. This teacher often teaches "to the middle of class." The YAC teacher has a set of lesson plans that can be reused with little or no change year after year and will teach the same way regardless of any change in the characteristics of the students who enter the classroom each year. This "one size fits all" approach predictably results in a range of grades.

The MAC Teacher's Philosophy

The MAC teacher's worldview is that competition leads to wars, whereas cooperation allows everyone to survive and prosper. Competition between students is viewed as a deterrent to a positive learning environment. A low anxiety level leaves the mind relaxed and open for learning. Competition breeds fear, anger, and frustration, which close the mind off to learning. When students are not competing for grades, all students have an equal chance to be successful and get an A. Grading on a curve is antithetical to the belief system of this teacher, who favors absolute grades. The MAC teacher will subscribe to one of the other methods of grading, all of which compare the student's achievement to some absolute expectation.

The MAC teacher believes that there may be a range of innate ability in humans, but all students can learn, although some may take a little longer or have unique learning needs. A student's first attempts in the learning process may contain many mistakes, but it is the teacher's responsibility to use that assessment feedback to adjust the teaching so that the student can be a successful learner at some later point. A MAC teacher who believes strongly that students should not be penalized for mistakes while learning may choose the selective scores method of grading, where only the final or best student work is judged for mastery.

When reviewing students' test scores or grades, MAC teachers reflect on their teaching and how they might improve their techniques in the future with students who received low grades. They believe that students should take ownership of their learning, but they understand that the teacher is the adult, the professional whose job it is to reach and teach all students.

This dichotomous view of the YAC and the MAC teachers risks oversimplifying how teachers think, but it has some measure of truth. The point is that personal beliefs are entangled with a teacher's method of grading. Getting teachers to reflect critically on their grading practices can raise emotions because of the link to general beliefs.

Five Basic Grading Methods

Five basic methods for assigning report card grades, specifically traditional letter grades (A, B, etc.), will be considered in this chapter. However, the discussion can apply to other grade symbols, such as performance standards or levels, like "Advanced (4)," "Proficient (3)," "Basic (2)," and "Below Basic (1)." Current use of performance standards or levels comes from the format and use of a rubric to judge student work, usually on a single performance task. Performance levels, labeled with a word or number, are combined with descriptors of what student performance looks like at each level to form a rubric, a scale of qualitative performance. Judges rate student work in comparison to the rubric and model work that exemplifies each level. A rubric provides explicit, public criteria for judging student work or "performance tasks."

The five basic methods are: grading on a curve, average scores, combination scores, selected scores, and gain scores. Grading on a curve can be applied to one assessment to convert scores to letter grades, or some total score from several assessments to derive a composite grade. The other four methods are appropriate for combining data from several assessments into a composite grade. It will be argued that grading on a curve is always inappropriate, and certain applications of other methods often used by teachers also are inappropriate.

Method 1: Grading on a Curve

Grading on a curve is a method of assigning relative grades to students. Thus, the grade indicates a student's ranking compared to other students. It is based on the flawed notion that the laws of nature dictate that student achievement approximates a normal curve, a bell-shaped spread of test scores. While many phenomena in nature approximate a normal curve, it is not *de facto* true of student achievement. A statistical formula is employed in an attempt to transform original test scores into a type of relative score that will take on the shape of the normal curve. Table 3-2 presents a summary of grading on a curve and its disadvantages.

Table 3-2. *Grading on the Curve*

Interpretation	Procedure	Advantages/Disadvantages
The letter grade indicates student performance in comparison to other students. The grade may reflect one final test score or a set of test scores.	• *Grading on a Normal Curve*: A statistical formula is applied to students' scores. The distribution of scores determines the percentage of students assigned each letter grade. • *Grading on the Teacher's Curve*: The teacher sets the percentage of students for each letter grade, ranks the scores, and assigns grades.	*Advantage:* None, really. *Disadvantage:* A grade represents a student's rank but not what was learned; an A in a class of low achievers may be a C in a class of high achievers. The method fosters competition rather than collaboration among students to learn.

If you are unfamiliar with a normal curve or with histograms that graph a distribution of scores, draw a number line with short vertical lines and numbers extending across the line from 0 to 10. Above the middle score, 5, place ten vertical Xs, repeat with nine Xs above the 4 and 6, seven Xs above the 3 and 7, four Xs above the 2 and 8, two Xs above the 1 and 9, and one X above the 0 and 10. Draw a line connecting the tops of the Xs and you now have an adequate normal curve (Figure 3-1).

Figure 3-1. *Example of a Normal Curve*

No. of Xs											
10						X					
9					X	X	X				
8					X	X	X				
7				X	X	X	X	X			
6				X	X	X	X	X			
5				X	X	X	X	X			
4			X	X	X	X	X	X	X		
3			X	X	X	X	X	X	X		
2		X	X	X	X	X	X	X	X	X	
1	X	X	X	X	X	X	X	X	X	X	X
	0	1	2	3	4	5	6	7	8	9	10

Grading on a curve does not compare a score to a standard—some criterion of mastery, such as scoring at least 90% correct on a test to receive an A. Grading on a curve compares each student's score to the average of the group. If the score is very close to the average, the student will get a C, and the other grades are determined by the distance of the score from this average. This method uses a statistical formula to determine how many students will receive each letter grade.

When the distribution of original scores approximates a normal curve, the percentage of students receiving each letter grade is determined by the curve. A normal curve is a bell-shaped distribution of scores, a symmetrical curve with most scores near the center or average and fewer and fewer scores farther away from the average. Under a normal curve, 2% of students might be assigned an A, 14% a B, 68% a C, 14% a D, and 2% an F. A flatter curve would decrease the percentage at the center and increase the percentages at each end.

Grading on the teacher's curve is a variation in which the teacher arbitrarily decides what percentage of students will receive particular letter grades (e.g., A = 5%, B = 15%, C = 60%, D = 15%, F = 5%). The teacher ranks the scores and assigns grades according to the predetermined percentages. The highest test score will receive an A, regardless of whether it is 100% correct or 50% correct. The letter grade A simply denotes that the student had one of the highest scores in the class; it does not necessarily indicate mastery of the curriculum.

Suppose a high school teacher uses the curve method for a final exam for each of five classes, and overall achievement levels vary widely in some classes. It is possible for a student with an 80% correct score in the highest performing class to be punished with a C, while another student with an 80% correct score on the same test in the lowest performing class is rewarded with an A. Is this fair? Of course not. The letter grades do not indicate students' mastery level of the curriculum or say anything about actual learning.

Some principals audit teachers' distribution of grades to see if they are aligned with unwritten expectations for the percentage of As, Bs, and so forth (Stiggins, Frisbie, & Griswold, 1989). Some university professors of measurement use the curve method in their classrooms and encourage teachers to use it. These measurement specialists believe that teachers cannot write good tests. For that reason, they say that teachers should write tests with items that have a wide range of difficulty in order to spread out students' scores so that they can be reliably ranked and assigned grades accordingly. Since teachers cannot write tests to measure the curriculum, they should write tests to compare students to each other (Frary, Cross, & Weber, 1993).

It is certainly very difficult for anyone, including teachers, to create good multiple-choice questions. However, just because teacher-made multiple-choice tests might inaccurately measure the curriculum does not mean that teachers should continue to use poor tests and grade on a curve. It does not make sense to give an A as a course grade to a student who got the highest score—which might be only 50% correct—on a final exam that poorly measured the course curriculum, measured other things, or measured nothing at all. The highest score on a poorly designed test still leaves in doubt whether the student mastered the important concepts and skills in the course curriculum. Using a bad test is wrong, and grading on a curve is wrong, and we all know that two wrongs do not make a right.

Teacher-developed bad tests can be avoided by teachers selecting from good tests and test-bank items developed by professionals, such as traditional tests and performance assessments with rubrics found in some recent curriculum materials and now Web sites (e.g., http://problems.math.umr.edu has more than 20,000 high school math problems and solutions). Only the results from valid tests of student learning should be used to make decisions about students, especially when such decisions affect their promotion or retention at the end of the year. There is, quite possibly, no single test that is highly accurate for all students, so it is important to assess students as often as reasonable and use a variety of alternative assessments, each of which is at least fairly accurate.

Grading on a curve is antithetical to good instruction and assessment; it should not be used to assign grades on an assessment or to combine scores into an overall report card grade. Frary et al. (1993) miss the point of instruction and assessment. The goal of instruction is to support all students in learning key concepts and skills. Students have diverse learning needs, and it is the responsibility of a teacher to learn and use a variety of teaching strategies to help each student learn successfully. A teacher should have the expectation that each and every student can reach high standards and then work to make it happen.

Method 2: Average Scores

Average scores is perhaps the most common method for deriving report card grades from multiple test scores within a grading period. According to this method, several test scores are averaged together to produce a composite score for assigning letter grades. Complications arise when scores from different types of tests are averaged. There are two types of complications: (a) averaging scores from tests with different total possible scores (tests with different numbers of items), and (b) averaging *quantitative* scores from traditional multi-item tests (e.g., multiple-choice tests) and *qualitative* scores from performance tasks. Table 3-3 summarizes the

Table 3-3. *Average Scores*

Interpretation	Procedure	Advantages/Disadvantages
The letter grade indicates overall student performance throughout the term. Grades usually are based on scores from tests only but may include other learning indicators that are scored, such as student work and class participation.	• *Simple Average Scores*: The scores are averaged; these average or composite scores are ranked; and "cut scores" (ranges) are set to separate each letter grade. • *Weighted Average Scores*: Weights are assigned to each type of score being combined, usually according to its relative importance (e.g., 30% midterm exam, 70% final exam).	*Advantages*: Student is aware of the importance of each performance measure, which might be motivational. Multiple measures can be combined from various tests. *Disadvantages:* Failure on early tests might discourage the student from learning from mistakes and taking chances. It can disallow correcting past work for a higher score. Teachers may apply an incorrect method (see examples in this chapter).

advantages and disadvantages of two types of average scores, simple and weighted averages. Before we describe these two types, some comments will be made about the issues of deriving and using average scores.

Is averaging scores to derive a grade an objective measure when teachers have their own subjective notions about the grade to assign to each successive range of average scores? Consider the conversion of the average score from many tests to a composite letter grade on a report card. Even if teachers use the same tests and the same method of averaging scores, students' letter grades will not be comparable across teachers if the teachers use their own cut score criteria for letter grades. Suppose Melissa has a string of seven scores in the 90s—90%, 92%, 93%, 94%, 91%, 90%, and 92%. These average out to 91.71%. Table 3-4 shows three typical grading scales for three teachers (example and table are adapted from Canady & Hotchkiss, 1989). Suppose all three teachers gave the same test but, as is customary, used their own grading systems. If Melissa had Teacher X or Y, her grade would be a B, but if she had Teacher Z, her grade would be an A. This does not seem fair to Melissa, and it highlights the problem that grades across teachers do not reflect an absolute measure of mastery. Chapter 9 discusses this issue in more depth from the perspective of standards-based grading.

Table 3-4. *Three Typical Grading Scales*

Teacher X	Teacher Y	Teacher Z	Letter Grade
95–100	93–100	90–100	A
88–94	85–92	80–89	B
81–87	77–84	70–79	C
75–80	69–76	60–69	D
0–74	0–68	0–59	F

Should all test data in a grading period be included in the average score to derive a grade? To motivate students to always try hard on every test, the teacher tells the students that all (or most) test scores will be entered into the grade book, and the average scores will be converted to letter grades on the report card. However, students may become cautious or unduly anxious when tests administered early in the learning process are combined with results at the end. Students with failing test scores early on may become discouraged and give up rather than learn from their mistakes and be judged by test results after trial-and-error learning.

Canady and Hotchkiss (1989) advocate allowing students to drop their lowest grade or one test during a grading period, under the assumption that no one, including students, performs at peak level all the time. Dropping one or two "bad hair day" scores can still be considered as an option in the average scores method, rather than the selected scores method (discussed below). The intent is to include most scores, those that reflect accurate measures of student learning. One score that needs long and hard consideration before inclusion is a zero. A zero can have a devastating effect. Add a single score of zero to Melissa's average of 91.71, and it drops to 80.25. Look again at Table 3-4. Now Melissa would receive a D from Teacher X, a C from Teacher Y, and a B from Teacher Z. I am not advocating that any very low scores be dropped, just pointing out the impact on the average score.

What sources should be included in deriving the average score? Some teachers give equal weight in their grading systems to tests, pop quizzes, student work, and homework. Pop quizzes are a coercive strategy to get students to study, and they punish students who the teacher suspects are unprepared on a particular day. Pop quizzes should not substitute for good teaching or more appropriate means of motivating students, nor should the scores be included in the final composite grade. If student work that is part of learning activities is graded, it can raise students' anxiety and fear of discovery learning and of taking risks. Feedback *not* in the form of grades should be given for student work, or a teacher should consider another method, such as selected scoring. If student class work and homework are meant to reinforce and practice newly presented concepts and skills, then they should not be used as assessments and included in the final report card grade.

Some teachers add "extra credit" points to the total scores or points for effort or general class participation and behavior. This does a disservice to students when their test scores rightly show that they did not learn certain key concepts and skills and the extra credit tasks do not help students to master those concepts and skills (Frisbie & Waltman, 1992). Sometimes the extra credit work is barely, or not at all, related to the key concepts and skills that are supposed to be the basis of the grade. Not everyone agrees with my position, but I believe it is logical and fair to students.

The average score should reflect multiple measures of what was learned, not what was beginning to be learned combined with what was finally learned. This discussion points out that the average scores method can be used in a mathematically correct way but still result in an unfair outcome for the student or have an unintended negative impact. In short, teachers must carefully decide which types of student performances should be included in the composite score and what weight each measure should have (Canady & Hotchkiss, 1989).

Now that we have discussed the issues of converting average scores into grades and what types of data should be averaged, let us move to the technical issues and methods of averaging scores. Why go to the trouble of using the same score scale for tests of different length and averaging the scores? Why not just add the raw scores from the tests together and set cut scores for letter grades (e.g., 180–200 = A, 160–179 = B) that are based on the total score rather than the average score? The test with the lowest number of points automatically has the least weight in the total score, but it may be the most important measure of what was taught. Suppose a 45-minute, 50-point multiple-choice test is combined with a 2-hour, 4-point performance task that integrates the most important concepts in the course. Obviously, it is absurd to add them together for a scale from 1 to 54, but it is also bad practice to create tests with specific numbers of items just to be able to add the scores. Tests should have enough items to assess what ought to be assessed, not equal numbers of items.

There are obvious situations in which the average scores method is appropriate—that is, averaging multiple test scores instead of using only a final, comprehensive test score to determine report card grades. For example, a fourth-grade teacher, Ms. Wright, is using a mathematics book in which conceptual strands are the focus of each textbook unit and each of the seven units contains a valued performance assessment. Ms. Wright does not think it is appropriate to give fourth-grade students a comprehensive, lengthy test at the end of the year to cover all of the strands. Instead, she decides to assess students after each unit of study and combine the results as an overall measure of their mathematics achievement for final grading.

Simple Average Scores

Simple average scores is one version of the basic method of averaging scores. Let's start with the example of Mr. Rong and then return to Ms. Wright. Suppose Mr. Rong, a high school science teacher, gives a midterm exam worth 50 points and a final exam worth 100 points. He records the number correct in his grade book for each test. At the end of the semester, he averages the two scores and bases his grades on that composite score. This is wrong, because it gives the final exam twice as much weight (because it has twice as many items) as the midterm, which was not his intention. To correctly average two scores from tests with different numbers of items, Mr. Rong should average the *percentage* correct scores, not the *number* correct. Using the same score scale—in this case, percentage correct— gives equal weight to both tests. On the other hand, if he did want to give the final twice as much weight, his original method would be fine.

Correctly interpreting the composite, average score is not always straightforward. If the final exam covered the same content that was on the midterm (in addition to new materials), then the average score reflects more about the concepts common to both tests than it does about the remainder of the final exam's content. It is assumed that both tests fairly and accurately measured the intended key concepts and skills. If this assumption is not true, then the result can be "garbage in, garbage out." If you develop a test that turns out to be bad, throw it out. Do not go on to the next version of averaging scores (weighted averages) in the hope of giving less weight to a bad test.

Averaging Scores From Traditional and Performance Assessments

Let's return to the case of Ms. Wright to discuss a more complex application of simple averaging. Suppose she uses two types of assessments during the grading period: (a) traditional computation tests with many short-answer items that range from easy to difficult, and (b) performance assessments from (textbook) curriculum materials, with a four-point rubric matched to the district's performance standards (4 = Advanced, 3 = Proficient, 2 = Basic, 1 = Below Basic).

How can Ms. Wright average scores from a task with a total of 4 points and a test with a total of 45 points? First, let's look at what she should *not* do, because many teachers and school districts use certain inappropriate techniques. A common mistake is to treat rubric scores from performance assessments as if they were real numbers rather than symbolic numerals, and then convert the scores to percentages correct and average them with true percentages correct from traditional tests. The lesson to be learned here is that apples are not oranges; sometimes a number is really a number and sometimes it is a symbol of something else, such as performance levels.

For a very long time, teachers have given traditional tests that have many items, such as multiple-choice items or math computation items. The traditional test yields a number correct (called a raw score) or a percentage correct. This is an example of *quantitative* data; some psychometricians also call it *interval* data. If each item was assigned 1 point, then a score of 45 is truly 5 points higher than a score of 40. These numbers (number of points, number of correct items) are numerical; they involve counting. Let's call these numbers "apples" or "real numbers."

Now many teachers are using performance tasks with rubrics as an authentic assessment of in-depth understanding and real-world application. Numbers are assigned to each performance level of the rubric instead of using the labels; for example, "Advanced (4)," "Proficient (3)," "Basic (2)," and "Below Basic (1)." The numbers are a shorthand notation, a useful symbol for recording ratings in a grade book or into a computer database; a one-digit number takes up much less space than a word. A rubric has performance levels that describe qualitative, not quantitative, differences in student performance. The labels (e.g., the number 4 or the word "Advanced") for the performance levels are *qualitative* data; some psychometricians use the term *ordinal* data. The difference between a 3 (Proficient) and a 1 (Below Basic) is not 2 points; the difference is the quality of the student work, not the quantity. On a writing task, the difference between a 3 and a 1 is not having written two more paragraphs, or making two fewer spelling errors. Let's call these rubric numbers "oranges" or "symbolic numbers."

As we all know, apples are not oranges, and they should be mixed only in a fruit salad. So a quantitative, number-correct score from a traditional test should not be averaged with a qualitative rubric score from a performance assessment. Nor should an attempt be made to change an orange into an apple. A rubric score should not be converted into a percentage correct so that the teacher can average percentages from traditional and performance assessments as if they were now on the same scale of measurement.

Arbitrarily converting rubric scores to percentages is wrong; for example, 4 = 90%, 3 = 80%, 2 = 70%, and 1 = 60%. First, the "distance" or difference from one performance level to the next is not equal, at least not quantitatively. Second, a rubric score represents a range of performance (e.g., from low to high Proficient), so it should not be converted to a specific percentage correct. Third, it is a far stretch of the imagination to equate the difficulty level of a performance assessment with that of a traditional test. A rubric score of 1 converted to 60% correct is not comparable to a 60% correct on a traditional test, or a 61%, a 59%, or a 50%. Converting rubric scores to percentage correct is inappropriate, and combining the inappropriate percentage correct from a performance assessment with an appropriate percentage correct from a traditional test is also inappropriate.

Now we return to Ms. Wright's situation of averaging qualitative scores from performance assessments with quantitative scores from traditional, multi-item tests.

While she knows that it is wrong to convert the rubric scores into percentage correct, she also knows that it is permissible to convert a test's number correct or percentage correct to performance levels. A *quantitative* score can be converted into a *qualitative* score; but it results in a loss of information. Specific information about number or percentage correct can be collapsed into more general information about intervals, or ranges, of scores, indicating performance levels. An interval of *quantitative* scores can indicate a *qualitative* level of performance. Instead of stipulating that a student had a specific score (e.g., 83%), the information is reduced to stipulating that the student had a Proficient score (e.g., in the range of 80%–90% correct).

Ms. Wright teaches in a standards-based school district, and she supports the idea of giving students assessment feedback in terms of their performance in relation to the district's performance standards. So Ms. Wright converts the traditional tests' numbers correct to performance levels aligned with her district's performance standards.

It is crucial that Ms. Wright does not arbitrarily set the score ranges, or cut scores, on the traditional tests. She knows that she must set the cut scores on each multi-item test to match the district's four performance levels. The technically sound procedure for setting cut scores is for Ms. Wright to look at each test item and decide if it could likely be answered correctly by a Below Basic student; if not, then by a Basic student, a Proficient student, or an Advanced student? An easy way to do this is to order the items in terms of their difficulty level and then start counting. She adds the items that Below Basic students should get correct, and that becomes the cut score between Below Basic and Basic. She takes that cut score and adds the number of the items for Basic students, and that becomes the cut score between Basic and Proficient. She repeats the process for the cut score between Proficient and Advanced.

Ms. Wright is enrolled in a master's degree program and earned an A in her statistics course, so she is aware that tests have measurement error. Since tests are not perfectly reliable, an examinee's "true ability score" might not be the actual score on that test on that day of administration. She decides to lower each of her tentative cut scores by 1 point to allow for error and give the benefit of the doubt to the student. If her test had closer to 100 points, she would have lowered the cut scores by 2 points.

Ms. Wright set meaningful cut scores based on her school district's performance standards, which have descriptors that guide teachers in setting score ranges for a traditional test that will reflect the level of rigor in the performance standards. *The essence of the procedure is to determine what range of test scores best represents the performance of each of the four levels of students.* The key to setting cut scores for performance levels or letter grades is to move away from arbitrariness and make an essentially subjective process as objective, logical, and defensible as possible. Teachers should not arbitrarily set cut scores—for example, 91% to 100% = Advanced, 81% to 90% = Proficient, and 71% to 80% = Basic. Arbitrarily setting cut scores loosely reflects the performance standards, and the problem is further compounded when one test is more difficult than another, yet they have the same cut scores.

At the end of the term, there are two ways that Ms. Wright can calculate an average score to assign report card grades. She can use the simple average scores procedure to sum the scores (all natural or converted scores are now in the range of 1–4 to reflect the district's performance standards) across the tests for each student and divide by the number of scores. This average score has the same score range of 1–4 as the original performance levels—a nice feature. While Ms. Wright's school district focuses on content and performance standards, it has not yet moved from traditional letter grades for subject domains (e.g., reading, writing, and mathematics) to standards-based grades. She creates a "decision table" to transform average scores into report card grades, where a B is considered a solid, proficient grade-level achievement and C is a basic, fundamental achievement of many but not all key concepts and skills. Table 3-5 presents the cut scores that Ms. Wright used to convert composite scores to letter grades (1.25, 1.75, 2.75, and 3.75 are the actual cut scores). This is one example, not the only set of cut scores that can be selected.

Table 3-5. *Converting Average Scores to Letter Grades*

Average Score	Letter Grade
3.75–4.00	A
2.75–3.74	B
1.75–2.74	C
1.25–1.74	D
1.00–1.24	F

Oranges cannot be converted into apples, but Ms. Wright just averaged qualitative scores, representing performance levels, into a quantitative number (with two decimal places, no less). That would be wrong if Ms. Wright stopped here and reported scores like 3.75 as if they reflected a quantitative measurement scale. But she went on to convert the "quasi-quantitative" scores back into score ranges to represent performance levels, or grades. This is permissible, and the results will be fairly similar to those using a strictly qualitative method, such as the combination scores method discussed below.

One problem in using the average scores method with performance assessment ratings is that the average of two widely discrepant scores yields a performance level unlike either of the two individual assessment scores or levels. For instance, a "Proficient (3)" averaged with a "Below Basic (1)" yields a "Basic (2)," but neither piece of student work was Basic, and the original scores are not apparent in the mathematical formula of averaging scores.

Weighted Average Scores

Weighted average scores is the second version of the basic method of averaging scores. It is the most frequently recommended method for criterion-referenced approaches in which test scores, based on the same scale, are weighted and averaged to yield a composite score. Weighting involves judging the importance of each test and then assigning numerical values to reflect each test's importance. Suppose a final test with 50 points is deemed to be twice as important as a midterm test with 30 points. Multiply the final test score by 2, add the midterm score, and divide the total by 130 ($50 \times 2 + 30 = 130$) to derive the average percentage correct. Another variation is to multiply the percentage correct for the final test by 2, add the percentage correct for the midterm test, and divide the result by 3.

Stiggins et al. (1989), in a small survey study, found that high school teachers varied in their methods of "averaging" scores—from subjective guessing based on vague symbols and comments in the grade book to a visual scanning of a line of scores. Often scores were combined from tests with different numbers of items, instead of placing all test scores on a common scale. No teacher correctly combined the scores.

Ms. Wright thinks that three of the math tests are relatively more important than the other four, so she decides to use the weighted average scores procedure to give more importance to these three. She would like them to be twice as important as the other four tests. To do this, she multiplies each score by its weight—2 for each important test and 1 for each less-important test. Then she sums the weighted scores and divides by the sum of the weights ($2 + 2 + 2 + 1 + 1 + 1 + 1 = 10$) to yield the weighted average score. If done correctly, this composite score will have a possible range of 1–4. Then she sets cut scores to assign letter grades. The resulting grade reflects more about a student's performance on the three more-important assessments than on the other four.

The weighted average scores method is not a solution when one test is good and the other is bad; they do not average to an "okay" composite score. In such a case, one test accurately measured what students know and can do, and the other test did not. I am not saying to discard low test scores. If the test was valid, but the students did not learn enough to perform well, then their poor performance alone is not a justification for discarding the results. However, if the students performed poorly because the teacher tested them on content not taught, then we have a bad test, bad instruction, or both. In this situation, the teacher should throw out the test results and learn from the experience: *It is fair to assess well what has been taught well.* Discarding some test results in a composite grading score will be addressed in the selected scores method below.

Method 3: Combination Scores

The combination scores method is appropriate when blending data from several performance assessments or when performance assessments are combined with number or percentage correct from traditional tests converted to performance levels. A set of criteria, or decision rules, are used to combine the scores from various assessments to determine a composite grade. There are many options, but this chapter will consider only three models: the *compensatory* model is appropriate for two or three assessments, and the *minimum general* and *minimum specific* models are appropriate for more than three performance assessments. Appropriateness has to do with the ease of setting up the decision table, not with mathematical properties. These three options are similar in nature to the "frequency of scores" method

Table 3-6. *Combination Scores*

Interpretation	Procedure	Advantages/Disadvantages
The letter grade indicates overall student performance throughout the term. Grades are based on multiple measures, and criteria define grades in terms of minimum scores. Minimum scores are based on a judgment that accounts for each test's accuracy and importance—a personal or group, rather than arithmetic, weighting method.	• *Compensatory:* A high score on one test can offset a low score on another test. • *Minimum General:* For a set of multiple measures, students must meet or exceed a set of minimum scores to be assigned a particular grade. • *Minimum Specific:* In the set of multiple measures, each test is assigned a minimum value, and students must meet or exceed the set of minimum values to be assigned a particular grade.	*Advantages*: Multiple measures can be combined from various tests using a matrix that visually defines the criteria for combining scores and assigning grades. *Disadvantages*: There is no allowance for individual differences, unless differential standards are set (e.g., a particular test may be more accurate for some students but not others).

presented in chapter 4. Table 3-6 presents a summary as well as the advantages and disadvantages of this method.

Compensatory Combination Scores

The compensatory model is appropriate when there are only two or three assessments involved. A traditional multi-item test, with scores like number or percentage correct or percentiles, are converted to performance levels by using arbitrary or meaningful (standards-based) cut scores, or all the assessments are performance ones with rubric scores.

The model shown in Table 3-7 uses a math performance task with a 4-point rubric. The other measure is a mathematics test with many items that yield a percentage correct score. Percentage correct scores are grouped into intervals, which in this example are arbitrary. The cells in the matrix show the grade the teacher

Table 3-7. *Grading Decision Model, Performance Assessment and Test*

Math Task Rubric Score	Math Test With Percentage Correct Scores				
	0–24	25–49	50–74	75–89	90+
4	C	C	B	A	A
3	C	C	C	B	B
2	D	D	C	C	B
1	F	D	D	C	C

decided to assign each combination of scores. For example, a student with a Math Task score of 4 and a Math Test score of 90% is assigned a letter grade of A. This matrix is a decision model, a set of criteria for assigning grades to combinations of results. It is a compensatory model because a low score on one assessment can compensate for a high score on the other assessment. For example, students are assigned a grade of C based on a high Math Task score and low Math Test score or, conversely, a low Math Task score and high Math Test score.

This compensatory model with a matrix is much simpler when both measures are performance assessments with, for example, 4-point rubric scores. The matrix in Table 3-8 is an example of assigning grades in which a B is considered to represent a rubric score of 3 (Proficient), and a C is a 2 (Basic).

Table 3-8. *Grading Decision Model, Two Performance Assessments*

Performance Assessment A	Performance Assessment B			
	1	2	3	4
4	C	B	B	A
3	C	C	B	B
2	D	C	C	B
1	F	D	C	C

Table 3-9 presents the layout for three performance assessments in a decision matrix. This is a little more complicated. The teacher must look at each triple combination of scores and decide the appropriate grade. Beyond three assessments, using a matrix to visually set grading criteria becomes too unwieldy. One of the two following models is better suited to more than three measures.

Table 3-9. *Partial Grading Decision Model, Three Performance Assessments*

Assessment A	Assessment B	Assessment C			
		1	2	3	4
4	4				
	3				
	2				
	1				
3	4				
	3				
	2				
	1				
2	4				

Minimum General Combination Scores

In the minimum general model, the teacher decides what the lowest score or combination of scores can be on a set of performance assessments to achieve each grade. It is similar to the compensatory model in that low scores can compensate for high scores, but scores can only be "so low." Table 3-10 presents a simple set of minimum scores needed for each letter grade. For five performance assessments, each using a 4-point rubric, a student receives an A if no more than one score is as low as Proficient (i.e., at least four Advanced scores and one Proficient score). For a C grade, a student must have at least two Proficient scores and three Basic scores. Some other possible score combinations would have to be determined for each letter grade; Table 3-10 shows only a simple set. For example, the teacher must decide if a student with a set of three Proficient, one Basic, and one Below Basic should receive a C or a D.

Table 3-10. *Minimum General Model*

Grade	Number of Assessments at Each Performance Level			
	Advanced	Proficient	Basic	Below Basic
A	4	1		
B		5		
C		2	3	
D			2	3
F				5

Minimum Specific Combination Scores

In the minimum specific model, the lowest score is determined for each specific assessment. This is appropriate to use when assessments vary in difficulty, importance, or timing (e.g., an assessment at the beginning of the term may have a lower minimum score than an assessment given later). Table 3-11 presents an example of assigning specific minimum scores to each of five performance assessments in order to receive particular letter grades. In this example, a student is allowed a

Table 3-11. *Minimum Specific Model*

Grade	Number of Assessments at Each Performance Level			
	Advanced	Proficient	Basic	Below Basic
A	2, 3, 4, 5	1		
B	2	3, 4, 5	1	
C		2, 5	1, 3, 4	
D			2, 5	1, 3, 4
F				1, 2, 3, 4, 5

relatively lower score on Assessment 1 because it was given near the start of the term. Assessment 2 was a relatively easy test, so a higher score is necessary to receive a B. Assessment 5 was a cumulative test of key concepts covered in the reporting period, so it was relatively important and a student must be at least Proficient on it to receive a B or C grade on the report card.

Method 4: Selected Scores

In the selected scores method, a teacher or student chooses the student work that best, or most accurately, represents that student's final stage of learning. Not all test scores are included. Table 3-12 outlines the key features of this method.

Table 3-12. *Selected Scores*

Interpretation	Procedure	Advantages/Disadvantages
The letter grade indicates the student's overall, highest level of performance for the term. Grades usually are based on the best student work or test scores that cover key concepts and skills.	• The teacher sets criteria for inclusion—what scores or student work will be included and how a grade will be assigned from the combination of evidence. • The student may select best work for inclusion, often as part of portfolio assessment, with the teacher making the final determination of a grade. • *Connoisseur:* The teacher uses professional judgment to review the student's best work to arrive at a grade. • *Cumulative:* One of the options of the average scores method is used to determine the final grade.	*Advantages*: Early mistakes while learning do not affect the final grade. Student involvement in the grading process fosters meta-cognition and responsibility for learning. Portfolios provide evidence for a grade as well as rich parent feedback and student motivation under certain conditions. Specific pieces may substitute for a final exam and still cover the curriculum. *Disadvantages*: This method may present a problem of comparability unless standards are used; portfolios require extra management skills and time.

When portfolios are used, students acquire the ability to reflect on their learning, select pieces, and write a justification for their selections as an introduction to the portfolio. The chosen pieces represent best work—that is, the student's highest level of mastery. Several pieces of information are selected because the teacher knows that any one assessment has limitations in what it can measure; multiple measures provide more information and more accuracy. When the content area is writing, the guideline may be to select the best work from each type of genre covered during the year. Some pieces may have been produced on demand, and others through a process of drafting and revising.

Each assessment should have been scored and feedback given to students immediately. At the end of the school year, the scores and accompanying comments facilitate the selection process. There are two ways for combining scores under the selected scores method: *connoisseur* selected scores and *cumulative* selected scores.

In the connoisseur selected scores option, the teacher uses professional judgment to review the student's best work and mentally arrive at a letter grade. It is better if this judgment is grounded in a rubric or performance standard. When the student is the "junior connoisseur" and judges his or her own work, there should be a rubric or other descriptors to guide the student's judgment. As in teaching any other skill, the teacher should provide guided practice on individual assessment pieces during the year to prepare for portfolio assessment at the end of the school year. The student presents his or her grade and justification to the teacher, who may hold a short conference. The teacher will always be the final judge for formal grading.

In the cumulative selected scores option, one of the two types of the average scores method is used to determine the final grade. The assessment pieces are selected, and a simple or weighted average score is computed and converted to a letter grade.

Method 5: Gain Scores

According to the gain scores model, the final grade represents progress over a period of time, not a year-end achievement level. A student's achievement at the beginning is compared to achievement at the end, and a determination is made whether the gain in learning was "enough" to warrant a particular letter grade. Gains are defined by a premeasure and a postmeasure—perhaps an actual test administered at two different times. There are three basic types of gain scores that can be used to assign grades: *idiosyncratic* gain scores, *expectations* gain scores, and *criterion* gain scores. Table 3-13 summarizes gain scores and their advantages and disadvantages.

Idiosyncratic Gain Scores

In the idiosyncratic gain scores option, the teacher takes into account all that is known about the student: academic achievement at the beginning and ending levels, effort, attitude, background and history, special learning needs. The teacher determines whether the gain was, for instance, "tremendous" for that particular student and deserving of an A. Another student in the class may have made the same gain, maybe even from the same starting level, but for other reasons particular to that student, the teacher may decide that the gain only deserves a B. The actual progress made may or may not be educationally significant or meaningful. For example, a student may have finally begun to read but still be several grade levels below actual grade placement; however, it was discovered that the child has severe dyslexia and has overcome behavioral and emotional problems resulting from years of frustration with trying to read.

Table 3-13. *Gain Scores*

Interpretation	Procedure	Advantages/Disadvantages
The letter grade indicates the student's growth or progress for the term. Grades may be based on one pre- and posttest assessment instrument but more often on a developmental scale or general judgment about student work from two time periods.	• Pre/Post: A pretest score is subtracted from a posttest score (using the same or equivalent test), and the gain score is converted to a letter grade. • General student performance at the beginning of the year is compared to year-end performance and a judgment is made. • In the *Idiosyncratic* method, the teacher makes a decision for each student without applying the same scoring criteria for all students. • In the *Expectations* method, each teacher has personal expectations about what students should know and grades all students in his or her class accordingly. • In the *Criterion* method, the same standards are used across teachers for all students.	*Advantages*: Recognizes great achievement gains for a student who otherwise would receive a low letter grade for year-end achievement below grade-level standards. Especially appropriate for judging primary grade students using a developmental scale; for English language learners to report English progress; for certain special education students in terms of IEP goals; for students struggling below grade level. *Disadvantages*: The grade represents gains but may be interpreted by the student and parents or others as year-end grade-level performance. This is not a problem if it is represented as a separate grade from year-end achievement.

Expectations Gain Scores

Expectations gain scores are based on the teacher's personal expectations of the students: Grades are determined by the teacher's judgment of how well the students measured up to these. All students are held to the same expectations, more or less, about what content and skills should have been learned during the year.

Criterion Gain Scores

The third option, criterion gain scores, is the best choice, for it uses a standard against which each student's progress is compared. On a norm-referenced test, such as the SAT-9, achieving at the 50th percentile in third grade and then at the same percentile in fourth grade represents a year's growth. A gain of zero, in terms of year-to-year percentiles, is considered a year's growth because the student had the same relative standing compared to each grade's norm group. A positive gain score (e.g., +5 percentile points) indicates accelerated learning, while a negative gain score indicates slow learning. Differential standards may be set by the district, such as how many levels on an English-language development scale a student is expected to gain, depending on the student's beginning level, age, and perhaps other factors. In this option, a wider range of people than just the teacher sets the expected level(s) of progress.

In a standards-based assessment system, students might be expected to progress from a low performance standard at the beginning of the school year to a higher standard by the end of the year. For example, with four performance levels, a student might be expected to start at the second level, Basic, and progress during the year to at least the third level, Proficient. A student starting at the first level, Below Basic, would be below what is expected at the start of the grade level and might need interventions to accelerate progress to at least Proficient by the end of the year.

Criterion gain scores is preferred because it is much more objective and linked to some notion of standards than idiosyncratic or expectations gain scores. It is suggested that gain scores alone should not be reflected in the grades on a report card, nor should they be combined in some fashion with actual achievement status. Instead, a report card should show grades for achievement status, and, if progress also is to be reported, then grades for progress should appear on a separate area of the report card.

Which Grading Method Is Right for Me?

The simple yet indefinite answer to which method is right for any given teacher is "the grading method that most accurately reflects what students know and can do, compared to grade-level content and performance standards, while fostering students' motivation to continue learning." As noted earlier, the method you choose will be influenced by your philosophical approach to teaching and your worldview. What does all this mean, and is there a clear way to make a wise choice? The simple answer is "yes."

Table 3-14 identifies the type of student information that the teacher should use in determining a grade and the type of judgment that the teacher will make. The table shows a matrix that matches the type of information (left column) with the type of judgment (center column), leading to the appropriate method of combining student data (right column).

Type of Information

Affective characteristics such as effort, attitude, interest, and personality are factored into grades by some teachers, but the disadvantages of doing so often outweigh the advantages. Students' attitudes about learning influence their achievement, but the teacher should not try to factor attitudes into a grade. What is communicated or miscommunicated when a "low achiever" gets an A because he or she tried hard, and a "high achiever" gets a C because he or she did not appear to try hard? Should the "high achiever" be penalized because the teacher's presentation style and pace do not match the student's? Tardiness and absenteeism might be related to attitudes and also should not be part of the grade. If a student is absent from most of the classes and still does well on the final exam, this may simply indicate the lack of a challenging curriculum, and grades should not be used to punish students who are "turned off" by the teacher.

Table 3-14. *Matrix for Identifying Methods of Combining Data*

Type of Information	Type of Teacher Judgment		Method of Combining Student Data
Affective (e.g., effort, attitude)	Subjective	Idiosyncratic	Selected
		Expectations	Selected
Academic achievement	Subjective	Idiosyncratic	Selected, Gain
		Expectations	Average, Selected, Gain
	Objective	Class rank	Grading on a curve
		Arbitrary	Average, Combination, Selected, Gain
		Standards-based	Average, Combination, Selected, Gain

Grades for academic achievement include any indicators of academic learning as evidenced by student work, assessment results, and participation in academic discussions and collaborative tasks. A teacher might use some mixture of affect and academic achievement in grading, but these are best evaluated separately and reported as separate grades. Many educators agree with Stiggins et al. (1989) that "grades should indicate how much students have learned rather than an estimate of how much they are capable of learning or how much they have learned in relation to their judged ability level" (p. 8).

Teacher Judgment

Subjective judgment does not rely on explicit criteria but is made solely in the teacher's head and thus is not obvious to students or parents. *Objective judgment* is based on explicit criteria: the rules of scoring can be shown to students and parents. Judgments involving affective factors are subjective, for teachers do not objectively measure students' efforts and attitudes and then use that data to assign grades. Affect, when it is considered, is factored into the grade subjectively.

Idiosyncratic judgments are subjective—the teacher treats each student uniquely, taking into account several factors to reach a conclusion about grading. Effort may count more for one student, whereas academic achievement may be all that counts for another student in the same class for the same teacher. Judgments based on a teacher's expectations are made when the teacher applies one set of criteria to all students, but the judgments are made in relation to the teacher's personal expectations about how good is good enough or what type of information will be included to assign letter grades. In this case, teachers in a school do not use the same criteria for grading, nor do they openly share with each other what they do use.

Arbitrary judgments are objective—they are based on public criteria applied to all students, but the cut scores used to classify students for grading are not aligned with grade-level performance. The teacher arbitrarily decides to set cut scores at intervals of ten (91% to 100% correct = A, 81% to 90% = B, etc.) without regard to whether the cut score is truly a logical divider between an A and a B or between Proficient and Basic.

Standard judgments, on the other hand, are based on common, consistent criteria across all teachers, and *standards-based judgments* are based on a district's content standards. This type of judgment is recommended when report card grades are part of the district's standards-based accountability system for reporting to the state. In this case, teachers will be using academic student information—objective performance criteria that are standards-based.

Let's say that you are a fifth-grade teacher. For the content area of writing (three genres), you are going to use year-end writing samples, because you want to measure what students have learned after a year of teaching. You will use the selective scores method of grading because you want to ignore the earlier writing samples, when students were in the process of learning to write better, and select the best student writing samples for each genre. For the content area of mathematics, you gave unit assessments that focused on key conceptual strands throughout the year, so you will use the average scores method of computing a composite score for conversion to grades, based on district performance standards for setting cut scores.

Many school districts across the nation are developing a standards-based assessment and accountability system to comply with Title I legislation and state policy. At the heart of such a system are assessments that are reliable, with consistent scoring of performance assessments by teachers. When report card grades are used as one of a district's multiple measures, there should be proof that grading is consistent across all teachers. Only the last row in Table 3-14 identifies the conditions and method of grading that are appropriate for a standards-based system of accountability. Any other row or combination of rows will either not reflect district content and performance standards or not provide comparable data and grades across teachers. Chapter 5 presents a real example of a district moving toward a system of standards-based grading. The district described is continuing to work toward meeting the conditions for reliable standards-based grading. Two major steps toward consistency are the district's attention to staff development and using staff meetings to discuss results and plan instructional improvements.

Summary and Conclusion

This chapter discussed five methods for combining scores from multiple assessments and then converting the composite score to a letter grade. Grading on a curve was discouraged. The current situation of report card grading appears to be rather messy in some, perhaps many, districts. Grading has been an almost taboo topic of discussion in many school districts until now, when districts are faced with the obvious disconnection between teachers' grading systems and a district standards-based accountability system.

Teachers need to think carefully about the grades they put into their grade books and how they reach a decision about the composite grade to put on a report card. Were the assessments accurate measurements of what the student knows and can do? Should grades or scores during the learning process be included in the final report card grade, or just test scores at the end of the lesson? Ongoing assessment is important in order to provide both teachers and students with feedback so they can adjust their plans and practices. Assessment during the learning process should not hinder a risk-free, experimental learning environment. One safeguard is to provide multiple assessment opportunities to motivate students to keep striving for success; if a student receives a low score, he or she is given another opportunity.

Combining multiple measures from different types of assessments during the year is a worthy goal. Many educators agree that no one assessment is best for all students or is able to measure a domain or standard completely; multiple measures are needed for better accuracy. In the quest for multiple measures, let us get on board but not go overboard.

We will conclude with a list of simple "do's and don'ts." Table 3-15 presents recommendations for practices to avoid in the left column counterbalanced by practices to use in the right column. This table highlights key ideas to be considered when a teacher is going to plan a grading system.

Some last thoughts and words of wisdom are drawn from a few of the many articles and books in the literature. Frisbie and Waltman (1992) present nine fundamental questions of concern when developing a grading plan, including what components should be included in a final grade, what method should be used to derive a grade, and how should one account for other factors that can influence the philosophy of grading. Marzano and Kendall (1996) discuss a variety of grading issues and options within a standards-based or standards-referenced system, including advice about planning a grading model for both the individual teacher and the school district. Reeves (1998) succinctly addresses all facets of a standards-based grading system and sums up the most important rule in three words: "Tell the truth."

> We tell the truth about what we expect of students. We tell the truth about the differences between their present performance and those standards. We tell the truth about the time and effort it will take to close the gap. And we tell the truth about the progress that students make toward the goals the community has established. (p. 77)

Wiggins (1996) questions the method of averaging scores and argues, "Let us report complex performance by its major elements, and summarize the meaning of the data in a brief narrative—just as occurs on the back of a baseball card" (p. 146).

Finally, Stiggins (1994) addresses many important issues about grading and concludes with two final guidelines:

Table 3-15. *Do's and Don'ts*

Don't	Do
Keep your grading system personal and private from students, parents, other educators	Collaborate with other teachers or, better yet, serve on a district committee to establish standards for grading so that students are treated fairly and equitably and grades have universal meaning aligned with content and performance standards.
Grade on a curve	Assign grades based on academic achievement, according to performance standards.
Include nonacademic information about the student in your academic grading system	Only include academic information in your academic grading system.
Use arbitrary criteria (e.g., cut scores at 90, 80, etc.) to convert score ranges to grades	Use performance standards to convert score ranges to grade symbols so that the symbols reflect explicit descriptors of student performance. Include evidence for each student, preferably integrated into a portfolio, at least for teacher-parent conferences.
Include scores from all student work and assessments in a composite score for assigning grades	Include only scores from accurate assessments, either (a) discarding low scores from a few bad tests or "bad days" before combining scores for the student, or (b) selecting best performances and scores from a set of tasks and tests that measure the same content.
Give all tests, homework, and projects equal weight	Weight scores according to their relative importance in measuring key concepts and skills, putting all scores on a common scale (e.g., four performance levels, or percentage correct) before combining them. Number and percentage correct scores can be collapsed into performance levels, but not vice versa.

(1) You need not assign a grade to absolutely everything a student produces. (2) Your challenge is not to rank students in terms of their achievement...when we become the outstanding teachers we are all capable of being, everyone will end up at the very top of the list. (p. 394)

I recommend that teachers (a) clearly identify for students what they are expected to learn and how well, (b) teach in ways that provide opportunities for all students to learn, (c) assess in ways that allow all students to show what they have learned, and (d) apply a grading system that accurately sums up a student's academic learning. Ideally, this grading system would be consistent across all teachers and reflect the district's content and performance standards.

For those readers interested in moving away from traditional report card grading systems to a standards-based system in their school district, chapter 5 presents a district model; chapter 9 discusses what a standards achievement report might look like and what issues to consider in the change process.

References

Canady, R. L., & Hotchkiss, P. R. (1989). It's a good score! Just a bad grade. *Phi Delta Kappan, 71* (1), 68–71.

Frary, R. B., Cross, L. H., & Weber, L. J. (1993). Testing and grading practices and opinions of secondary teachers of academic subjects: Implications for instruction in measurement. *Educational Measurement: Issues and Practice, 12* (3), 23–30.

Frisbie, D. A., & Waltman, K. K. (1992). Developing a personal grading plan. *Educational Measurement: Issues and Practice, 11* (13), 35–42.

Marzano, R. J., & Kendall, J. S. (1996). *A comprehensive guide to designing standards-based districts, schools, and classrooms.* Alexandria, VA: Association for Supervision and Curriculum Development.

Reeves, D. B. (1998). *Making standards work.* Denver, CO: Center for Performance Assessment.

Stiggins, R. J. (1994). *Student-centered classroom assessment.* New York: Macmillan.

Stiggins, R. J., Frisbie, D. A., & Griswold, P. A. (1989). Inside high school grading practices: Building a research agenda. *Educational Measurement: Issues and Practice, 8* (2), 5–14.

Wiggins, G. (1996). Honesty and fairness: Toward better grading and reporting. In Guskey, T. R. (Ed.), *Communicating student learning* (ASCD Yearbook, pp. 141–177). Alexandria, VA: Association for Supervision and Curriculum Development.

Grading and Standards-Based Assessment

Kathleen Busick

4

> *I have a dream that assessment will be put to use honoring what children can do rather than destroying them for what they can't do.*
>
> —Roger Farr

Grading for What Kinds of Accountability?

In chapter 3, John Carr described letter grading systems and their rationales, and he suggested the characteristics of grading systems that would be compatible with standards-based instruction and assessment. This chapter picks up where Carr left off and expands on the description of such grading systems and practices. Specific examples from real school districts will be used to illustrate the principles of good standards-based grading.

Grading is most frequently justified on the grounds that the public and parents deserve to know how students are doing (the so-called "accountability" function of grades). In this chapter I will emphasize a different form of accountability and argue that the most important functions of grades are to contribute to student learning and improve the quality of teaching. In her book *Assessment for Learning* (1995), Ruth Sutton underscores the importance of the first function:

> Marking for accountability is fine, but the first accountability is to the child who's done the work and to [his or her] improved learning. . . . [The] ultimate aim is to offer pupils clear feedback which will help them to improve their [meeting of] standards. (pp. 65–66)

The question of what constitutes clear feedback is at the heart of this chapter. Sutton notes that "the use of codes and grades for feedback is of very limited help in improving learning unless all those involved know precisely what the grades mean" (p. 82). Her observation captures one of the major themes of this book, that the meaning of grades is often unclear to the "consumers" of grades.

Wiggins (1998) speaks to the second function—improving teaching excellence:

> [A]ny hope we have of ever being excellent teachers depends on accountability, because at the heart of accountability—not the arbitrarily imposed accountability you may have experienced but true accountability—. . . is an idea that . . . feedback and self-adjustment play a crucial role in any performance. Performers—including teachers—learn and improve from feedback. . . . [O]ur eventual success depends on our ferreting out student responses and adjusting our performance, not just theirs, in light of results. True accountability thus involves the obligation of teachers to learn from assessment of student performance (teacher results) in the broadest possible sense (are we achieving our goals) and to act on that learning in a timely and effective way. (pp. 289–290)

When standards define the broad goals of learning, then accountability must provide useful information about student work and the impact of teaching in relation to those standards. If the grade is expected to reflect attainment of, or progress toward standards, then the codes or symbols used—be they letters, numbers, or descriptive words and phrases—must have behind them clear descriptions of what each symbol means. Although some educators believe that all grades should be banned, it seems to me that clear communication about learning—both progress of a student's work over time and the relationship between a student's current work to standards and appropriate benchmarks—is an essential responsibility of educators. Whether that communication takes place in the form of traditional grades or in some other form (e.g., portfolio evenings, student-led parent conferences, schoolwide celebrations of student learning) is where we exercise choice. Failing to communicate with clear, accurate, and honest information about learning is not an option. To ban grades entirely would be an overreaction to a flawed practice. We have an obligation to communicate about student learning, especially in an era of standards. It may not be so much the symbol A or F that is the problem, but rather the fact that there is often no common meaning behind the symbol.

One difficulty with many current grading systems is that they rely on a single number or letter to convey too much information (something that has been alluded to in the preceding chapters). A parallel problem occurs when states or districts rely on a single score to communicate student achievement in reading, writing, mathematics, or other subject areas. Some educators are getting around this problem by using multiple scores and more complex reports on student achievement. In North Dakota, new voluntary state assessments are developed directly from standards, and results are communicated on a multipage form that lists each standard and associated benchmarks and provides a score (0–4) for each benchmark. The use of a single score is considered inappropriate to communicate about standards-based learning.

Characteristics of a Standards-Based Grading System

An ideal standards-based grading system would use information about learning gathered from sound assessments of valued learning targets that are embodied in local, state, or national standards. It would be connected directly to high-quality instruction to provide feedback to students and teachers that promotes progress toward the essential knowledge, skills, and capabilities defined in standards. If grading and reporting do not relate the grades back to standards, they are giving students a mixed message. Students are being told, "Here's what we really want you to learn (the standards and benchmarks), but we're going to grade something else, and we're going to report it in a way that isn't going to tell you anything about where your work is in relation to those standards." If standards define the learning that is essential for students' success in their schooling and their future, then our grading practices must reflect and illuminate those standards.

The information conveyed by grades must be understood by the students themselves as well as by teachers, parents, and the larger community. In a standards-based system, grading must communicate clearly about each student's learning in relation to the essential learning valued by the community. Students who are being held accountable for working toward challenging standards need to know the strengths of their work in terms of those standards. They also need to know the areas of their work that need attention and additional effort in order to reach those standards. A grade that simply labels the student's work as worthy of a B does not provide useful information—unless that symbol is tied to a clearly articulated description of what a B stands for within a standards-driven classroom.

In places where standards are the guideposts for curriculum, instruction, assessment and reporting, an observer is likely to see the following:

- Students involved in using standards and benchmarks to develop scoring guides that will be used to assess their work
- Instructional planning that uses standards and benchmarks to guide unit development
- Teaching strategies that are selected with the standards in mind
- Scoring guides that reflect the essential dimensions or traits of a performance that meets the selected standard(s)
- Grading that is based on comparisons of student work with clearly defined descriptions of levels of performance that meet the standards, as well as how the work looks as it moves toward the standards
- Scoring that provides useful information that feeds progress toward the standards

Shifting the Grading Question

When educators think about parents and grading, they often worry about the question foremost in parents' minds: "What grade did he or she get?" In standards-based systems, the questions that parents are encouraged to ask are "What has he or she learned about _____?" or "How well can he or she reason, write, communicate, work with others, or problem-solve?" Each of these questions arises from shared knowledge of what constitutes achieving or mastering a standard or set of standards.

Grading to Support Standards-Based Learning

The various conventional approaches to grading must be evaluated in terms of how well each supports clear and accurate communication about student learning in relation to standards. Grading on a curve, for example, is fundamentally inconsistent with standards-based learning because it uses the range of student performance as a standard rather than using well-defined, subject-related standards that are held constant across students. Assuming that grading is primarily a communication system that informs decisions and actions, the following questions should help to determine which grading strategies make sense:

1. Does the grading system enable its users—students, teachers, parents, community—to know how a student's current work compares with broad, challenging, and long-term standards? Does it help to identify strengths that students and teachers can build upon as the learning continues?

2. Is information from the grading system useful for classroom and school decision making?

3. Does the grading system lead to standards-referenced goal setting and action?

Excerpts From District Grading Schemes

Tables 4-1 and 4-2 (Regional Educational Laboratories [REL], 1998) are adapted from the progress reports of two different elementary schools. They capture student progress toward standards in rather different ways. The report form in Table 4-1 conveys information that allows the student and the parents to understand to what degree the student is meeting grade-level expectations, in a way that the report form in Table 4-2 does not. One might ask where on the way toward mastery of standards—essential knowledge, skills, habits of mind—is this student's work in mathematics? However, from the report form in Table 4-2, one can get a more detailed idea of the specific skills and behaviors being evaluated and see what the next level of performance is expected to be.

Table 4-1. *Dos Rios Elementary School Progress Report*

Mathematics		
Problem Solving	4	
Mathematical Connections	3	Key
Reasoning	3	4 = Exceeds expectations for grade level
		3 = Effectively demonstrates
Quantity and Number		2 = Demonstrates some of the time
		1 = Needs more time and practice
Number Sense	3	NA = Not assessed at this time
Concepts of Whole Numbers	4	
Whole Number Computation	3	

Table 4-2. *Waialae Elementary School Progress Report*

Reading
The shaded section of this sample from a Reading Continuum indicates the reading behaviors most characteristic of the student's current work.

Emergent	Beginning	Developing	Expanding	Mature
• Enjoys being read to • Is curious about print	• Chooses to read • Reads simple books	• Chooses books independently • Uses pictures to predict words	• Selects and reads books with confidence • Chooses from a wide variety of written materials	• Reads a wide range of materials • Reads to learn rather than learning to read • Makes thoughtful personal responses to texts

The following excerpt from a narrative report yields yet another picture of student learning:

> Tina loves to read and is keen to try challenging books. She is determined to figure out what is written and uses a variety of skills such as sounding out, picture cues, recognizing words she knows and making sense from the rest of the text. She is now able to read books such as *Clifford and the Grouchy Neighbors* and simply needs practice and opportunities to build upon and refine her reading abilities. (Colleen Politano, Wishart Elementary School, British Columbia)

This report is an example of important detail that communicates well to parents, and it should be usable by the teacher and the student to help set goals for the latter. All three examples represent early steps toward grading and reporting that communicate the meaning behind the summary symbol. Table 4-3 illustrates the informational power of a narrative description linked to a standard, as opposed to simple numerical information.

Students who learn to use assessment information to help set goals are, in effect, taking charge of their own learning. A fifth grader in a school in Oregon wrote the following:

My writing goals:

> I want to be more careful about the words I use. I need to choose words that help my reader picture and feel what I'm writing about. To do this, I'm going to keep adding to my new words list and ask the librarian to help me pick out some books that have really exciting words.

Table 4-3. *Content Standard: Mathematics as Problem Solving*

Useful	Versus	Limited Use
Thomas can pick out the essential information in a problem, can generally come up with a plan for solving the problem, can select the appropriate mathematical tools and procedures to use, but has difficulty communicating about how the problem was solved.		The student got 76 of 100 points, which = C.
55% of my students scored 2 (out of 5) or lower on the trait of math communication.		55% of my class received a C last quarter.
Action: Give students the problem-solving rubric along with samples of problem-solving responses. Model, with one sample, how to use the continuum for math communication to identify examples of strong and weak communication.		*Action:* ?

Using Rubrics in the Process of Grading

Analytical rubrics, scoring guides that are used to evaluate major traits, characteristics, or dimensions of student performance, can help us to develop pictures of student learning in its true complexity. Writing rubrics, for example, often provide scoring information about a variety of traits: how well the *idea* behind the writing is developed and supported; how the *organization* of the writing contributes to meaning for readers; the choice of *words* the writer has made and how well those words bring the central idea to life. The rubric in Table 4-4 (REL, 1998) is used to assess students' development of ideas and content. A rubric like this, linked to standards, can be extremely useful to teachers and students in analyzing what the student needs to work on and what the teacher can provide instructionally.

Converting Rubric Scores to Grades

How can the rich detail provided by high-quality rubrics for individual performance assessments be reduced to a summary grade? Faced with that question, Linda Elman, testing coordinator for a school district in the state of Washington, responded with a letter to teachers. Figure 4-1 reproduces excerpts from Elman's letter. The variations that Elman describes are in harmony with the intent of rubric-based scoring and with treating rubric scores as qualitative data, which they are.

All of these methods allow teacher judgment to be brought to bear and all of the complexity of student performance over a grading period considered. It is possible, of course, to report student achievement in terms of rubric scores and not convert them to grades. However, this practice may lead to too many reporting "points." Writing, for example, might be scored on as many as six traits or dimensions, so some districts might decide that conversion from multiple scores to fewer scores is necessary. There are districts that do use rubrics directly as a basis for assigning grades, so, for example, a student might receive a 3 on a 4-point scale as a grade for reading (see chapter 5 for a variant on this practice).

Table 4-4. *Ideas and Content Development*

---

5 *This paper is clear and focused. It holds the reader's attention. Relevant anecdotes and details enrich the central theme.*

- The topic is **narrow** and **manageable.**

- The writer seems to be writing from **knowledge** or **experience;** the ideas are **fresh** and **original.**

- **Insight**—an understanding of life and a knack for picking out what is significant—is an indicator of high-level performance, though not required.

- **Relevant, telling, quality details** give the reader important information that goes **beyond the obvious** or predictable.

- The reader's questions are **anticipated and answered.**

- Reasonably **accurate details** are present to support the main ideas.

3 *The writer is beginning to define the topic, even though development is still basic or general.*

- It is **easy to see where the writer is headed,** although more information is needed to "fill in the blanks."

- The writer seems to be drawing on knowledge or experience, but has **difficulty going from general observations to specifics.**

- Ideas are **reasonably clear,** although they may not be detailed, personalized, accurate and expanded enough to show in-depth understanding or a strong sense of purpose.

- **Support is attempted,** but it doesn't go far enough in fleshing out the key issues or story line.

- The writer **generally stays on topic** but does not develop a clear theme.

1 *As yet, the paper has no clear sense of purpose or central theme. To extract meaning from the text, the reader must make inferences based on sketchy or missing details. The writing reflects more than one of these problems:*

- The writer is **still in search of a topic,** brainstorming, or has not begun to define the topic in a meaningful, personal way.

- Information is very **limited** or **unclear.**

- The text may be **repetitious** or may read like a collection of **disconnected, random thoughts.**

- **Everything seems as important as everything else;** the reader has a hard time sifting out what the writer is trying to say.

Figure 4-1. *Linda Elman's Letter*

February 7, 1997

To: Teachers
From: Linda L. Elman, Testing Coordinator
      Central Kitsap School District, Silverdale, Washington
Re: Converting Rubric Scores for End-of-Quarter Letter Grades

Introduction

There is no simple or single way to manipulate rubric scores so that they can be incorporated into end-of-quarter letter grades. This paper contains a set of possible approaches. Or you may have developed a process of your own. Whatever approach you choose to use, it is important that you inform your students about your system. How grades are calculated should be open to students rather than a mystery. In addition, you need to make sure that the process you use is reasonable and defensible in terms of what you expect students to know and be able to do as a result of being in your classes.

In all cases, you might not want to use all papers or tasks that students have completed as the basis for your end-of-quarter grades—you might choose certain pieces of student work, choose to emphasize certain traits for certain pieces, let students choose their seven "best" pieces, etc. You might want to score only certain traits on certain tasks.

You might consider placing most emphasis on works completed late in the grading period. This ensures that students who are demonstrating strong achievement at the end of a term are not penalized for their early "failure." It also encourages students to take risks in the learning process. Whatever you choose to do, you need to have a clear idea in your mind of how it helps you to communicate how students are performing in your classroom. In the end, what you need to have are adequate samples of student work that will allow you to be confident about how well students have mastered the skills that have been taught. (Do you have enough evidence to predict, with confidence, a student's level of mastery on his or her next piece of work?)

Down the road we will want to convene a group of teachers to come up with a common acceptable and defensible system for converting rubric scores to grades. In the short run, here are several methods that can be used to convert rubric scores to letter grades.

Method

The method described here can be used with any tasks, papers, or projects that are scored using rubrics. The example is from writing assessment, but the methods identified here are not restricted to writing. In the table below we have Johnny's scores on the five pieces of writing we agreed to evaluate this term on all six traits.

Johnny's Writing Scores on Five Papers

Johnny's Scores	Ideas and Content	Organi-zation	Word Choice	Sentence Fluency	Voice	Conven-tions	Total
Paper 1	3	2	2	3	1	4	15
Paper 2	4	2	3	4	3	4	20
Paper 3	5	4	5	5	3	4	23
Paper 4	4	4	4	4	2	4	23
Paper 5	5	5	5	5	4	4	28
Totals	21	17	19	21	12	19	109

Frequency of Scores Method. Develop a logic rule for assigning grades. The following are just four of many possible ways you could go about setting up a rule for assigning grades in writing.

To get an A in writing you have to have 50% of your scores at a 5, with no scores of Ideas and Content, Conventions, or Organization below 4.

To get a B you have to have 50% of your scores at a 4 or higher, with no Ideas and Content, Conventions, or Organization below 3, and any other score below 3 counterbalanced by a score of 4 or higher.

or

In this class, in writing,
Mostly 4s and 5s is an A
Mostly 3s and 4s is a B
Mostly 2s and 3s is a C

or

To get 100% in writing you have to have 50% of your scores at a 5, with no scores of Ideas and Content, Conventions, or Organization below 4.

To get 90% in writing you have to have 50% of your scores at a 4 or higher, with no Ideas and Content, Convention, or Organization below 3, and any other score below a 3 counterbalanced by a score of 4 or higher.

or

To get a C in writing, all work must be at a 3 or higher. To get an A or a B, students need to choose five papers, describe the grade they should get on those papers, and justify the grade using the language of the six-trait model and specific examples from the written work.

Depending on how the rule finally plays out, Johnny might either get an A (mostly 4s or 5s) or a B (lots of 4s or 5s, but more 4's than 5's) or 90% (there is one 3 in Conventions for the writing part of his grade). Or he might get an A by citing specific examples from the written work and the six-trait rubric that show he really understands what constitutes good writing [the standard] and is ready to be a critical reviewer of his own work.

Conclusion

Once you, as teacher, arrive at a method for converting rubric scores to a scale that is comparable to other grades, the responsibility is on you to come up with a defensible system for weighting the pieces in the grade book to come up with a final grade for students. This part of the teaching process is part of the professional art of teaching. There is no single right way to do it; however, whatever is done needs to reflect evidence of students' levels of mastery of the targets of instruction.

What Grading Systems Are Currently Being Used?

In chapter 3, Carr discussed commonly used grading systems. Other systems that are being used by some districts are described below.

Profiling as Grading. A student is described in terms of his or her strengths and weaknesses rather than given a single score, either in number or letter form.

Progress/Growth Grading. Student grades are based on progress over time, both in terms of how the student is meeting standards and in terms of growth relative to his or her own past performance ("ipsative" grading—grading compared to oneself).

Selected Work Grading. Students submit what they consider to be their best current work through a portfolio, exhibition, or other demonstration of learning. Letter grades, scores, or descriptions of levels of quality are determined using rubrics that define what the body of work must contain to be considered to have achieved a particular level.

Descriptive Grading. A narrative addressing important areas of learning is written about each student. Although some would not consider this approach to be "grading," it is increasingly being used, especially in primary school levels to convey more clearly what students are doing at a particular time in terms of valued learning.

On-Standard/Not-Yet Grading. Some school systems have agreed to provide information that indicates whether student work has met the standards for particular kinds of assignments, exceeded the standards, or has not yet met the standards. Reports are based on this scale and no formal "grade" is given until the work has met the standards of quality.

Continuum. A developmental scale (usually for each content area) is used to plot a student's level of achievement. Table 4-2 is an example of a continuum.

Some of the approaches described above are more compatible than others with a standards-based grading system. Each approach is grounded in assumptions about the purposes of grades, the kinds of student work that should be included, and what counts when summarizing learning within a period of time. Table 4-5 shows some of the more common types of grading practices, likely sources of information used to determine the grades, assumptions underlying each approach, and some thoughts about the value and limitations of each in relation to standards-based education.

Table 4-5. *Grading Practices*

Grading Strategy	Underlying Assumptions	Benefits	Drawbacks	Compatibility With Standards-Based Learning
Using Rubric Scores	Grading should be based on clearly defined descriptions of what work looks like as it moves toward the standards.	Good rubrics give students a clear picture of their learning targets.	Rubric scoring is time-consuming. Judgments have to be made in reference to the dimensions of the rubric. (A teacher may want to add or subtract dimensions.)	Using well-constructed rubrics that clarify learning targets, that describe how work develops as it moves toward standards, and that enable students to assess work in progress is an approach to grading that is most consistent with standards-based learning.
	Increased knowledge of the criteria on which judgments will be based will improve student learning and quality of work.	Providing rubrics for work in progress can help students improve prior to grading.	Poorly constructed rubrics are no more useful or effective than existing testing strategies.	
	Students need clear knowledge of what it takes to achieve a set of standards at various stages of development.	Students develop the language needed to communicate about their learning and the quality of their work.	Determining how to convert from rubric scores to grades can present problems.	
	Students can "own" the criteria and use them to improve their work.	Analytical scoring can show students the specific strengths of their work and areas needing more attention.	Rubrics in their early stages of development often use language that is not meaningful to students—thus limiting the benefit of the rubric in making the learning targets clear.	
	Scoring must be based on the dimensions and traits of an excellent performance.	Generalized rubrics can be used across multiple tasks, providing sufficient samples to make valid inferences about standards attainment.	When too many dimensions are included, or too many points are placed on the scale, rubrics become cumbersome and difficult to use.	
	When performance assessment is the appropriate method for particular learning targets, Yes/No or Right/Wrong scoring is not possible.		Rubrics that offer narrow and very specific details about what *has* to be included to attain a particular point on the scale can limit students' expectations of themselves and define excellence narrowly—missing and minimizing the quality of approaches to assignments that are not conventional.	

Grading Strategy	Underlying Assumptions	Benefits	Drawbacks	Compatibility With Standards-Based Learning
Portfolio Grading	Student work has value beyond grades. Grading is not the primary purpose for gathering student work. Learning and improving from collecting, selecting, reflecting, and self-assessing can contribute significantly to the quality of student work. The process of thinking through how to present yourself as a "scientist" or as a "writer" is a valuable skill. Comparing work over time provides a useful and valuable perspective on student learning. Grading decisions should be made from careful examination of selected work that is focused and specific to the learning targets.	Grades derived from portfolios offer immediate evidence of the learning that is behind the grade. Progress—growth toward the standards over time—is made tangible. The process of collecting, selecting, and reflecting on work in relation to standards is itself a learning experience. There is a body of evidence available for others—parents, other teachers—to use to make good decisions about where student work is in relation to standards. The grade is made tangible with work that demonstrates particular levels of achievement. Students can use the portfolio to communicate about their learning and set goals for future work.	Grades based on portfolio entries may not reflect the actual quality of student work, especially if students themselves do much of the selecting and are not yet clear about criteria. Students who select work that they like or that they learned a great deal from to place in their portfolio may find their grade deflated. When the portfolio collection represents samples from throughout the grading time period, the current performance of students in relation to standards can be misrepresented. Start-up of a portfolio system requires time, energy, and communication with students, parents, and others. Without students' taking part in developing or using the criteria themselves, the benefits to students are limited. Using portfolios for grading when students and teachers are themselves learning about portfolios is inappropriate and limiting. Portfolio purposes can sometimes be so vague that students don't know why they're collecting, have only a limited sense of what should be included, and don't know how to use the work in progress to improve. Portfolios are only as good as the assessments used to generate the evidence and the uses to which the work is put.	When the portfolio system is standards-based and includes work selected specifically to illustrate movement toward benchmarks and standards, portfolio grading is compatible with standards-based learning. When the portfolio is not focused, but is primarily a collection of activity worksheets, tests, etc., it's not worth the time it takes, and it is not consistent with standards-based learning and grading.

Grading Strategy	Underlying Assumptions	Benefits	Drawbacks	Compatibility With Standards-Based Learning
Cumulative Points Grading	Students need to know specifically how much each assignment is worth so that they can use their time and effort on those assignments that are more important that others. Some assignments, or parts of assignments, are not as important as others. Work beyond expectations should increase student grades by providing extra points toward the cutoff score.	Students know where they are in relation to the grading requirements throughout the grading period. It's possible to weight assignments, giving more value to those that demand more from students and limiting the amount that can be earned for early assignments or assignments that are primarily scaffolding for more challenging later work. Assigning points for following a procedure, using the proper headings on a paper, etc., can assure some measure of success for students who may have failed in the past. The scaffolding embedded in some points schemes helps students to get a clearer picture of expectations.	Students can sometimes focus on accumulating points, rather than learning. Determining what counts for each assignment is time-consuming and open to much variation among teachers. Assigning points for assignments without a scoring guide is often arbitrary—students often don't know what's the difference in work that received 10 points versus work that received 9 points. The *quality* of the work produced is sometimes secondary to format and the "presence" of certain pieces (title, headings, indentation, etc.).	As with many other approaches to grading, the meaning behind the points can make for compatibility with standards, or can make this strategy incompatible with standards-based learning and grading. If the awarding of points is based on clear criteria that define the differences between each point level, then this can be a compatible approach. (Often, however, when trying to define what constitutes 11–14, e.g., points, meaning gets lost.)

Grading Strategy	Underlying Assumptions	Benefits	Drawbacks	Compatibility With Standards-Based Learning
Averaging Grades/ Scores/ Points	An average score provides the most accurate picture of learning because it indicates where the majority of the student's scores fall within a time period. All student assignments should count toward the final grade. It's important to convert raw scores into averages (or some common scale) in order to accurately include assignments that have been scored differently.	With enough assignments, a few poor scores won't bring down the entire grade. Students know in advance that all their work will be included in their grades. A common scale enables use of data that have been scored in different ways.	Early work that reflects students' initial confusion or misunderstanding of important concepts is counted and lowers the grade even after students have mastered the learning that was the target of the unit. Students know that if they do poorly at first, there's no way to get a high grade. If their effort and your teaching pay off, it won't be reflected accurately in the grade. With a limited number of assignments, the average score can be inflated or deflated by a single extreme score.	Averaging that includes all student assignments during a marking period is generally not compatible with standards-based learning and grading because it does not communicate clearly and accurately about where the students' work is in relation to standards and benchmarks. When missing assignments are counted as zero in determining grade averages, the information about standards is even more likely to be misrepresented.
Grading on a Curve	There is a normal distribution of student abilities that should be matched by student grades. Some students must fail. Only a few As should be awarded. Teaching cannot overcome "innate" ability. Student work will improve with competition for scarce grades. It's more objective to award grades by using a distribution along the bell curve.	Setting cutoff scores for various grades makes the grading process quicker than many other approaches to grading.	Grades based on the bell curve do not accurately reflect learning in relation to standards. The underlying assumption that teaching excellence and student effort cannot result in improved learning dooms students to failure. What appears to be "objective" is actually often very "subjective," as scores awarded for assignments like essays, reports, projects, and investigations may be based on unknown criteria. Comparisons of students to each other do not provide useful information about student attainment of standards.	Grading on a curve is incompatible with standards-based learning. It is based on a completely different set of assumptions about students and their capabilities and cannot provide information about standards attainment.

Summary

Any survey of current literature on assessment (and, to a lesser extent, grading) reveals a tremendous level of activity across the country related to aligning assessment with standards. In this chapter, I have suggested that we can provide useful, timely, and honest communication about learning through our grades when there is clear meaning behind the symbols. This can be the case only when the assessments themselves are based on clear purposes, explicit targets are embedded in the standards, and there is a careful match between the kind of target and the forms of assessment. We can provide high-quality information about learning when we have multiple measures and ways for students to learn from their assessment experiences. Finally, we can draw upon the potential for assessment to deepen and enhance the learning itself when we honor what students bring to the classroom and our assessments build on their diverse gifts. To be sure, this is a lofty vision, but it is a worthy one, and we have the capacity to bring it about.

References

Farr, R. (1996). I have a dream about assessment. *The Reading Teacher, 49* (5), 424.

Regional Educational Laboratories. (1998). *Improving classroom assessments: A toolkit for professional developers.* Portland, OR: Northwest Regional Educational Laboratory.

Sutton, R. (1995). *Assessment for learning.* Salford, England: RS.

Wiggins, G. (1998). *Educative assessment: Designing assessments to inform and improve student performance.* San Francisco: Jossey-Bass.

How to Design a Model Standards-Based Accountability System

5

Louise Bay Waters

The Cabello–New Haven (CA) District has designed a unique developmental approach to standards-based assessment through a process of research and collaboration. According to our own research as well as input we have had from the U.S. Department of Education and the RAND Corporation, ours is one of the few comprehensive standards systems to incorporate a developmental perspective with the more traditional accountability features of "high standards for every student." Similarly, it is one of the few approaches to utilize standards and assessment information systematically across many facets of education. The process of creating this model has increased our professionalism as individual educators as well as our professional cohesion across classrooms and schools and between schools and the district office.

Overview

The District

For a number of years, teachers at Cabello Elementary School in Union City, California, have been grappling with how best to teach and assess a very heterogeneous student population. Cabello serves 912 students in grades K–4. Like that of the rest of the New Haven Unified School District, the student population is extremely diverse. Roughly 26% of the students are Filipino, 18% West Asian (Afghan and Indian), 15% Asian (primarily Vietnamese), 12% European American, 11% African American, and 6% multiracial. Thirty-five percent of the students receive free or reduced-price lunch, 20% receive Aid to Families of Dependent Children (AFDC), and 37% have a primary language other than English.

The New Assessment System

Six years ago, teachers began collaboratively evaluating student work samples and discovered an even greater academic heterogeneity than they had anticipated. They found that there was almost as much variability in skill levels within a given class as between classes. Since then, they have researched and designed a comprehensive, schoolwide, student assessment and reporting system. The system includes clear descriptions of seven different performance levels (from "Pre-Readiness" through "Independent"). These performance levels may be attained by students at any grade level but are benchmarked as goals for certain grades. Tied to the performance levels is a system of authentic assessment, parent reporting, and schoolwide data analysis through a database that includes all 912 students. Cabello's child-centered, developmental approach to standards-based assessment is now being implemented districtwide at all elementary schools and is the prototype for revisions taking place in grades 5–12.

The New Haven model has three major components:

- A standards-based assessment system evaluating student progress against standards
- A developmental report card reporting progress against the standards
- A database pulling together assessment, demographic, and intervention information for multiple uses

Table 5-1 details the components of the model.

Table 5-1. *The New Haven Standards-Based Assessment System: A Comprehensive, Child-Centered, Developmental Approach*

Assessment System	Report Card	Database
• Specified grade-level standards in reading, writing, and math that meet or exceed California State Standards • A standards-based continuum that evaluates student progress against seven developmental levels that are benchmarked to the grade-level expectations • Charts providing anchor samples of student work and explanations of key indicators of the standards • Student work portfolios to assess and document progress • Teacher observation portfolios to assess and document progress containing anecdotal records of classroom observations, running records, conference notes, etc.	• Reports of performance against standards using rubrics • Communicates to parents along with: √ Explanation charts √ Student-led portfolio conferences √ Video √ Parent meetings	• Contains report card data of performance against standards as well as demographic and intervention information • Programmed for common disaggregations (grade level, gender, ethnicity, etc.) • Incorporates state standardized test and district performance test data and is programmed to weight these and the report card data for a multiple-measure assessment against standards • Used for: √ Identifying at-risk students and targeting interventions √ Program evaluation and accountability √ Decision making and resource allocation √ Supporting instruction

Creating a Standards-Based Assessment System

Beyond the "Grade Level" Paradigm

In 1993–94, as part of the Program Quality Review process,[1] the Cabello faculty began analyzing student writing samples against grade-level anchor papers. (Anchors are student papers that exemplify a particular level of performance vis-à-vis specified standards.) During this analysis, the academic heterogeneity that teachers knew existed in every class became clearly documented. We then began discussing the implications of such a range of student performance. If the optimal point of instruction is just beyond the student's current skill level (Vygotsky's "zone of proximal development"), this variability meant that it was not sufficient for a teacher to simply teach the "third-grade" curriculum. Similarly, it meant that a report card system based on grade-level criteria with traditional grades did not adequately report achievement to parents of a wide range of students. Nor did it describe the next instructional level to teachers and parents or motivate students to move forward, no matter what their current level of accomplishment.

In response, the faculty decided to develop a new assessment and reporting system. The purpose of this system was to report student achievement clearly, relative to standards that were consistently applied across teachers. Report card performance levels were to be tied to specific grade-level expectations, in order for parents to be able to see whether a child was at, above, or below grade level. However, the major emphasis was reporting progress against specific criteria at whatever the child's level. For this reason, factors such as attitude, participation, and attendance were to be excluded from performance evaluation, which was designed to report academic progress only.

Designing the Report Card

To accomplish this rather ambitious goal, teams of teachers first began to define levels of achievement in writing (from Pre-Readiness through Independent), followed by reading and math. Over the summer, they designed a pilot report card and set forth ideas for collecting report card data. With permission from the superintendent, 13 teachers decided to pilot the report card for the 1994–95 school year. Refinement continued over the year by the faculty as a whole. In the summer of 1994, Cabello teachers were joined by representatives from the other five elementary schools in the district for another refinement of the report card process, as well as the development of anchor papers and a handbook for teachers explaining the report card and the developmental levels according to which students would be judged. In school year 1995–96, the District gave permission for all Cabello teachers, along with a small group of teachers from each of the other schools, to use the new system.

---

[1] The Program Quality Review process is a periodic survey and critique of the educational programs within a district, conducted by a team of educators under the auspices of the California State Department of Education.

Aligning Performance Criteria With Outside Standards

The following summer, 40 teachers reexamined the report card in light of the latest California Draft Content Standards, standards from the major curriculum groups (like the National Council of Teachers of Mathematics), the Michigan *Omnibus Guidelines* (a standards document), and achievement standards from British Columbia, Washington, and Oregon. Based on this thorough review, another revision of the pilot report card took place. In addition, the committee designed three large posters for each participating classroom, one each in reading, writing, and math. Each poster had a paragraph description of the performance levels (Pre-Readiness, Readiness, Beginning, Early, Developing, Intermediate, and Independent) as well as an anchor paper representing student work for that level. It also specified end-of-year, grade-level achievement expectations from the Beginning level at the end of first grade to the Intermediate level at the end of fourth grade. In school year 1996–97, the pilot continued with all of the teachers at Cabello and about half of the teachers in the other five elementary schools.

Integrating All the Pieces

In the spring of 1997, the district decided to integrate the Cabello system with the development of District standards, the math and language arts textbook adoption process, and the new draft accountability system for the state of California. This was the task of the Report Card Committee for the summer of 1997. The task for the summer of 1998 was to once again revise both the standards and the report card to reflect the new, final state standards and to provide anchors and explanations for teachers assessing against these. Developing a standards-based reporting option in a political climate of ever-changing standards has been a challenge in and of itself. Central to the success of this process and its sustainability over many years has been the district's willingness to grant flexibility to one site and then—something that is even more unusual—to build upon the work of that site to radically alter districtwide practices.

Parental Input in the Process

Throughout the process, parents of the Cabello School Site Council reviewed and gave input on the report card and related parent education materials and framed them in terms understandable to parents. The School Site Council is a diverse group in itself, quite representative of the cultural and ethnic mix of the school community as a whole. Its members include parents from the European American, African American, Filipino, West Asian, and Hispanic communities. The Site Council also conducted surveys to find out about parents' attitudes and needs. The responses to these were overwhelmingly positive. As a result of their review of the needs of parents, the Site Council suggested clear explanations, charts with examples, multilingual materials, a parent-education video, and parent information nights. These suggestions were incorporated into the work of the committee. An excerpt from the Explanation Charts for writing is shown in Figure 5-1.

Figure 5-1. *Report Card Explanation Chart*

Early
(End of Second Grade Standards)

> Dear Teacher,
> I am George. I like
> computers Do you have a computer
> in your room? I am good at
> computers. I want to learn to
> wright in cursive! I know how
> to wright my name in cursive
> Watch I will show you. Watch me
> George there you see!
> I hope you are a nice
> I hope you are cool! Do you
> like pretty flowers? I will give you a
> beutefull flower.
>
> Love,
> George

Organization

- Writes on a topic with related ideas.
- Sequences ideas in a logical order.
- Presents a message that is understandable.
- Uses simple or patterned sentences.
- Uses some adjectives or descriptive phrases.
- Organizes ideas into simple paragraph when appropriate (includes main idea sentence and supporting sentences).
- Begins to use writing process (e.g., may do simple prewriting, edit for capital letters).
- Begins to consider audience and purpose.

Grammar

- Writes a complete sentence with correct word order.
- Writes sentences with subject-verb agreement.

Punctuation and Capitalization

- Uses correct ending punctuation (. ! ?).
- Begins to use commas correctly (especially in a series, in dates, and in friendly letters).
- Begins to use quotation marks and apostrophes correctly.
- Uses capital letters at the beginning of a sentence, for the word "I", and for names (applies some other capital rules inconsistently).

Spelling

- Correctly spells early level words in writing.
- Correctly spells short and some long vowel patterns in one-syllable words in writing.
- Begins to use other spelling patterns in writing (e.g., controlled "r", consonant blends, and digraphs).
- Finds conventional spelling by referring to simple resources such as word walls or word banks.

The New Haven Pilot Report Card and Assessment System

Collecting Data on Students

Each Cabello teacher collects student data in two types of portfolios—a student work portfolio and a teacher observation portfolio. The purpose of both portfolios is to document student performance against standards. The portfolios provide evidence for the performance reported on the report card, and, in this way, they are analogous to the teachers' grade book in the traditional reporting system.

Student Work Portfolio

The student work portfolio includes samples of student work from various projects and assignments as well as ongoing records, such as reading response journals, writer's workshop journals, or math journals. In order for the portfolio to contain enough work samples for the teacher to assess consistent performance at a given level adequately, teachers must preplan assignments so that they include the opportunity to evaluate multiple facets of a standard or more than one standard. For instance, a social studies research project would provide an opportunity to assess writing conventions and expository writing, in addition to certain social studies standards. If it had been planned to include summaries of multiple sources of information (as in note cards or an annotated bibliography), it would also provide an opportunity to assess reading comprehension. By including prewrites and edited drafts, teachers could assess the editing process. In other words, when teachers carefully identify the assessment goals of an assignment and include samples of the work in the portfolio, the portfolio becomes a thoughtful source of diagnostic and assessment information, not simply a collection of work.

Teacher Observation Portfolio

The second type of portfolio, the teacher observation portfolio, has a similar purpose. It too seeks to document student progress against standards. However, in this case, it includes teacher observations rather than student work products. These observations may take numerous forms. They may include informal reading inventories, observational surveys, various tests of dictation and reading and mathematics readiness, and "running records" (a system of reading assessment for accuracy and types of errors). They may also include notes from reading, writing, or mathematics conferences with students, recording the thought processes the students use in solving problems or discussing stories they have read. Finally, they may include anecdotal notes taken while teachers are moving around the room observing independent or group work. Again, the teacher can record notes on the problem areas, points of confusion, and instances when a student demonstrates use of a skill (such as properly using phonemic analysis while trying to figure out how to spell a new word in journal writing time). These notes, along with the work samples from the student portfolio, provide evidence that students have internalized certain skills and are able to apply them in multiple contexts.

Some teachers keep clipboards of computer labels for making notes during cooperative math groups, independent reading, or any other time when they have the opportunity to observe students at work. Others have charts with students' names and observable indicators ("tracks from left to right," "understands one-to-one correspondence"), prewritten with space for notations. Teachers use both of these sources of data to evaluate students against the performance criteria and work samples on the Report Card Explanation Charts and described in the New Haven standards. The purpose of these observations and work samples is to document the level of performance of each student at each of the three marking periods. Figure 5-2 shows examples of a teacher-made observation checklist. This can be used to make notes on multiple students' work at one point in time, such as during an independent writing period. It can also be used in conjunction with a writing portfolio to look at one student's work at multiple points during the year.

Figure 5-2. *Assessing Reading Concepts*

NAME				
Recognizes own name				
Recites short poems, rhymes, & songs				
Identifies & produces rhyming words				
Points to words with one-to-one matching				
Matches words in print				
Names all upper- & lower-case letters				
Uses pictures to make predictions about story				
Retells & responds orally to literature				
Blends v-c sounds orally to make one-syllable words				
Matches all consonants & short vowel sounds				
Reads one-syllable & high frequency words				

Adhering to the Rubrics

The reporting of student progress is done on the pilot report card, which shows not only the level at which a child is working but also specific skills within that level. In turn, each skill is evaluated against a rubric as Emerging, Progressing, or Accomplished. All students K–4, including special education and limited English-proficient students, receive reports using the same performance standards. Thus, a below-grade-level second grader (with the second-grade expectation of Early level) might be at the Beginning level in reading and writing and the Readiness level in math. Another student, an average second grader, might be at the Early level in all three areas. A fourth grader new to this country with limited English could be at the Beginning level in reading and writing and the Intermediate level in math. The reporting process makes these developmental views of students evident in a way that traditional grades do not, and consequently we have fewer misunderstandings among teachers, parents, and students about what a grade means.

Because the assessment system reports academic achievement and social skills, behavior, and work habits separately, the latter three factors do not affect the performance level reported. Therefore, even though a student might do messy work and turn in homework erratically, if high-level skills have been obtained, they are so reported. Problems the student has in the other, nonacademic areas are reported on a separate part of the report card. We believe that this practice makes sense within a developmentally focused assessment and reporting system, where the purpose is to describe a child's academic knowledge and skills. Table 5-2 shows a portion of the report card and a rubric for judging student performance. The third-grade portion has been coded as it would be for fall, winter, and spring.

We are in the process of designing systems to monitor and increase the reliability of teacher assessment against the report card standards. This will include practice sessions where grade-level groups of teachers examine the student work and teacher observations for a given student and then assign and compare "grades." Later we hope to design a more formal system to establish an interrater reliability of 70% or better at each school site.

The Database

A unique feature of Cabello's assessment system is the database. Demographic data and performance and intervention information are collected for all students in a FilemakerPro database. The database includes not only the performance levels in reading, writing, and math but also information about whether a student is at, above, below, or more than a year below grade level (at risk). Specific criteria have been established for what constitutes above, at, below, and at risk for each grade level each term. This information is used by teachers to make instructional decisions, by teachers or administrators to target specific interventions, and by all concerned to make sure no students are falling through the cracks. Figure 5-3 shows a sample printout from the database, the class roster given to each teacher in September.

Table 5-2. 1998–99 New Haven Pilot K–4 Student Progress Report on Progress Toward Grade-level Standards

Performance Levels

- ● Can use skills and concept consistently (90%) in a variety of ways
- ⊗ Can sometimes use skill and concept, but not consistently
- ⊘ Beginning to use skill and concept with close monitoring
- ○ Not covered at this time

Each section below is marked across Fall / Winter / Spring columns for both Reading and Writing.

End-of-Year Goal — Independent

Reading: Independent-level readers have mastered the skills from the preceding levels. They are able to read and respond to complex literature as demonstrated in their reading log and language arts portfolios.

Writing: Independent writers have mastered the skills from the preceding levels. They are able to put them together to produce quality extended writing as demonstrated by projects in their language arts portfolios.

Fourth Grade — Intermediate

Reading:
Reads text at the Intermediate level
Comprehends test at the Intermediate level:
- ● Comprehends basic plot
- ● Recognizes cause & effect, fact & opinion, compare & contrast
- ● Makes, confirms, or revises predictions
- ● Relates what is read to prior knowledge & experience
- ● Recognizes sequence of events or actions
- ● Describes and analyzes characters & setting
- ● Identifies theme or author's message

Writing:
Writes with content & organization appropriate to Intermediate level:
- ● Writes for a variety of purposes
- ● Organizes ideas
- ● Uses details, descriptions, & examples
- ● Conveys a clear message
Uses Intermediate level spelling in writing
Uses Intermediate level punctuation & capitalization
Uses Intermediate level grammar

Third Grade — Developing

Reading:
Reads text at the Developing level
Comprehends test at the Developing level:
- ● Comprehends basic plot
- ● Recognizes cause & effect, fact & opinion, compare & contrast
- ● Makes, confirms, or revises predictions
- ● Relates what is read to prior knowledge & experience
- ● Recognizes sequence of events or actions
- ● Describes and analyzes characters & setting
- ● Identifies theme or author's message

Writing:
Writes with content & organization appropriate to Developing level:
- ● Writes for a variety of purposes
- ● Organizes ideas
- ● Uses details, descriptions, & examples
- ● Conveys a clear message
Uses Developing level spelling in writing
Uses Developing level punctuation & capitalization
Uses Developing level grammar

Second Grade — Early

Reading:
Reads text at the Early Level
Comprehends test at the Early Level:
- ● Comprehends basic plot
- ● Recognizes cause & effect, fact & opinion, compare & contrast
- ● Makes, confirms, or revises predictions
- ● Relates what is read to prior knowledge & experience
- ● Recognizes sequence of events or actions
- ● Describes and analyzes characters & setting
- ● Identifies theme or author's message

Writing:
Writes with content & organization appropriate to Early level:
- ● Writes for a variety of purposes
- ● Organizes ideas
- ● Uses details, descriptions, & examples
- ● Conveys a clear message
Uses Early level spelling in writing
Uses Early level punctuation & capitalization
Uses Early level grammar

First Grade — Beginning

Reading:
Reads text at the Beginning level
Retells stories using beginning, middle, & end
Identifies character and setting from stories
Recognizes topic in nonfiction
Reads high-frequency words
Reads common word families
Uses phonics to help read new words
Uses pictures & language structure to read new words
Identifies letters, words, & sentences

Writing:
Writes multiple sentences for a variety of purposes
Uses Beginning level punctuation
Uses Beginning level capitalization
Uses phonics in writing
Spells Beginning level high-frequency words

Kindergarten — Readiness

Reading:
Reads one-syllable & high-frequency words
Matches all consonant & short-vowel sounds to appropriate letters
Blends vowel-consonant sounds orally to make words or syllables
Retells and responds orally to literature
Uses pictures to make predictions about story content
Names all uppers & lowercase letters
Matches words in print
Points to words with one-to-one matching
Identifies and produces rhyming words
Recites short poems, rhymes, & songs
Recognizes first name

Writing:
Writes a simple sentence
Writes consonant-vowel-consonant words
Uses phonics in writing
Writes first name correctly
Reads and explains their writing & drawings

Figure 5-3. *Fall Classroom Roster*

Tchr	Gr	ID	Name	Sx	BD	Prim Lng	Ethnic	Rd Sp	Rd GLC Sp	R/R Lev	Rd Star St	Dist Rd T	Wr Sp	Wr GLC Sp	Wr Star St	Dist Wrt T	M Sp	M GLC Sp	M Star St
Gerk	4	20506	Tommy	M	10/7/88	English	White	I/A	G	26+	006	004	D/P	B	007	003	I/A	G	007
Gerk	4	21033	Anna	F	9/7/88	English					007	003			007	002			006
Gerk	4	23227	Mark	M	1/21/88	English	White	I/A	G	26+	005	002	I/P	G	006	003	I/A	G	005
Gerk	4	23255	Charles	M	6/25/88	Tagalog	Filipino	I/E	B	26+	005	001	I/P	G	006	003	I/P	G	004
Gerk	4	23386	Stephanie	F	5/16/88	Ilocano	Filipino	I/P	G	26+	004	003	D/P	B	007	002	I/P	G	005
Gerk	4	23411	Samirn	M	1/1/88	Farsi/Argh	West	D/P	B	26+	002	003	D/P	B	005	003	I/P	G	004
Gerk	4	23571	Michelle	F	2/7/88	English	White	I/A	G	26+	006	004	I/A	G	007	004	I/A	G	007
Gerk	4	23586	Justin	M	5/16/88	English	White	I/A	G	26+	006	004	I/A	G	005	004	I/A	G	006
Gerk	4	23760	Stephanie	F	11/21/88	Vietnamese	Asian	I/A	G	26+	006	004	I/A	G	007	003	I/A	G	007
Gerk	4	23787	Arternio	M	7/3/88	Spanish	Hispanic	I/P	G	26+	002	002	I/P	G	004	003	I/P	G	004
Gerk	4	23804	Lyndsay	F	10/11/88	English	White	I/A	G	26+	005	003	I/A	G	006	002	I/A	G	006
Gerk	4	23812	Elsa	F	9/4/88	Tigrena	Black	I/A	G	26+	005	003	I/P	G	008	002	I/P	G	005
Gerk	4	23973	Diane	F	9/26/88	Tagalog/Pi	Filipino	I/A	G	26+	006	003	I/A	G		004	I/A	G	
Gerk	4	24107	Susan	F	8/15/88	English	Filipino	I/A	G	26+	007	003	I/A	G	007	004	I/A	G	006
Gerk	4	24116	Elaine	F	4/17/88	Tagalog/Pi	Filipino	I/E	B	26+	002	002	I/P	G	005	003	I/A	G	004
Gerk	4	24255	Skunder	M	3/10/88	Farsi/Afgh	West	D/P	B	26+	003	002	I/P	G	006	002	I/A	G	004
Gerk	4	24389	Megan	F	6/18/88	English	Hispanic	I/A	G	26+	005	003	I/P	G	007	003	I/A	G	006
Gerk	4	24403	Justin	M	7/11/88	English	Pac Isle	I/A	G	26+	004	002	I/P	G	005	004	I/A	G	006
Gerk	4	25325	Ada	F	2/24/88	Spanish	Hispanic	D/P	B	26+	005	003	I/P	G	006	001	I/P	G	006
Gerk	4	25369	Maria	F	9/16/88	Tagalog/Pi	Filipino	I/A	G	26+	006	002	I/A	G	008	004	I/A	G	007
Gerk	4	26540	Alexandria	F	2/20/88	Dutch	White	I/A	G	26+	007	004	I/A	G	008	003	I/A	G	006
Gerk	4	27057	Usman	M	10/22/88	Farsil/Afgh	West	I/E	B	26+	004	001	I/P	G	005	002	I/A	G	006
Gerk	4	27667	Talei	F	5/18/88	English	Black	I/A	G	26+	005	004	I/A	G	005	004	I/P	G	004
Gerk	4	28171	Daniel	M	4/24/88	English	Hispanic	D/P	B	26+	005	001	D/P	G	005	002	D/P	G	004

Key to Abbreviations

Tchr = teacher
Gr = grade
ID = student identification number
Sx = sex
BD = birthday
Prim Lng = primary language
Ethnic = ethnicity
Rd Sp = reading (spring)
Rd GLC Sp = reading grade-level comparison (spring)
R/R Lev = running record level
Rd Star St = reading Star test stanine (state norm-referenced test)
Dist Rd T = district reading test (1–4 rubric)
Wr Sp = writing (spring)
Wr GLC Sp = writing grade-level comparison (spring)
Dist Wrt T = district writing test
M Sp = math (spring)

MGLC Sp = math grade-level comparison (spring)
M Star St = math Star (SAT 9) stanine

(under Rd Sp, Wr Sp, and M Sp)

Report Card Levels (left of slash)
Pr = Pre-readiness
R = Readiness
B = Beginning
E = Early
D = Developing
I = Intermediate
Ind = Independent

Performance Levels Within Each Report Card Level (right of slash)
E = Emerging
P = Progressing
A = Accomplished

Using the Database to Identify Students at Risk and Target Interventions

By analyzing the data in different ways, we are able to identify students who might need special assistance. For instance, in a school with a large number of students whose primary language is not English, we have often missed students with special needs whose lack of progress has been attributed to limited English proficiency. With the database, we have found three different ways of sorting the data that help us to identify these students. First, when we sort limited English-proficient students by enrollment date, we can see students whose achievement lags behind those who have been in the school the same amount of time. A second sort, by last name, helps us to find disparities in achievement within a family. Finally, sorting by scores from the student's primary-language assessment (e.g., Spanish, Tagalog) allows us to look for students who are not progressing in English who also have weak primary-language skills—an indicator of a possible basic language processing problem. We have also used the database to target students for tutoring during our Extended Day program. In addition, we utilize report card information detailing what aspects of a standard a student is working on in order to help structure the tutoring sessions.

Using the Database for Program Evaluation and Accountability

Thanks to countless volunteer hours by a parent, we now have programs in place to analyze our data and graphically present it so that it is easily understood. This presentation of performance against standards both raises and responds to parent and teacher questions. For instance, after an initial look at data, teachers questioned whether achievement results were depressed by our significant limited English-proficient population or by transience. In response, we have created the "standard student"—one who is not limited English-proficient, who is not special education, and who has been enrolled in the school at least 2 years. The word *standard* is used in a statistical sense, as in the term "standardized." That is, we want to be cautious not to compare students from unlike groups with each other.

Indeed, eliminating students from these populations did have an impact on the data on performance levels, but not as significantly as had been anticipated. In the 1997–98 school year, the high kindergarten and first-grade reading performance, coupled with a look at the new California state standards, raised questions about whether our expectations at these grade levels were too low (see Figure 5-4 a and b). Upon reflection, we raised our standards for 1998–99.

Multiple Measures

Again thanks to our volunteer consultant, we have been able to integrate data from district performance tests and the new state SAT-9 standardized tests (STAR) into our database. Our consultant has developed a program to weight and combine these measures to produce the required California and Federal Title I reports on student performance relative to standards, using multiple measures.

These reports have helped us to identify those students, districtwide, who are the most at risk and should be targeted for summer school and other interventions.

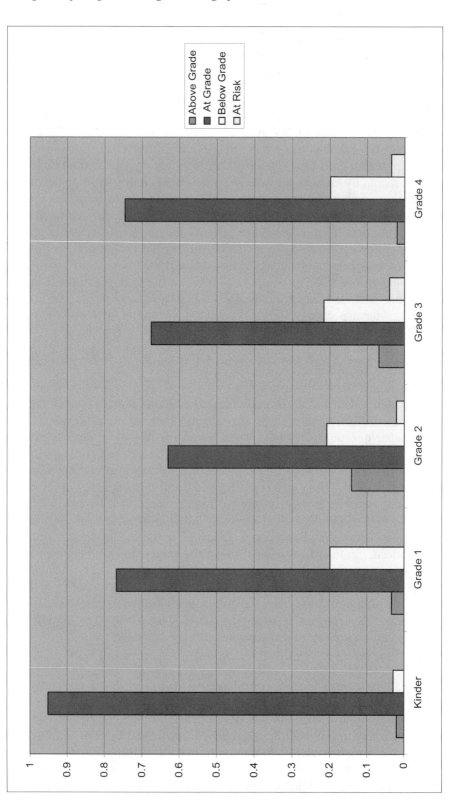

Figure 5-4a. Cabello Spring '98 Reading Report Card—All Students

Figure 5-4b. Cabello Spring '98 Reading Report Card—Standard Students

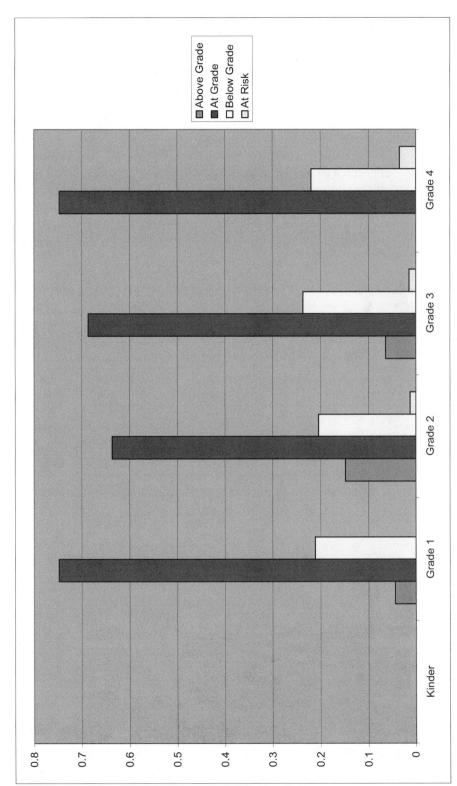

These are students scoring below the 32nd percentile in STAR, getting a 1 on the District Performance Test,[2] and more than a year below grade level in classroom work, as measured by the report card. Being able to readily compare these three measures has helped us to maintain the integrity of all three by seeing whether or not they are consistent and helping us to analyze inconsistencies that did appear. For instance, when we examined the three measures disaggregated by ethnicity, we found that African American students scored significantly lower on the SAT-9 than on the District Performance Test or on the report card. In response, we created a test prep club targeted at African American students and led by African American staff. Continued cross-referencing of the three should also greatly increase the reliability of the process. Of course, there is always the possibility that for some reason a student's true performance levels are discrepant. In such a case, it would be important to find out why. (Table 5-3 shows the multiple measures matrix and lists the score ranges for each, representing "above grade level," "at grade level," "below grade level," and "at risk.")

Table 5-3. *Multiple Measure Assessment: Language Arts*

District Performance Test		Standards-Based Report Card		SAT-9 State Test		Overall Performance
Reading	Writing	Reading	Writing	Reading	Writing	
4	4	4	4	4 56+	4 56+	21–24	Above Grade Level
3	3	3	3	3 50–55	3 50–55	18–20	At Grade Level
2	2	2	2	2 40–49	2 40–49	12–17	Below Grade Level
1	1	1	1	1 39 or lower	1 39 or lower	6–11	At Risk

It has become clear to us that having a grading system that produces reliable, consistent grades is necessary for a district to be able to justify using grades as a component of an accountability system. Without reliable, standards-based classroom assessment data, grades cannot be taken seriously as performance indicators. Educators will be forced to rely on external standardized measures that may not reveal the true performance of their students or much about the success of their instruction.

---

[2]There are district-developed assessments in each of the major content areas (reading, writing, and mathematics) for each grade level. They are scored on a four-point rubric, with 4 representing above grade level, 3, grade level; and 2 and 1, below grade level.

Using the Assessment System for Decision Making and Resource Allocation

The availability of data through the database system and the relative ease of disaggregation (i.e., of analyzing the data on various subpopulations independently) make program evaluation an ongoing part of the decision-making process. Formally, this occurs periodically in connection with the School Accountability Report Card (required by the state), the School Plan, the Program Quality Review, and the principal's reports to the faculty. On an informal level, the ongoing assessment and diagnosis in which teachers engage continually impacts the allocation of time and money. This was seen most dramatically 2 years ago when Cabello turned down $20,000 from the district for take-home computers for fourth-grade Title I students. Instead we requested (and were allowed) to spend the money on Beginning and Early level take-home science reading books for third- and fourth-grade classes. We were able to make an intelligent decision based on our own data and to convince the district that we knew what we needed on the basis of that data.

A Worthwhile But Demanding Process

The process of developing and carrying out an assessment, accountability, and reporting system such as ours entails ongoing and often intensive effort. We believe the effort is worth it because of the improved decision making we already observe in action. The following represent decisions related to time and budget made at Cabello during just one month, October 1997:

- Use of faculty meeting time to evaluate student writing portfolios against standards and anchors and the subsequent critique of these
- Staff approval of extended-time pay for additional teams of teachers to review the writing anchors (felt to be too easy) and rubrics (too unclear)
- Staff decision to design standardized test preparation strategies given the lower performance of Cabello students on standardized (as opposed to authentic) assessment measures
- First-grade teachers' request to DynEd Corporation for five sets of *Let's Go* software for students at the Readiness and Pre-Readiness levels (software was donated)
- Purchase of more transitional Beginning/Early and Early/Developing home reading books in response to an e-mail request to the principal
- Fourth-grade use of Wednesday morning collaboration to look at meaningful language arts activities to use with various levels of students while guided reading groups are working with the teacher
- Second- and third-grade multiage teachers' use of collaboration time to arrange their math curriculum so that students could readily flow back and forth between the two curricula as needed
- Kindergarten use of collaboration time to discuss supporting high-end children who are already reading (and a subsequent request for more kindergarten home reading books)

Using the Assessment System to Support Instruction

Perhaps the most fundamental use of the assessment system is the ongoing teacher utilization of assessment information as a tool for instructional planning and parent communication (see Busick's number one priority for an accountability system in chapter 4). Examples of the system's effects on instruction are as follows:

- At the beginning of the year, each teacher receives a database (Figure 5-3) detailing the levels of each student's performance in reading, writing, and math. This is used to design guided reading groups, target appropriate computer software, and assign home reading levels in September. Ongoing authentic assessment against the standards helps the teacher to continually modify these groupings.

- All classrooms have libraries of home reading books that are color-dotted to correspond to the report card levels. Students select from the appropriate books each night.

- An extensive literacy center has big books, small group sets of books, and "Wiggle Works" CD-ROMs color-dotted for individual intervention and for use with guided reading groups. One whole section is devoted to sets of science books organized by reading level in order to integrate science and reading.

- Kindergarten and first-grade teachers make their own big books at the Readiness level to be used for shared reading. This is their response to the lack of appropriate commercial big books. In general, commercial ones are designed for reading aloud and are written at too high a level for beginning readers to actually interact with the print.

- All students are assessed with running records several times each term. This, in addition to ongoing assessment of classroom work in relation to the standards, allows teachers to target instruction even within whole-class lessons. For instance, knowing which beginning consonants a child can read allows the teacher to call that child up to participate successfully in an interactive writing lesson.

- The anchors for the writing standards are used for student self-evaluation, and the report card indicators are incorporated into editing checklists.

- Students share their portfolios with their parents during student-led parent conferences in the fall. Once the student has taken the parent through the work and the parent has seen the wall charts with performance anchors, the teacher presents the actual report card and explains the student's performance level. By this time, the report card information is not a surprise.

- Report Card Explanation Charts, with details and anchors of the standards, and the report card itself are important components of Student Study Team meetings with parents. This information makes it much easier for parents to see that their child is below grade level (which is usually the case when a child is reviewed by the Team). These sessions have become more problem solving in nature, with finger-pointing virtually eliminated.

- Assessment information is used by teachers to identify students needing Extended Day tutoring and/or homework support.
- The database is used to identify lower-grade children for upper-grade "reading buddies."
- The database is used in forming classes to make sure that there are clusters of students with similar reading levels, so that no one high or low student is isolated. It is also used to make sure that every non-English-proficient student is paired with a fluent-English peer of the same primary language.

Summary

Developing a comprehensive system such as the one in the New Haven District may sound like a daunting task, and none of the participants in the process would want to suggest otherwise. It is, however, a deeply rewarding process because of the benefits it confers on a district. We can truly say that we now have a system that gives us the information we—teachers, administrators, students, and parents—need to understand how our students are doing and to target specific actions to address specific needs. By using developmental indicators and benchmarks, we focus on what students can do, and we are not faced with rationalizing a grading system that doesn't really communicate what we actually know about our students' achievement and development.

We created a standards-based assessment system that includes a report card that reports progress against the standards. In addition, we have developed a complementary database that integrates assessment, demographic, and intervention information for multiple uses. In doing so, we involved teams of teachers for developing different parts of the system and the Cabello Site Council. The system includes the use of two types of portfolios in which to collect samples of student work and other evidence of progress; it also includes a set of rubrics and grade-level benchmarks by which to record progress. A Parent Handbook was developed to support their understanding of the new accountability system.

Of course, our journey is not over, and, in fact, in many ways it has just begun. We have had to spend the last few years continually revising our standards and report card to meet changing state expectations. This has meant that we have had to step back from our focus on the actual process of student assessment. We hope we can now return to developing sophistication and consistency in our staff in terms of embedded, authentic assessment and high-quality, standards-based performance tasks. We also need to expand the use of the database as a research tool from one that is now used primarily by administrators to one used by teachers as well.

Finally, we need to use the power of the database to take hard looks at our program. Which types of instruction and which interventions are resulting in the greatest gains in student achievement? In the past we have avoided this topic by saying that norm-referenced tests were not accurate measures of students' achievement, especially for low-performing students. Now, however, if we have a consistent, reliable, standards-based classroom assessment system and the means to quantify these results, we can no longer avoid questions of accountability. Our answers can no longer be anecdotal, based on our philosophical or programmatic allegiances.

On a Personal Note . . .

I became interested in the development of an alternative assessment system at Cabello before I became principal there. In fact, my experiences as a parent were a major impetus for my getting involved in assessment. I have two sons who went through Cabello. One was a gifted student who generally got straight As. He spent little time on his homework, and I was unable to get him to see the point in refining what he was doing. Why should he? He already knew he was getting an A. To me, the traditional report card did a disservice to him and artificially limited his learning.

My second son was also very intelligent but in addition was learning disabled and had been diagnosed with attention deficit disorder (ADD). By fourth grade he was barely reading. He had a special education individual education plan that allowed his grades to be modified, which meant that he got C–s, with a statement on his report card about the modification. When graded, his daily work was generally C or below (or a sad face in the years when faces, not grades, were used). Not only was the content of his work incorrect, but the work was generally sloppy, often incomplete, and frequently lost. Throughout elementary school he refused to look at his report card and generally threw his papers away as soon as they were returned. I once found one crumpled up on the street a block away from school. He considered himself stupid and believed that his grades "proved" it. Beyond this, his grades gave me no information about his work. Even though it said C–, he obviously didn't know what was being taught; but nothing showed me what he did know. So for me, the traditional report card gave me no information about what either of my sons knew and was actually demotivating for both.

Avoiding Bias in Grading Systems

Elise Trumbull

6

Bias: A lack of objectivity, fairness, or impartiality on the part of the assessor or evaluator, the assessment instrument or procedures, or in the interpretation and evaluation process, that leads to misinterpretation of student performance or knowledge.

—National Forum on Assessment, 1995

Much of the literature on bias relates to testing and not grading per se. Of course, a substantial portion of a grade usually depends on various types of tests or assessments. This chapter briefly reviews traditional conceptions of bias and fairness in testing and then turns to examining how bias may creep into the grading arena. As a judgment-based process, grading is potentially susceptible to numerous forms of bias. However, armed with some knowledge of major pitfalls and a willingness to monitor their grading processes, teachers can avoid bias in grading.

Traditional Definitions of Bias

While validity usually refers to the accuracy of test score interpretations, *bias* has been traditionally thought of as a quality of a test or assessment that interferes with validity (Shepard, 1982). In the simplest terms, bias works by favoring some people over others on the basis of an attribute or attributes unrelated to the construct being evaluated. A biased test leads to wrong conclusions about the abilities or learning of certain test takers. For example, if poor readers could successfully solve mathematics word problems orally, a written test of mathematics word problems would be biased against them (Shepard, 1982). It would not lead to valid conclusions about their mathematics ability. Similarly, a test given in a language with which a student is not yet proficient would be biased against that student (Duran, 1989; Olmedo, 1981). Accurate inferences about the student's knowledge or skills could not be made. In both of these cases, students have not been given equal opportunity to show what they know (Lam, 1995). The result is a distortion in assessment results (Camilli & Shepard, 1994). Test *misuse*, such as using a visual-motor test to determine reading aptitude, is distinguished from test *bias* and is probably a less common problem.

Fairness in Testing

There is a fine line between the concepts of *unbiased* and *fair.* Fairness is more often associated with test use—that is, the consequences of testing—but some measurement experts have suggested that bias extends to test use (e.g., Shepard, 1982). If students have not had the opportunity to learn what they are being tested on, it would not be fair to make judgments about their learning ability on the basis of that test. Or, if a test has differential predictive validity—that is, when it wrongly predicts that members of particular subgroups will or will not be able to attain the desired criterion performance that the test purports to predict—it is biased. For example, some standardized tests predict that minority students will do worse than they actually do in college. The ACT (American College Testing) test is not a good predictor of college success for many minority students (Myers & Pyles, 1992), who often do better than the tests predict. Although men outscore women on the SATs (now called the Scholastic Assessment Tests), which are intended to predict first-year college grades, women actually get better college grades (including when matched for courses at similar universities) (Neill, 1997b).

Concerns for fairness in assessment would lead to a careful examination of the effects of tests and assessment practices on students, including wrongful predictions about their future success and foreclosure of opportunities of which they might well have taken advantage. Students should be given the benefit of the doubt in cases where clear decisions about their achievement or ability cannot be made because of the ways in which test scores and grades can narrow chances for students later in life. Thus, fairness is more than a technical concept: it has ethical ramifications. We should say that simply because an assessment (or a grading practice) has an adverse impact on students does not mean that it is biased (Camilli & Shepard, 1994). However, most educators would probably agree that we do not want our grading practices to have adverse affects on students.

In most grading systems, the students who attain the highest marks on the basis of individual achievement are rewarded with the highest grades. But a system based purely on achievement may rankle educators and parents alike because of concerns for fairness and equality. One way to address the equality issue is to ensure that students have equal opportunities to learn. Failing that, one could adjust grades to reflect that inequality. Perhaps the *fairest* balance in grading, responding to the dual values of equality and achievement, is struck by grading according to effort. "'[E]ffort grading' is more equalitarian than criterion- or norm-referenced systems because it distributes rewards according to a criterion which everyone allegedly has an 'equal' opportunity to meet" (Hiner, 1973, p. 359). This solution is inherently unsatisfying to educators, particularly those trying to implement standards-based systems of instruction and assessment. Nevertheless, the example is very useful in illustrating a tension around the concept of fairness.

A Continuum of Bias and Fairness

As Shepard (1982) has observed, there is a range of types and degrees of bias in testing. At one extreme are tests that clearly disadvantage certain students because of their content or the way they are constructed (as with English-language tests for limited English–proficient students, which may be invalid on both counts). At the other end, there are tests that penalize students whose ways of knowing or experiences are far from those of the "mainstream." In such cases, issues of bias and validity intersect with concerns for equity and social justice. Tests may be seen as a vehicle for perpetuating inequities, and teachers may decide that, in good conscience they cannot use them, or they may use test results more judiciously to protect students from expected consequences.

Sometimes fairness comes into conflict with needs for comparability across students (see examples regarding "special populations" in chapter 7). By making accommodations or changes in assessment, whether in the design of the assessments or in the scoring and interpretation, we may lose comparability in both assessments and grades. Weighing the consequences of alternatives should be done in advance so that all involved have a sense of what is being gained and lost.

Bias: Possible at Any Point in the Assessment Process

Bias can be introduced into the assessment process at any point: in the selection of content, in the design of a test or assessment activity, in the process of administration, in setting scoring or grading criteria, in the interpretation of a score or grade, or in the uses to which a score or grade is put (the consequences of assessment) (see Table 6-1). Although test content is most frequently targeted as the source of bias, ways of administering assessments or gathering information about student learning can also prejudice outcomes. For instance, some students simply will not perform at their best on an "on-demand," timed, written test. Part of fairness is ensuring that students *do* have opportunities to show what they have learned.

In this book we are focused on helping teachers to make valid, defensible judgments about students' learning based on good evidence. In doing so, we hope to identify practices that also result in fair outcomes for students. Part of fairness has to do with how students perceive grading practices. Students—whether female, minority, or general education with special education students in their classes—may believe that they are not graded according to the same criteria as others (see, e.g., Frierson, 1986; Gersten, Vaughn, & Brengelman, 1996; Newstead & Dennis, 1990). Even when this proves not to be the case, if there is student suspicion, it may be worthwhile to institute practices such as occasional blind grading (where students are not known to the grader) to reassure students. As Newstead and Dennis say, "any assessment system must not only be fair, but [must] be seen as fair" (p. 138).

Table 6-1. *Sources of Assessment Bias*

- *Content of a test or assessment task*: This usually refers to content that is likely to be more familiar to certain students than others on the basis of personal experience or privileged status. It could also refer to curriculum that certain students have not had the opportunity to learn. In some cases, the content is actually offensive to students on the basis of their cultural or religious beliefs or because of stereotypical depiction of a person or group.

- *Form or design of a test or assessment task*: A test or assessment may penalize certain students because of its format (e.g., multiple choice, true/false, essay), modality (e.g., oral or written), language (e.g., the ways questions are worded), or other feature. Concerns about form could extend to informal assessment techniques such as group or individual questioning.

- *Administration of a test or assessment task*: The procedures used to elicit a performance from students may penalize some over others. For example, English-language learners will more likely be penalized by a timed test that requires considerable reading and/or writing. Students used to working together or discussing their thoughts with each other may find individual performance more demanding. Poor physical conditions of administration would presumably penalize any student.

- *Setting scoring or grading criteria:* Rubrics or scoring guides as well as implicit criteria used by teachers may be biased because they give too much value to less important aspects of performance that are influenced by linguistic and cultural differences. For example, small grammatical or spelling errors may sway scorers of English language learners' papers to assign unduly low scores. Oral-based written rhetorical styles of African American students may be graded as deficient if rubrics are too restrictive.

- *Interpretation and use of test or assessment scores or grades*: Decisions may be made about a student on the basis of a test or course grade that is not justified. For example, if a test routinely excludes students from a certain group, but it is known that with relatively little extra support many of those students would succeed in the program, denying admission may not be fair. Or, if a teacher concludes that a student who uses rhetorical structures from another literate tradition (and has been graded down because of that) is incapable of learning the conventions valued in school, that would be a serious misinterpretation of a student's likely ability.

Traditional Methods for Dealing With Test Bias

Statistical Techniques

Test bias has been dealt with largely by statistical methods. Measurement experts conduct analyses to determine whether a test favors one group over another—boys over girls, Caucasians over African Americans, and so on. If bias is detected, adjustments may be made either in the test or in the ways that scores are computed or interpreted. Note that bias in tests is always dealt with in terms of groups, not individuals (Camilli & Shepard, 1994). The problem of poor predictive validity mentioned above can be corrected statistically by having different cutoff scores for the subgroups that are penalized by the test in order to bring up the proportion of those passing or reaching an acceptable score to be more in line with the proportion likely to succeed on the ultimate criterion (Thorndike, 1971).

Bias Reviews

Subjective analyses of test content to determine whether the answers to some items are too dependent on specific kinds of sociocultural experiences have also been conducted. Panels of teachers from different ethnic and racial groups who are convened to review all items on a test may conduct such analyses. Reviewers usually scan for content that might be not only too dependent on particular life experience but also offensive to certain test takers. Ethnic stereotypes, lopsided representations of historical events, and condescending depictions of a group may be identified. Themes or topics that appear neutral to a person from the dominant society may be taboo for certain students. For example, some animals are considered sacred by the Navajo, and asking a traditional Navajo student to write an expository piece on these animals could be inappropriate. These kinds of concerns are probably less applicable to classroom teachers or even to school districts than they are to developers of widescale tests, because teachers know their own communities. However, alertness to possibly offensive or inappropriate material is important. Textbooks, reference materials, publishers' tests, and periodicals used in the classroom may be sources of such bias. Grading is, after all, part and parcel of curriculum and instruction. Fair grading depends on equity in access to curriculum and to instruction that is meaningful and engaging (and not offensive) to each student.

Another aspect of content that might be overlooked is its potential interest level. As Neill (1997a) comments, when students are not given open choices about what to write about or are confined to "sanitized" topics, those from "nonmainstream" communities may be disproportionately disengaged. Those who have learned the "school game" of accepting "the bland, the decontextualized, the irrelevant" (most likely middle-class White students) will have a testing advantage in such situations (p. 1). These are, to some degree, speculations, but there is no doubt that student motivation to perform intersects with interest level and meaningfulness of material on assessments, with certain effects on performance (Anastasi, 1990). It is clear that in order to meet the needs for both culturally appropriate and interesting material, teachers need to know students and their cultures.

Bias reviews have been largely confined to standardized tests that are used on a wide scale and generally scored by machine or by scorers other than a child's own teachers. Of course, a bias review cannot eliminate inequalities in educational opportunity, which are the greatest source of difference in performance on standardized tests. Bias is present when inferences about students' ability to learn are made on the basis of an assessment that tests students on skills or knowledge that they have not had the opportunity to learn. Here is where concern for social justice usually triggers questions about the fairness of assessment systems.

Bias in Grading

With grading, there are both greater opportunities to reduce bias (because of the knowledge teachers have of their students) and greater risks of introducing bias (because of unconscious prejudices or judgments teachers may bring to bear). Table 6-2 summarizes possible sources of bias in grading.

Table 6-2. *Major Sources of Grading Bias**

- Performance bias (teachers' idiosyncratic valuations of particular skills)

- Expectancy, based on past performance or some student characteristic (as opposed to evidence of learning)

- Culture- and language-based biases:
  — favoring certain communicative styles
  — relying on assessment formats that disadvantage some students
  — judging performance on the basis of oral response in a group
  — overreliance on on-demand assessment
  — overuse of timed tests
  — lack of knowledge of "non-American" or "non-mainstream" styles of writing
  — overemphasis on low-level errors in written language
  — failure to recognize the language demands of assessments (e.g., in math)

- Racial bias

- Gender bias

* All of the sources of bias in assessment listed in Table 6-1 also feed into grading. Here I list particular sources of bias with which teachers are likely to grapple. Some are particular instances of categories listed in Table 6-1, with some explanation as to how they may play out in the classroom. In addition, these biases are often interrelated. Racial bias and culture- and language-based biases may operate simultaneously, for, in reality, language, culture, and race are intertwined.

In the first instance, performance bias, teachers need to consider specific steps to construct or modify assessments to be appropriate for their students: They can ensure that different kinds of assessments and indicators are used, leading to a more realistic and complex depiction of student learning; they can avoid tests that are not well matched to the learning experiences of their students; and they can annotate student work, explaining the conditions under which it was undertaken and interpreting the meaning of a score or grade. In the second instance, expectancy, teachers need to be conscious of avoiding the introduction of bias into assessment and grading by virtue of holding prejudices about individuals or groups.

As with standardized tests, bias can be a function of the design of the instruments (formal and informal) that teachers use to assess students. But it can also be part of the bigger picture of expectations. Grading is a judgment-based process, more complex than assigning a score on a test. Of course, many of the current performance-based assessments require considerable teacher judgment, and teacher biases have to be addressed head-on through scoring training that promotes adherence to specific criteria. In fact, scoring trainings are excellent opportunities for teachers to recognize their own biases or, more broadly, the values that underlie their grading practices (Koelsch, Trumbull, & Farr, 1995).

Teachers' Personal Biases

Teachers may make unwarranted judgments about students on the basis of gender, ethnic or racial group membership, religion, proficiency with English (or use of standard dialect), perceived ability, behavior, appearance, family background, personal dislike, past performance, disability, medical condition, or any other student characteristic. In some of these instances, biases are based on stereotypes (the expectation that people from a certain group will perform a certain way); in others, they are based on subjective knowledge of individual students. They may be conscious or entirely unconscious. In any given case, more than one bias may be operating at the same time, and they may even work in opposite directions (Newstead & Dennis, 1990). For example, a teacher may expect more of boys academically yet penalize them when grading time comes because of their conduct.

The language of education itself may unwittingly lead to bias about students, sometimes the very students we think we are most committed to supporting. Think of the implicit expectations conveyed by labels like "disadvantaged," "underprivileged" (a little dated but still used at times), or "at-risk." We may want to ask ourselves whether these terms serve any good purpose. Goodwin and Macdonald (1997) speak eloquently about the problem of expectations and terminology:

> What seems clear is that a teacher's belief in children's capacity to learn and worthiness has a bearing on the quality of instruction children receive. While children of color should be perceived as efficacious, capable, and unique by their teachers, in reality they are more typically seen as incapable, inferior, and invisible. This is implicit in the labels assigned to children of color (and their families)—at risk, limited English proficient, disadvantaged, culturally deprived, developmentally delayed, dysfunctional, underclass—and the less-than-high-class education they are offered. (p. 218)

Performance Biases

Certain teachers may seize upon particular aspects of performance to the exclusion of more important ones. Handwriting legibility is a notorious factor in unduly elevating or depressing the grades of students (e.g., Sweedler-Brown, 1993). Neatly written papers are often awarded grades they do not deserve, and papers written with poor handwriting are routinely graded down, despite otherwise good quality. In one recent study (Sprouse & Webb, 1994), teachers identified more spelling errors in less legible spelling tests of fourth graders. They overlooked errors in legible test samples and scored them as having *fewer* errors than they actually contained! In this study, teachers also gave strong essays of eighth graders in the legible condition an average score of 93.8 and the same essays in the less legible condition an average score of 75.3. Furthermore, they showed gender bias by more frequently attributing the less legible handwriting to a boy than a girl.

It is not a total mystery why poor handwriting should be a cause for lower grades. After all, by definition it is hard to read, so teachers may not be able to get to the content readily because of the form. More likely, the problem with less legible papers is that they take noticeably longer to read; and teachers may simply get frustrated with ploughing through them. Nevertheless, it *is* a serious problem when a less important skill influences a grade more than what most would consider a much more important set of skills. Similar problems arise with regard to an overemphasis on spelling, punctuation, paragraphing, and the like. While these skills are important, most educators believe that they should not influence a grade more than a student's ability to mount a cogent argument or spin a good yarn.

"Expectancy"

Many of the sources of bias are traceable to *grading on the basis of expectations rather than evidence*. Numerous research studies have shown that expectancy based on beliefs about students' abilities or past performance can lead teachers to biased judgments about the performance of those students (Brophy & Good, 1986; Good & Brophy, 1984; Irvine, 1991). Babad (1985) found that teachers who were asked to grade a worksheet that was completed by a student described as "excellent" were significantly more likely to give a higher grade than those who were told that the student was "weak."

Perhaps more interesting is the fact that when Babad analyzed which teachers were influenced by the prejudicial information, he found that they were most likely to be inexperienced and/or dogmatic in their beliefs. In addition, the most conventional teachers, as judged by the style of organization of their classrooms, were the most biased. Those who preferred a "frontal" or lecture mode gave an average grade of 81 (on a 100-point basis) to the "excellent" student and 60 to the "weak" student—for the same paper. Teachers preferring an "open classroom" style of classroom organization gave mean scores of 65 to *both* students.

Babad reasoned that inexperienced teachers were less secure in their own judgments and thus more likely to be influenced by outside information—that is, the "excellent" or "weak" label. With regard to the greater bias exhibited by more dogmatic individuals, earlier research has shown that people with authoritarian personalities (whether associated with right-wing or left-wing ideologies) believe themselves to be more objective, reasonable and *less* biased than nondogmatic, less biased people (see, e.g., Babad, 1979; Babad, Inbar, & Rosenthal, 1982; Rokeach, 1960). Because they hold these beliefs about themselves, they may, ironically, be *less* on the lookout for their own biases.

Biases Based on Language, Culture, and Race

Like everything else that human beings create, assessment and grading are cultural phenomena. The ways they are carried out are influenced by culture-based beliefs about how knowledge is acquired and how children and adults or students and teachers should behave vis-à-vis each other. Many of the immigrant students in U.S. schools have had classroom experiences very different from those of native-born American students. Even if such students are fortunate enough to enter bilingual programs where their language and academic needs are addressed, they will still have to learn the norms of U.S. classrooms. They will have to learn who is allowed to talk when and what can be talked about; they will absorb the rhythms of moving from group to individual work; they will gradually acquire an understanding of the rules for using school property such as books and pencils; and they will learn how to demonstrate what they have learned through the means teachers use. All of this will take time, and in the meanwhile, there are endless opportunities for misunderstanding between student and teacher (Arias & Casanova, 1993; Greenfield, Raeff, & Quiroz, 1996).

Communicative Style Differences

Beyond more subtle forms of racial bias related to behavior and values are potential biases based on communicative style, both oral and written. Ball (1992, 1997) has shown how African American rhetorical styles of writing are more negatively evaluated by European American teachers than by African American teachers. European American teachers are likely to be unfamiliar with African American styles and simply judge students who use them to be deficient in writing or speaking skills, as opposed to skilled in a different way. These teachers tend to be biased against African American forms of narrative organization (Ball, 1997). This example demonstrates that teachers need to be extremely careful not to jump to conclusions about students' abilities on the basis of performances that are different from what they expect. This is not to say that students do not need to master forms that meet different (more "mainstream") criteria (Delpit, 1995); they do. It is, rather, the inferences made about students that need to be questioned. White students whose differences in language use and form may be class based are susceptible to similar bias.

Different Responses to On-Demand and Multiple-Choice Testing

If we know that a student's home culture stresses waiting to perform a task publicly until one has firmly mastered a skill, we may decide that it is not fair to expect the student to perform it on demand at an arbitrary point in time. This same cultural value may make it difficult for students to engage in guesswork on a multiple-choice test—a strategy that students from the "mainstream" culture will use to their advantage (Estrin & Nelson-Barber, 1995). This is the case for many American Indian students, particularly those who live in intact traditional communities. There are differences in ideas about what it means to "select the best answer." Many American Indian students are taught to respect all points of view, that any response to a question can have some merit. It may be extremely hard for them to choose one response to the exclusion of all others, and they may take much longer than their dominant-culture peers to complete a test that requires this of them. Multiple-choice tests are also not advised for English language learners (see below). They may be more easily fooled by tricky language that appears to provide the right answer (plausible distractors) or not recognize synonyms (when language in the stem of the question is not repeated exactly in the correct answer).

   If we cannot avoid using multiple-choice tests with such students, we may need to identify other forms of assessment that are more compatible for the student and use them in combination with multiple-choice tests. In this way, we can get another perspective on a student's learning and make more informed inferences. The same is true of the on-demand characteristic of testing. It may be reasonable to allow students some choice in *when* they will take a test—that is, to determine their own readiness. This may not be practical at times, but when it is, it may lead to different outcomes for students.

Differences in Ways of Displaying Knowledge

Much of assessment is done informally, in the course of instruction and classroom activity through questioning by the teacher. Direct questioning, with the expectation of a response from a single student followed by an evaluative comment by the teacher, is not a universal educational practice, although it is common in U.S. classrooms (Cazden, 1988; Mehan, 1979). In some cultures, students are permitted to answer as a group (Eriks-Brophy & Crago, 1993; Jordan, 1985). Students from certain cultural backgrounds may be uncomfortable displaying their knowledge in front of the whole group because such displays are considered too competitive or self-centered. Teachers have in the past interpreted such behavior as "shyness," but it goes well beyond individual personality traits (Dumont, 1972). It is reflective of a culture that places more emphasis on the well-being of the group than on the achievement of the individual, so the communicative style is in harmony with an important value.

This reticence to display knowledge in a group has been documented among Asian Americans, immigrant Latino Americans, and American Indians. Because of this particular cultural difference, judgments about some students' understanding may be way off the mark. In that case, the students from cultures that encourage speaking out and individual displays of knowledge will be advantaged, from an assessment perspective. Of course, it is to students' benefit to learn how to use "mainstream" forms of communication and participation as well as those of home. Carroll, Blake, Camalo, and Messer (1996) use the term "surfing between cultures." However, it is a serious threat to validity and fairness in testing and grading to confuse behaviors that are functional in the student's home environment with lack of capability.

Standards

Another possible source of bias or unfairness vis-à-vis students from nondominant cultures, races, ethnicities, or social classes has to do with the standards themselves. In the context of the example of cultural difference cited above, one might want to examine the language arts standards used by districts. If, for example, the only acceptable narrative structures described in standards are those of the dominant Euro-American culture, we could infer that they are biased against students from cultures that stress other narrative forms. Not all stories have a beginning, a middle, and an end and plots that follow a problem-solution pattern (Heath, 1982; Michaels, 1981). While Americans may feel most gratified by a story that has three episodes, American Indians tend to prefer four, Chinese five, and other Asians two sets of two (Söter, 1994).

Language Differences

Differences in performance by language-minority students are not simply attributable to differences in familiarity with English. They are intimately intertwined with culture-based expectations and experiences. Different social and cultural backgrounds bring with them differences in the ways in which language is used, differences in dialects (and their social status), and differences in problem-solving approaches.

English language learners, especially immigrants, may have serious sociopolitical and economic realities that differentiate them from their "mainstream" peers, and real differences in opportunities to learn may be associated with those realities. Some students may not have had formal schooling or may have missed several years of school. Students' choices of writing topics in language arts or history/social science may make teachers cringe; they may find such topics inappropriate or morally disturbing. A personal reaction of this sort should not interfere with evaluating a student's skills and learning. It is not the teacher's job to Americanize students or to correct students' views that may be based on experiences or beliefs that are frightening or repulsive to the teacher (Carroll et al., 1996), yet it is certainly difficult for teachers to set aside feelings that can be engendered by such writing.

Immigrant students from collectivistic cultures that stress orderliness, conformity, compromise, caring, and family may not automatically tune into typical American narrative themes related to individual achievement, responsibility, control of one's environment, and individual rights and choices (Trumbull, Greenfield, Rothstein-Fisch, & Quiroz, in press). Should their teachers grade these students down when they fail to make the "right" literary interpretations? Perhaps some of the examples offered here seem extreme; perhaps the teachers most likely to be teaching immigrant students will know about these cultural differences and take them into account. However, many newcomers to our schools are not accommodated by full-time programs taught in their native languages or by culturally knowledgeable teachers. These kinds of concerns are real in many communities and should be addressed.

Written Language Issues

Students who are still learning English (even those who have been redesignated from special programs into English-only instruction) are also disadvantaged by demands for articulate oral responses in a group. Even the constraints of time—the expectation to respond quickly—may prevent a student from successful participation in discussion or question-answer sessions. Time is a factor in writing as well. Students writing in their second (or third) language may need extra time to revise and edit; otherwise, they may not complete assessments.

At times, students may actually do better on a written assessment, even though writing is in some ways a higher level language skill. Given adequate time, on a written assessment the student can review what he or she has written and make revisions, and any errors will not be heard by all 25 or 30 classmates. At the same time, judging what an English language learner knows based on written language presents its own problems. It can be difficult to distinguish between normal developmental patterns in acquiring English as a second language and those that suggest actual learning problems (Langdon, 1992; Leki, 1992; Valdés, 1991). Writing is, of course, the principal medium of formal assessment. But teachers, even those with some training in working with English language learners, may have difficulty in both (a) assessing a student's writing and (b) evaluating student learning expressed through writing.

Some further cautions about grading the written work of English language learners can be culled from the literature. Students using English as a second language (orally or in writing) may never reach nativelike proficiency, but some errors are more important than others. Oddly enough, some of the least important errors, in terms of ability to express an idea so that it can be understood by others, are also some of the most noticeable. Scorers of English language learner students' writing have to be warned not to be so distracted by them as to lower a grade inappropriately. For example, a study by Sweedler-Brown (1993) showed that the more "article errors" an essay contained, the lower a score it received on a sentence-structure scale. (A typical article error would be, "My family and I went to park on fourth of July.") Moreover, sentence structure scores were highly correlated with the overall score given to the essays. Articles are difficult to master for speakers of languages that do not use them. They must be almost "unhearable," simply because they are short, unstressed words that contribute relatively little to sentence meaning. Teachers of English as a Second Language (ESL) courses, because of their training, have a sense of how much importance to place on such errors. They recognize that nonnative writers of English will probably never use fully idiomatic English and that some kinds of grammatical errors will persist. With this perspective, they grade on what they consider to be far more important factors, such as organization, development of ideas, paragraph development, and expressiveness. However, the general education teacher may grade unfairly on the basis of his or her sense of what the language ought to sound like.

One recommendation is to not grade English language learner and native speakers' writing side-by-side, in order to reduce comparisons. Otherwise, English language learner errors become conspicuous. Sweedler-Brown (1993) suggests that grading should involve a "skillful balancing of complex variables, as it generally does when applied to native speakers' writing" (p. 14). This balance gets disturbed when graders untrained in how to evaluate the writing of English language learners slip into an error focus. If teachers do not understand why students make certain kinds of errors, not only their grading will be thrown off but also their ability to determine from assessment what needs to be done next instructionally.

Confusing Language Learning and Academic Learning

We need to heed a general warning with regard to assessment and grading of any student who is a speaker of English as a second language: It is almost impossible to separate language from academic achievement. More often than not, educators have *overestimated* a student's proficiency with English (probably because conversational competence develops early on and fools us into thinking the child "speaks English"). At the same time, we have frequently *underestimated* students' cognitive abilities, attributing delayed academic progress to lower ability (Mercado & Romero, 1993). The result has been overplacement in remedial programs, a similar pattern to what is seen with African American students. Extreme caution must be exercised to ensure that unreliable assessment and grading practices do not perpetuate such outcomes. Finally, we must repeat that it is not only English language learners but those who are learning the "mainstream" dialects who may be penalized by teacher and test bias.

Language Demands of "Nonlanguage" Tasks

When students are solving verbal problems in a second language (English), they need to divide "their time and attention between the task of decoding the linguistic statement of a problem and applying cognitive strategies and previous knowledge to the interpretation and solution of a problem" (Duran, 1989, p. 579). Teachers may not realize how dependent cognition is on language, even in seemingly non-verbal tasks or assessments. Mathematics assessments are a case in point: Even though most of the visible work is completed using only mathematical symbols and procedures, much of the mental work is likely to be language dependent. If the student has not accurately interpreted the question or problem (posed in English) to begin with, he or she will have difficulty solving it. In the case of math, the "little" words that indicate relationships among content words (such as *of, from, in, on, for, by*) have to be interpreted precisely. Otherwise, minor confusions can lead to complete misunderstanding of a problem. Consider the difference between "Take one-tenth *from* 100," and "Take one-tenth *of* 100." Determining the student's mathematical skills independent of his or her language skills is incredibly challenging; hence the potential for grading bias.

Racial Bias

Racial bias is especially pernicious and persistent in our society. A frightening proportion of the White population of the United States still believes that African Americans are less intelligent than Whites or that their dialect of English is an inferior language (Hilliard, 1997). A person's perceived racial identity may be the stimulus for instant bias. Lowered expectations of students based on race can set up a nasty cycle in which teachers fail to see students' capabilities and undervalue their performances. At the same time, students are not blind to lowered expectations and may internalize them, eventually fulfilling the expectations (Steele, 1992). Numerous studies point to the unfortunate fact that children of color are less likely to have positive experiences in schools or with teachers (see citations in Goodwin & Macdonald, 1997; Nieto, 1992).

Perceptions of racial prejudice against African Americans in grading are widespread (see, e.g., Frierson, 1986), and certainly value conflicts between African American students and their White teachers may cause what could be interpreted as inequities in grading (Smith & Borgstedt, 1985). Bias against students because of race or ethnicity may be confounded with prejudice about language or ways of using language. As Smitherman (1998) notes, schools and teachers see themselves as the guardians of the national tongue. In this capacity, they often have little tolerance for nonstandard forms of English, which they see as deviant and deficient rather than merely different. They may regard African American children in particular as having poor vocabularies and being generally nonverbal. An ironic state of affairs, given the rich verbal traditions of African American vernacular English (Black Dialect) (Smitherman, 1998).

Gender Bias

Several studies have shown grading bias against female students (Bernard, 1979; Deaux & Traynor, 1973; Lenney, Mitchell, & Browning, 1983; Rudd, 1984; Spear, 1984). In Lenney et al., bias was identified in the absence of explicit grading criteria, but *no bias was detected in grading when criteria were well defined.* As women have entered graduate schools in professions that were historically male (medicine and law, for example), questions about possible gender bias in grading in these areas have been raised. For this reason, many of the studies on gender bias have been done with adult students.

However, contrary to expectations, many studies have *not* shown any identifiable bias against female students. One study showed that third-year female medical students actually obtained higher grades than male students in an ambulatory care training clerkship when they were graded by male supervisors (Wang-Chen, Fulkerson, Barnas, & Lawrence, 1995). Some studies on women's grades in communications courses suggested that female-specific patterns of communication were associated with higher course grades (Hughey, 1984; Hughey & Harper, 1983). According to the criteria for communicative competence, however, women actually *are* more communicatively compliant and competent than men, on the whole (Hughey, 1984), so their higher grades would not be a true case of bias. A study of middle school mathematics teachers (Wiles, 1992) also showed no evidence of grading bias.

Girls and women (like members of some nondominant sociocultural groups) often have a different response from boys and men to the dominant Western mode of education in the United States. According to some, women show less interest in the competitive grading system and to the organization of courses around rigid systems of tests and rewards (Davis & Steiger, 1993). Other research has shown that the traditional mathematics and science instruction—core subjects in determining access to higher education and many careers—alienates girls (Eisenhart, Finkel, & Marion, 1996). The typical analytical, decontextualized approach that teaches concepts, facts, and procedures in little relation to meaningful human and social realities apparently fails to engage girls. If this is true, we have to wonder about the meaning of the grades that girls receive in some courses—a reminder about the interrelatedness of curriculum, instruction, and assessment and grading. Girls' lower scores as a group on standardized tests, such as the SAT, may be due in large part to the fact that they take fewer higher mathematics courses.

While certain factors may lead to an underestimation of girls' abilities and lowered grades, others may lead to unfairly low grades for boys. There is good reason to believe that the more noisy, rambunctious behavior of boys leads to penalties in grading as well as overrepresentation in remedial and special education programs (Bennett, Gottesman, Rock, & Cerullo 1993; Brophy & Good, 1974). It is likely that similar behaviors have contributed to the overplacement of African American students in special education classes (Goodlad, 1984; Hilliard, 1990; Oakes, 1985).

Bennett et al. (1993) conducted a study with hundreds of K–2 students of mixed ethnicity in four schools in Ohio and New York to see whether students' behavior influenced teachers' assessments of their academic behavior. First, they gave students a brief battery of tests to get an independent measure of academic competence. They reviewed students' grades and behavior ratings on report cards and analyzed how these different measures were related. The researchers found that teachers' perceptions of students' behavior significantly colored their judgments of students' academic level. Students who were perceived to exhibit bad behavior were judged to be poorer academically than those who were perceived to have good behavior, regardless of academic skill and gender. But in grades 1 and 2, boys' behavior was perceived to be worse than girls, so their grades were more negatively affected. The results are especially striking, considering that grades purported to be separate from ratings of behavior and that the effects were seen across grade levels, schools, and different criteria for determining academic achievement.

Gender bias can therefore work both ways, by favoring or disfavoring either sex, but different performance characteristics and behaviors of males versus females may legitimately contribute to grade differences. It requires considerable vigilance and analysis to determine whether bias or legitimate difference is operating when gender differences in performances and grades are apparent. Perhaps if sexism were eliminated from our society and a broader range of curricular and instructional options were available, many of these differences would disappear.

Steps to Fairness

No type of grading system is free of the potential for bias, no matter how clear the standards by which students are to be judged. However, if teachers are aware of the ways in which all of the above-mentioned factors can contribute to bias, they can take conscious steps to promote fair grading practices. Many of the suggestions that follow are discussed in greater depth in other chapters, particularly chapters 3, 4, and 7.

Clarify Contexts and Criteria

The more a system can include information about *how* a student achieved as he or she did and can break down a student's performance into different components, the more fair and valid it will be. As discussed elsewhere in this book, single summary grades are not very informative. In addition, there is no such thing as a fair grading system that does not have an explicit set of criteria for judging student work (content and performance standards). Ideally, all teachers at a grade level, or teaching the same subject at a grade level, should use these criteria. If grades can be rationalized on grounds of criteria, evidence, and professional judgment (including knowledge of how linguistic and cultural factors influence student performance), then they are likely to be fair grades.

Make Students Privy to Expectations

To avoid bias in grading, as in assessment generally, it is important that all students understand what they are being graded on, when, how, and according to what performance expectations. This is a tall order for teachers to fill when they have students at different levels of English proficiency or immigrant students whose past schooling experiences are vastly different from those of American-born students. Immediate expectations cannot be the same, although long-term goals can be. It is only fair to share with students the criteria on which they are being judged. Sometimes sample performances from other students can be used to help students understand how the criteria are met.

Allow Students Flexibility in Assessment

Whenever possible, students should be allowed choice in the content, form, and timing of assessments. Ways of demonstrating knowledge must be many and varied if assessment is to be fair (Gordon, 1994; Malcom, 1991). Interest level affects engagement level and output; different formats and modalities of assessment elicit different kinds of performances, especially when students' languages and cultures differ from those of the dominant culture; and time issues (both amount of time and determination of when a test will be administered) affect the performance of some students unfairly. Teachers can vary assessment modes and formats (e.g., some timed and some untimed assessment opportunities) and analyze the differences in performance for an individual student on different indicators to see the conditions under which he or she performs well. However, in using different formats, teachers should let students practice with new formats before formally grading them.

Make Assessments Transparent and Linguistically Accessible

Tests and assessments themselves should be "transparent" (Farr & Trumbull, 1997). Their questions should be clear and not subject to linguistic trickery, and the criteria for a good performance should be explicit. The ways in which questions are worded or multiple-choice responses are ordered can penalize English language learners in comparison to their native English-speaking peers. For example, sentences with negatives are more difficult to process ("Which of the following was not a cause of the Civil War?"). When the second-best answer comes before the best answer to a multiple-choice question, English language learners will be distracted by it (and select it) more often than native English speakers at the same level of competency (Shepard, 1982). Bias reviews directed at content and vocabulary alone are likely to miss such problems.

Identify Susceptibility to Bias and Do Conscious Monitoring

Determining what leads some people to being more susceptible to bias is an important key to reducing bias. It is easy to assume that ignorance and misunderstanding are the most likely culprits. However, some research suggests that certain cognitive orientations may be at the root of susceptibility to bias in judging students' work. As in Babad's (1985) study, it appears that a certain degree of rigidity is associated with fixed biases. When the problem is unconscious attitudes (often born of ignorance), cultural awareness or sensitivity training can sometimes allow people to gain understanding and forge new attitudes.

Teachers who want to check their own tendencies to bias in grading can engage in conscious self-analysis in grading to surface hidden assumptions. Peter Elbow (1986) describes a technique he calls "movies of the reader's mind" (referring to the reader of student papers). Elbow suggests suspending all "measurement thinking" and claims to objectivity, and focusing on giving an accurate and honest account of what is happening in one's mind while reading a student paper (or judging any form of student work, for that matter). The idea is to pay attention to what is happening in one's thinking rather than drawing conclusions or beginning to make recommendations. Elbow speaks of the process as tapping "those perceptions or reactions which underlie judgments, conclusions, or advice" (p. 207). He adds:

> In trying to tell what happens to us as we read a piece of student work, we are not trying to produce a *fair grade*; we are not struggling to avoid subjectivity. Quite the contrary. But the procedure involves two kinds of *discipline* nevertheless: trying to tell the truth; and trying to ground one's reactions in specific details and accurate observations. (p. 228)

Develop a Knowledge Base

Many teachers who are teaching in "diverse" classrooms have not had access to the professional preparation they need to understand how language and culture influence student participation and performance in school. Whether teachers get this professional development formally or through association with other teachers who are from other cultures or who are trained in ESL techniques and cross-cultural communication, they need it if they are to teach, assess, and grade fairly. There is simply no way around it.

Work With Other Teachers

It has been suggested that blind marking or grading of student work (when a teacher other than the student's own teacher grades or when papers are graded without names) is one way to enhance fairness or at least the perception of it. This would certainly address one concern. However, real collaboration in grading with another teacher—as with scoring training for performance assessments—can help teachers illuminate hidden values that lead to actual bias. Elbow (1986), too, suggests using more than one observer to judge student work on occasion, for certain important judgments. He mentions the judging of doctoral dissertations by small committees as an example of this paradigm. When teachers meet regularly in grade-alike groups, it is not too much to expect that they will occasionally grade a set of each other's papers. This practice helps to align the criteria for grading and aids teachers in catching their own biases that sway them from the criteria (Estrin, 1993). When teachers from different grades mark each other's papers, there are real opportunities to discuss student development and to understand how the curriculum articulates across the grades.

Weight Assessments Judiciously

Moving away from an emphasis on tests and toward daily performance can work to reduce bias as well. As time-limited experiences, with associated pressure and demands for rapid language retrieval and production, tests can underestimate a student's learning. For this reason, schemes such as the Hawaii Algebra Grading Process have been developed to reduce bias while holding standards and expectations high (Regional Educational Laboratories, 1998). According to this process, daily work is more heavily weighted than tests. In fact, quizzes and tests count for only 8% of a student's overall grade. This emphasis parallels the goals of the instructional program: problem solving, daily application, and high engagement.

Use Multiple Measures and Multiple Scales

Teachers need to be sure that their grades are based on multiple measures—that is, on many indexes of student learning—but also on indexes that assess learning in different ways. For example, not only oral and written but also nonverbal means are important with English language learners—and, indeed, with many different kinds of students. Teachers need to attempt to separate language performance from other aspects of learning. Multiple measures may be necessary to get a broader picture of students' future possible successes (Shepard, 1982). In terms of multiple scales, perhaps the best examples have to do with written performances evaluated along several dimensions (Spandel, 1996). Again, with English language learners, it is important to distinguish performance on language mechanics and spelling from proficiency with advanced rhetorical and communication skills.

Consider Cultural Models of Assessing and Grading

In more collectivistic cultures, where there is less emphasis on individual achievement and more on how the group is doing, assessment may be done more frequently on a group basis. Many immigrant students from Latin America, Asia, Africa, and the Pacific come from highly collectivistic cultures. Teachers on the island of Rota in the Commonwealth of the Northern Marianas Islands (near Guam in the Pacific Ocean) say they often assess their students in group contexts. They provide opportunities for students to present orally or talk about what they are learning; some can show through drawing and using their drawings as props to talk about concepts. Teachers will ask some to participate in a group activity or presentation, some individually. One teacher said, "In the group, everybody will talk. When it comes to talking [in the group], they are really good!" Teachers wander around, listening in on small-group conversations. They have students evaluate each other as well (peer evaluation). In discussion, a teacher may ask, "What obstacles did you encounter?" They want to get students' own insights into their performances and their instructional needs.

Summary

Avoiding bias in grading depends on the same knowledge, skills, and attitudes as avoiding bias in assessment generally. Bias can be introduced into the assessment and grading process at any point: from the selection of content and design of an assessment to the interpretation of a student's performance and use of a score or grade.

Teachers have the opportunity to either reduce or increase the potential for bias in assessment. One common source of bias in grading is teachers' unconscious prejudices about students' abilities based on either their past performances or personal traits. The conditions of assessment and formats of assignments can bias outcomes in favor of certain students. Some students do not perform well under pressure of time or on formats that require black-and-white answers. Varying the ways of assessing can minimize such problems.

Preventing bias based on linguistic, racial, gender, cultural, or class differences depends on learning about students' backgrounds and on examining one's own attitudes. In particular, ways of using language vary by culture and class; and teachers may misjudge a student's ability because of differences in language use from what is expected in school. Studies of potential bias on grounds of race or gender have not shown any consistent pattern; however, it is important to remember that studies on bias are focused on (usually large) groups of students. Individual students in classrooms may be the "beneficiaries" of what is more properly called "prejudice," which results in lower expectations or misinterpretation of performance. We need only look to the language used to talk about students from nondominant backgrounds to recognize the low expectations and negative assumptions often made about students on the basis of race, language, and social class.

Not only documented cases of bias but also perceptions of bias need to be dealt with in schools. When students suspect that they are not being graded fairly, their ability to engage fully and to take the risks associated with learning new and challenging concepts is likely to be adversely affected.

Common standards of performance help to eliminate bias in grading. When groups of teachers agree on the most important aspects of performance to be evaluated, idiosyncratic grading practices (such as reducing a grade for poor handwriting) are minimized. Letting students know expectations and allowing them choices on how they will be assessed are two steps to reducing the potential for bias. Equally important is that teachers work together to both learn about students and share their own thoughts—to make their own thoughts conscious. They may find new ways of observing and assessing students in the process.

References

Anastasi, A. (1990). What is test misuse: Perspectives of a measurement expert. In *The uses of standardized tests in American education: Proceedings of the 1989 ETS invitational conference* (pp. 15–25). Princeton, NJ: Educational Testing Service.

Arias, B., & Casanova, U. (Eds.). (1993). *Bilingual education: Politics, practice, research, Part 2* (92nd yearbook of the National Society for the Study of Education). Chicago: University of Chicago Press.

Babad, E. (1979). Personality correlates of susceptibility to biasing information. *Journal of Personality and Social Psychology, 37*, 195–202.

Babad, E. (1985). Some correlates of teachers' expectancy bias. *American Educational Research Journal 22* (2), 175–183.

Babad, E., Inbar, J., & Rosenthal, R. (1982). Pygmalion, Galatea, and the golem: Investigations of biased and unbiased teachers. *Journal of Educational Psychology, 74*, 459–474.

Ball, A. F. (1992). Cultural preference and the expository writing of African-American adolescents. *Written Communication, 9* (4), 501–532.

Ball, A. F. (1997). Expanding the dialogue on culture as a critical component when assessing writing. *Assessing Writing, 4*, (2), 169–202.

Bennett, R. E., Gottesman, R. L., Rock, D. A., & Cerullo, F. (1993). Influence of behavior perceptions and gender on teachers' judgments of students' academic skill. *Journal of Educational Psychology, 85* (2), 347–356.

Bernard, M. E. (1979). Does sex role behavior influence the way teachers evaluate students? *Journal of Educational Psychology, 71*, 553–562.

Brophy, J. E., & Good, T. L. (1974). *Teacher-student relationships: Causes and consequences.* New York: Holt, Rinehart, & Winston.

Brophy, J. E., & Good, T. L. (1986). Teacher behavior and student achievement. In M. C. Wittrock (Ed.), *Handbook of research on teaching* (3rd ed., pp. 328–375). New York: Macmillan.

Camilli, G., & Shepard, L. A. (1994). *Methods for identifying biased test items.* Thousand Oaks, CA: Sage.

Carroll, P. S., Blake, F., Camalo, R. A., & Messer, S. (1996, December). When acceptance isn't enough: Helping ESL students become successful writers. *English Journal, 85* (8), 25–33.

Cazden, C. (1988). *Classroom discourse: The language of teaching and learning.* Portsmouth, NH: Heinemann.

Davis, F., & Steiger, A. (1993). *Self-confidence in women's education: A feminist critique.* Springfield, VA: EDRS (Document Reprodcution Service ERIC No. ED 372 999).

Deaux, K., & Traynor, J. (1973). Evaluation of male and female ability: Bias works two ways. *Psychological Reports, 32*, 261–262.

Delpit, L. (1995). *Other people's children.* New York: New Press.

Dumont, R., Jr. (1972). Learning English and how to be silent: Studies in Sioux and Cherokee classrooms. In C. Cazden, V. John, & D. Hymes, (Eds.), *Classroom discourse* (pp. 344–369). New York: Teachers College Press.

Duran, R. (1989). Testing of linguistic minorities. In R. Linn (Ed.), *Educational measurement,* (3rd ed., pp. 573–587). New York: Macmillan.

Eisenhart, M., Finkel, E., & Marion, S. F. (1996, Summer). Creating the conditions for scientific literacy: A re-examination. *American Educational Research Journal, 33*(2), 261–295.

Elbow, P. (1986). *Embracing contraries.* Oxford, England: Oxford University Press.

Eriks-Brophy, A., & Crago, M. (1993, April). *Transforming classroom discourse: Forms of evaluation in Inuit IR and IRe routines.* Paper presented at the annual meeting of the American Educational Research Association, Atlanta.

Estrin, E. Trumbull. (1993). *Alternative assessment: Issues in language, culture, and equity.* (Knowledge Brief No. 11). San Francisco, CA: Far West Laboratory.

Estrin, E. Trumbull, & Nelson-Barber, S. (1995). *Issues in cross-cultural assessment: American Indian and Alaska Native students* (Knowledge Brief No. 12). San Francisco: Far West Laboratory.

FairTest Examiner (newsletter). Cambridge, MA: National Center for Fair and Open Testing.

Farr, B., & Trumbull, E. (1997). *Assessment alternatives for diverse classrooms.* Norwood, MA: Christopher-Gordon.

Frierson, H. T. (1986). *Black North Carolina medical students' perceptions of peer and faculty interactions and school environment.* Paper presented at the annual meeting of the Southern Sociological Society, New Orleans.

Gersten, R., Vaughn, S., & Brengelman, S. U. (1996). Grading and academic feedback for special education students and students with learning difficulties. In T. Guskey (Ed.), *Communicating student learning* (ASCD yearbook). Alexandria, VA: Association for Supervision and Curriculum Development.

Good, T. I., & Brophy, J. (1984). *Looking in classrooms* (3rd ed.). New York: Harper & Row.

Goodlad, J. I. (1984). *A place called school.* New York: McGraw-Hill.

Goodwin, A. L., & Macdonald, M. B. (Eds.). (1997). *Assessment for equity and inclusion.* New York: Routledge.

Gordon, E. (1994, Winter). (no title). Paper presented at 1993 CRESST Conference, Los Angeles. In R. Rothman, Assessment questions: Equity answers. *Evaluation comment,* pp. 1–12.

Greenfield, P. M., Raeff, C., & Quiroz, B. (1996). Cultural values in learning and education. In B. Williams (Ed.), *Closing the achievement gap: A vision for changing beliefs and practices* (pp. 37–55). Alexandria, VA: Association for Supervision and Curriculum Development.

Hamayan, E. V., & Damico, J. C. (1991). Limiting bias in the assessment of bilingual students. In R. Kaplan (Ed.), *With different eyes.* Austin, TX: Pro-Ed.

Heath, S. B. (1982). *Ways with words: Language, life and work in communities and classrooms.* New York: Cambridge University Press.

Hilliard, A. G., III. (1990). Misunderstanding and testing intelligence. In J.I. Goodlad & P. Keating (Eds.), *Access to knowledge* (pp. 145–158). New York: College Board.

Hilliard, A. G., III. (1997). Language, culture, and the assessment of African American children. In A. L. Goodwin, & M. B. Macdonald, (Eds.), *Assessment for equity and inclusion* (pp. 229–240). New York: Routledge.

Hiner, R. (1973). An American ritual: Grading as a cultural function. *Clearing House, 47* (6), 356–361.

Hughey, J. D. (1984, November). *Why are women getting all those A's?* Paper presented at the annual meeting of the Speech Communication Association, Chicago.

Hughey, J. D., & Harper, B. (1983, November). *What's in a grade?* Paper presented at the annual meeting of the Speech Communication Association, Washington, DC.

Irvine, J. J. (1991). *Black students and school failure.* New York: Praeger.

Jordan, C. (1985). Translating culture: From ethnographic information to educational program. *Anthropology and Education Quarterly, 16,* 105–123.

Koelsch, N., Trumbull, E. E., & Farr, B. (1995). *Guide to developing equitable performance assessments.* San Francisco, CA: WestEd.

Lam, T. C. M. (1995). *Fairness in performance assessment* (Report No. EDO-CG-95-25). Washington, DC: Office of Educational Research and Improvement. Department of Education. ERIC Document Reproduction Service No. ED 391 982)

Langdon, H. (1992). Speech and language assessment of LEP/bilingual Hispanic students. In H. Langdon & Li- Rong Lilly Cheng (Eds.), *Hispanic children and adults with communication disorders: Assessment and intervention.* (pp. 201–271). Gaithersburg, MD: Aspen.

Leki, I. (1992). *Understanding ESL writers: A guide for teachers.* Portsmouth, NH: Boynton/Cook.

Lenney, E., Mitchell, L., & Browning, C. (1983). The effect of clear evaluation criteria on sex bias in judgments of performance. *Psychology of Women Quarterly, 7,* 313–328.

Malcom, S. (1991). Equity and excellence through authentic science assessment. In G. Kulm & S. Malcom (Eds.), *Science assessment in the service of reform* (pp. 313–330). Washington, DC: American Association for the Advancement of Science.

Mehan, H. (1979). *Learning lessons.* Cambridge, MA: Harvard University Press.

Mercado, C., & Romero, M. (1993). Assessment of students in bilingual education. In B. Arias and U. Casanova (Eds.), *Bilingual education: Politics, practice, and research* (pp. 144–170). Chicago: University of Chicago Press.

Michaels, S. (1981). "Sharing time": Children's narrative styles and differential access to literacy. *Language in Society, 10,* 423–442.

Myers, R. S., & Pyles, M. R. (1992, November). *Relationships among high school grades, ACT test scores, and college grades.* Paper presented at the annual meeting of the Mid-South Educational Research Association, Knoxville, TN.

Neill, M. (1997a, February 28). Internet Communication, K–12 Assessment Forum, p.1.

Neill, M. (1997b, March 11). Internet Communication, K–12 Assessment Forum, p.1.

Newstead, S. E., & Dennis, I. (1990). Blind marking and sex bias in student assessment. *Assessment and Evaluation in Higher Education, 15* (2), 132–139.

Nieto, S. (1992). *Affirming diversity.* New York: Longman.

Oakes, J. (1985). *Keeping track: How schools structure inequality.* New Haven, CT: Yale University Press.

Olmedo, E. L. (1981). Testing linguistic minorities. *American Psychologist, 36* (10), 1078–1085.

Regional Educational Laboratories (1998). *Improving classroom assessments: A toolkit for professional developers.* Portland, OR: Northwest Regional Educational Laboratory.

Rokeach, M. (1960). *The open and closed mind.* New York: Basic Books.

Rudd, E. (1984). A comparison between the results achieved by women and by men studying for first degrees in British universities. *Studies in Higher Education, 9,* 47–57.

Shepard, L. (1982). Definitions of bias. In R. Berk (Ed.), *Handbook of methods for detecting bias* (pp. 9–30). Baltimore, MD: Johns Hopkins University Press.

Smith, S. L., & Borgstedt, K. W. (1985). *Dynamics of interracial relationships involving White faculty in Black colleges: Review, systematization, and directives.* Springfield, VA: EDRS. (ERIC Document Reproduction Service No. ED 261 616.

Smitherman, G. (1998). "What go round come round": *King* in perspective. In T. Perry and L. Delpit (Eds.), *The real ebonics debate* (pp. 163–171). Boston: Beacon Press.

Söter, A. O. (1994). The second language learner and cultural transfer in narration. In C. K. Brooks (Ed.). *Tapping potential: English and language arts for the Black learner.* Urbana, IL: National Council of Teachers at English.

Spandel, V. (1996, July). *Working with student writers on 6-trait assessment.* Paper presented at Classroom Assessment: The Key to Student Success Conference, in Portland, OR.

Spear, M. G. (1984). Sex bias in science teachers' ratings of work and pupil characteristics. *European Journal of Science Education, 6,* 369–377.

Sprouse, J. L., & Webb, J. E. (1994). *The Pygmalion effect and its influence on the grading and gender assignment on spelling and essay assessments.* Master's Thesis, University of Virginia.

Steele, C. (1992, April). Race and the schooling of Black Americans. *Atlantic Monthly,* pp. 68–78.

Stiggins, R. (1997). *Student-centered classroom assessment* (2nd ed.). Upper Saddle River, NJ: Prentice-Hall.

Sweedler-Brown, C. O. (1993). ESL essay evaluation: The influence of sentence-level and rhetorical features. *Journal of Second Language Writing, 2,* 3–17.

Thorndike, R. L. (1971). Concepts of culture-fairness. *Journal of Educational Measurement, 8,* 63–70.

Trumbull, E., Greenfield, P. M., Rothstein-Fisch, C., & Quiroz, B. (in press). *Bridging cultures between home and school: A guide for teachers.* Mahwah, NJ: Erlbaum.

Valdés, G. (1991). *Bilingual minorities and language issues in writing: Toward profession-wide responses to a new challenge.* Berkeley, CA: University of California National Center for the Study of Writing.

Wang-Cheng, R. M., Fulkerson, P. K., Barnas, G. P., & Lawrence, S. L. (1995). Effect of student and preceptor gender on clinical grades in an ambulatory care clerkship. *Academic Medicine, 70* (4), 324–326.

Wiles, C. (1992). Investigating gender bias in the evaluation of middle school teachers of mathematics. *School Science and Mathematics, 92* (6), 295–298.

Grading and Special Populations

7

Henriette W. Langdon and
Elise Trumbull

> *There are two, largely polarized, schools of thought regarding grading practices for special education students. The first holds that standards ought to be absolute. . . . The second school of thought assumes a diametrically opposite position, calling for grading based primarily on individual effort.*
>
> —R. Gersten, S. Vaughn, & S. U. Brengelman
> *Communicating Student Learning*

Grading students from special populations, such as students enrolled in special education programs and those learning English as a second language, presents a conundrum. Should these students be graded in exactly the same ways as their fully English proficient and non–learning disabled peers? There is not as much literature on this complex and important question as one might expect. For that reason, Henriette Langdon conducted a study of grading practices with students enrolled in special education or English Language Development (ELD) programs in four schools in the San Jose, California, area. The results of this study are illustrative of the kinds of dilemmas teachers face, and they add to our understanding of problems associated with grading special education and ELD students.[1] Before turning to the study, let's outline out the issues and review what educators have done to address them.

Longstanding Issues in a New Context

As mentioned earlier in this book, with the move to establishment of standards for all of the disciplines, assessment and grading practices are once again being exam-

---

[1]Students whose first language is not English and who have not fully mastered English are usually referred to as "Limited English Proficient," or LEP, students. In this chapter we use the acronym ELD, to designate students who are still acquiring English. Some of these students may be close to "fully English proficient" (FEP) rather than LEP, yet still need language support.

ined. Of course, grades have always had consequences for students. Students pass on from one grade to another at least in part on the basis of grades. Admission to certain programs is dependent on grades, and grades are used as part of the decision-making process in college admissions. For students who do not fall into the so-called "educational mainstream," grades are also an important indicator of academic success and are a factor in decision making about program assignment. However, arriving at a fair and informative grading process—one that leads to equitable and successful outcomes—for students from special populations is a most challenging task.

Grades are a shorthand for communicating evaluative information about students' progress, growth, or achievement, but it is important to remember that grades are not an absolute index of student learning. They are, in fact, a translation or interpretation of test scores, observations, and other kinds of data gathered by teachers. Teacher judgment is always entailed in the deriving and assigning of a grade, and with "special populations," teachers may find that they need to look beyond the usual sources of data in order to make what they consider to be valid judgments about student learning. Alternatively, they may rely on the usual data but make allowances in how they interpret them to arrive at a grade.

Impact of the Standards Movement

Along with the advent of national and local efforts to establish clear and high educational standards in all subject areas, and the continued movement to mainstream students with disabilities into regular classrooms, has come a set of questions about how to grade such students (Bradley & Calvin, 1998; Bursuck, et al., 1996; Christiansen & Vogel, 1998). There are two populations of special education students: those who are mainstreamed or integrated into regular classrooms for the majority of their instruction, and those who are educated in separate classrooms with limited opportunities for mainstreaming. According to at least one study, the majority (74.3%) of students who are based primarily in special education classes are graded according to standards different from those for general education (Valdes, Williamson, & Wagner, 1990). Likewise, special education students who are integrated in general education settings are often graded according to somewhat different standards (Calhoun & Beattie, 1984; Pollard, Rojewski, & Pollard, 1993). For students with serious developmental differences or delays, it seems appropriate to modify standards or at least the expected rate and manner of achievement of standards. These students are probably most fairly graded *ipsatively* (with reference to their own past performance) on the basis of growth. However, with students who participate in the regular education curriculum, the picture is less clear vis-à-vis standards and grading practices.

Complicating the matter is the reality that the population of students with learning difficulties or disabilities who are mainstreamed into general education programs is not homogeneous, and any assessment and grading system needs to be flexible enough to account for that fact (Shriner, Ysseldyke, Thurlow, & Honetschlager, 1994).

Different Standards and Grading Methods for Different Students?

The question of whether to hold special education students and those still learning English to the same standards as general education students cannot be answered glibly. Advocates for students, vocal public groups demanding accountability, and many politicians have all argued in one way or another for equal expectations and equal treatment of all students (with the possible exception of seriously learning handicapped students). Public sentiment favors setting and maintaining higher academic standards. A recent report suggests that as much as 60% of the public believes standards have been set too low (Education Commission of the States, 1997).

A No-Win Situation?

Whether students with special learning needs are held to the same standards and graded in the same manner as other students or held to somewhat different standards and graded differently, the consequences can be quite negative. For example, when high school students with disabilities are graded in the same way as peers, they tend to have very low grade point averages, usually translating to grades of C+ to D (Donahue & Zigmond, 1990; Valdes, Williamson, & Wagner, 1990; Wood, Bennett, Wood, & Bennett, 1990). Such grades can be terribly demoralizing to students; far from motivating, they may discourage students to the point where they no longer try to do well. Many districts do have policies that allow modification of grades for students who have an Individual Education Plan (IEP)—60%, according to Polloway et al. (1994). One modification is to grade the student on the basis of his or her progress against objectives on the IEP. The possible downside of this practice is the devaluation of grades.

Inappropriateness of Some Criteria

Of course, grading criteria that make sense for regular education students may not apply well to students who are still learning English or students with special learning needs. When this is the case, teachers may make adjustments in their grading procedures. For example, one of the criteria for getting an A in a district surveyed by Austin and McCann (1992) is "speaks clearly and forcibly in discussions." As any teacher of students who are learning a second language knows, confident participation in classroom discussions may not be a realistic expectation until the student has considerable proficiency in that language. A statement about F work, mentioned by Austin and McCann, was "Written work is careless, untidy, inaccurate or incomplete" (p. 19). A learning disabled student may produce work that represents adequate understanding but that could be characterized by several of the terms in that statement. In some sense, student performance needs to be understood in the context of what is realistic for the student, given his or her particular developmental profile or special needs.

Getting to a Grade

Multiple Criteria

Most schools agree that multiple criteria should be used to arrive at a grade for any student (Austin & McCann, 1992). No single performance, even on a comprehensive final exam, should be taken as the sole index of student learning over a marking period. In the case of special education and ELD students, reliance on a single indicator may obscure critically important distinctions or variations in different types of performances. One need think only of the possible discrepancy in an ELD student's ability to represent a set of relationships visually or through a model versus through the language required for a timed essay exam.

Some districts have implemented portfolio systems in which a grade is based in large part on a cumulative portfolio score. By definition, portfolios entail multiple criteria and multiple measures (in the sense of different kinds of performances). In addition, portfolios have the flexibility to incorporate nontraditional products such as audiotapes, drawings, or even videotapes—forms of assessment that may show special education students' learning better at times than paper-and-pencil tasks. Of course, to work as an assessment tool, a portfolio ought to have clear guidelines for what gets included and how entries are evaluated (against what criteria). If the focus is on growth, the portfolio approach may be an excellent tool, because it typically houses performances collected at many points in time.

Multiple Grading Scales

A single symbol is greatly limited in power to communicate meaningful information, even if it represents only academic achievement. Some have suggested that students be graded along several dimensions represented by separate scales (Wiggins, 1998). Wiggins (1996) recommends that other components besides achievement be included in grades, such as the student's habit of mind—that is, persistence with difficult work; ability to clarify a task, organize an agenda, or ferret out unstated or unexamined assumptions; tolerance for ambiguity; and ability to take into consideration different points of view. He also proposes separating the concept of "normed" from "growth" grades. Thus, one set of grades would compare the student to age and grade-level peers, and the other would compare the student's performance against his or her own performance. This approach could be useful in communicating the learning or achievement of special education and ELD students.

Using Comparison Groups

A third scale is needed to answer the question "How does the student's progress (against standards or achievement targets) compare to that of *comparable students?*" (Wiggins, 1996). For example, ELD students exhibit predictable stages of second language development and predictable error patterns (varying to some degree according to what their first language is). Knowledge of these stages and patterns should be used to help gauge whether such a student's progress is adequate.

Criterion-Referenced Versus Norm-Referenced Grading

Regardless of the form of the grade report, the most common method of gauging and reporting students' progress is based on criterion-referenced assessments (Airasian, 1996; Gellman, 1995). All students who reach the criterion score for a given grade receive that grade on an assessment, or for a marking period as an average of assessments (in contrast to a norm-referenced system, in which the top 5% of scores count as an A, the next 10% a B, etc.). Teacher-made tests may be the primary source of data, but assignments of various sorts can, of course, be graded as well. Tests are intended to be closely linked to the curriculum taught, unlike published tests that often do not reflect the exact instructional experiences students have had.[2]

Curriculum-Based Assessment

Curriculum based assessment (CBA) has been touted as a valid form of student evaluation for special education students, because it yields so much more information than standardized tests and can detect student progress more sensitively than such tests (Farr & Trumbull, 1997). In CBA, an activity directly related to the curriculum is completed by the student while the teacher observes and applies certain evaluation criteria to the student's performance. The teacher may assist the student, but he or she makes careful notation of exactly what help the student required at what point. If applied systematically, CBA can be utilized to identify students with learning problems and follow their progress with specific interventions before referring them for a more comprehensive assessment (Fuchs & Fuchs, 1997).

The problem with all criterion-based systems is that the criteria on which students are to be judged have usually not been well specified (Gellman, 1995). What exactly are the skills and knowledge a student should master in order to get an A or a C on a test? Do teacher-made tests adequately examine the student's knowledge of the curriculum taught? These are questions that often cannot be answered satisfactorily.

Using Nonacademic Indicators in Grading

Effort, attitude, and behavior have been often used to boost students' grades and have been more frequently applied to the purpose of passing older students (Blount, 1997). More generally, they often are used to raise the grades of students who would otherwise fail or be graded very low (Seeley, 1994). In the 1960s, these variables were used to improve the grades of some students in order keep them in school so they would not be drafted. Effort, attitude, and behavior have also been used to improve the grades of athletes so they would be eligible for athletic schol-

---

[2]Performance assessments are also criterion-referenced: however, they are ideally designed to replicate or approximate the actual criterion performance a student might be expected to demonstrate under "real-world" conditions. For example, to demonstrate mastery of certain research skills for a science course, a student might be asked to design an experiment and carry it out.

arships (Owen, 1997). Again, especially in the case of students who have great difficulty attaining high grades through no fault of their own, the temptation on the part of teachers is to look for ways to encourage and motivate them through rewarding success in nonacademic aspects of school. There are two serious questions about such practices: Can one reliably identify effort? Does the practice of incorporating effort into a single grade "pollute" the grade (i.e., does such a grade communicate any real information about what a student knows and can do)? To address the problem of identifying effort, teachers often use classroom participation or homework completion. The second problem, however, is not easily resolved. A single grade that reflects a collapsing of information about nonacademic behaviors and academic achievement really communicates nothing useful in itself.

The Form of the Grade

The appropriateness of the form of a grade intersects with all of these concerns. While many teachers prefer checklists, narratives, or pass-fail grades to letter or number grades for students with learning disabilities (Bursuck et al., 1996), many districts apparently mandate letter grades (Polloway et al., 1994). Of course, some districts give multiple grades—grades for both academic achievement and effort or comportment (Blount, 1997; Bursuck et al., 1996). Developmental scales, which assign students to such performance levels as "emergent," " beginning," " developing," "proficient," and "advanced" are used by some districts. For special education students, in particular, a single symbol is unlikely to capture what is by definition likely to be an unusual performance profile. For example, a single grade for English or language arts may conceal a wide variation between reading and writing skills.

Making Accommodations in Assessment

"Adjusting" Grades

Teachers' expectations may vary from student to student, depending on what they see as a student's capabilities (Wiggins, 1996). A not uncommon practice among teachers is to adjust grades—and not just those of special education or ELD students—according to the student's ability. A separate grade may be given for effort, or effort may be factored into a single grade. Simply adjusting grades upward or giving credit for nonacademic aspects of performance would seem to reduce the meaningfulness of the grade. Students may suspect that their grades do not have the value that other students' grades have, and, indeed, the student may not be able to move into desired courses or programs on the strength of such grades. However, proponents of grade adjustment argue that students' true abilities are overlooked by traditional grading practices and that adjustment is justified.

Here is the root of much of the problem in deciding how to grade students from special populations: Teachers may not believe that it is fair (or revealing of students' learning) to simply use the same procedures they use with students in so-called "general education" programs. Because grades have such an impact on students' perceptions of their worth, many teachers would do anything to avoid failing a student (Blount, 1997). The inclination to give students some sense of success is surely a principal ingredient in the motivation to adjust grades. Elbow (1986) discusses the tension teachers experience as they are implicitly asked to be both judges of and advocates for students. It is no wonder that teachers of students with learning difficulties, language disorders, or language differences (ELD students) face a dilemma when it comes to how to grade them.

Modifying Assessments and the Assessment Process

Grade adjustment is just one form of accommodation. It is not only in tallying up the grade that teachers make adjustments or accommodations for students they perceive as needing special support. Teachers may strongly believe that they need to use different methods of assessment for different students (Geenen & Ysseldyke, 1997). For instance, a student with a reading disability may need to have directions to an assessment reworded or read aloud. Accommodations have to be made, but if different procedures are used or if different criteria are used to judge student progress or achievement, these should be made explicit. Some educators disagree with the common practice of annotating the report card to show when special accommodations for learning have been provided to students or when adjustments in assessment or grading have been made. Geenen and Ysseldyke state that " there should not be a special notation on the report card," which may be conducive to misinterpretations of the value of the grade. Others suggest the opposite: that traditional methods of grading do more harm than good to the student who is mildly handicapped, unless the grade is accompanied by the teacher's comment (Pennsylvania Department of Education, 1997).

This disagreement is emblematic of the tensions around the question of how to be fair to such students and yet communicate honestly about their achievement and growth. Students themselves (except perhaps for those who are extremely handicapped) are not blind to this tension. Nor are they exempt from the judgments of their non–special education peers who have their own sense of fairness about grading. Junior high and high school students tend to believe that everyone should be graded according to the same standards (Gersten, Vaughn, & Brengelman, 1996), and they are sensitive to exceptions to this practice. No matter how much teachers sugarcoat the grading pill, all students are susceptible to its effects. Nevertheless, districts need to come to a conscious decision about how they are going to deal with this issue—that is, whether grades for mainstreamed students who have IEPs will be determined on the same basis as those of general education students or through some modified process.

With the ever-increasing push to raise standards and hold them high for all students, there is also an increasing demand for students enrolled in special education to take the same tests as their peers who are in regular classes. The same policy is being applied in many cases to students who are not fully proficient in English. In California, for example, it is now a state policy to require all students, even those who speak little English, to take statewide achievement tests. To ensure that all students can participate in wide-scale assessments, certain accommodations may need to be implemented. They may range from providing more time to students to complete a given task, to modifying testing formats (e.g., changing from written to oral) and administering assessments in the dominant language of the student (which sometimes requires the development of new assessments). In no instance should a student be tested in a language in which he or she is not proficient. The results will not be valid, and the experience itself may be damaging to the student (see chapter 6).

Ensuring Accountability for *All* Students

Geenen & Ysseldyke (1997) suggest that assessments should be modified to make it possible for *all* students to be assessed. To them and many others in the field of special education, it is unacceptable to exclude groups of students who have difficulty completing assessments designed for the majority of students. Accountability data should include information about these students as well. It is not fair to exclude them, and their needs may not get public scrutiny. Of course, the data can be collected so that they can be disaggregated from the pool of results when necessary. The concern, then, is how much accommodation can be permitted in order to capture what the student really knows without violating the validity of the assessments. That is, if the assessment is changed substantially, it may no longer assess what it was intended to assess. The current trend is clearly to have all students take the same tests, unless a provision to the contrary is specified on the IEP. However, as Geenen & Ysseldyke note, because those IEPs are so individualized (and so many different kinds of accommodations could be required), results on students' tests would be very difficult to aggregate. Performances would not be comparable.

While accommodations would enable these students to participate in the data collection process, they do not address the fact that students with disabilities are more than twice as likely to drop out of school prematurely (Geneen & Ysseldyke, 1997). Therefore, group test data on older students do not reveal the true lack of success of the instructional system for an important subset of students, a fact that effectively reduces the accountability of districts.

The Need for Explicit Grading Policies

Making the purposes of grading explicit and establishing policies harmonious with these purposes are crucial steps for school districts. The goals of fairness and accountability demand that districts think long and hard about how they will address this issue. As is discussed in different ways throughout this book, these purposes and policies depend to some degree on one's views of student learning and on the perceived purposes of schooling. Austin & McCann (1992) crystallize an important part of the decision-making process surrounding grades: They suggest that schools need to decide whether they want to grade on the basis of achievement (if the purpose of school is to ensure that students *master* certain knowledge and skills) or on the basis of effort and progress (if the purpose of school is to *develop* skills). If school is a place to provide multiple programs and track students, then grades must differentiate students in terms of their performance from other members of the class, grade, or age group. A related and equally important decision (or set of decisions) for a district is about what students' grades will be based on and whether all students will be graded on the same basis.

Even when school districts have policies that permit grading special education and/or ELD students differently, such students will not automatically attain a greater grade point average. However (according to the logic of proponents of this approach), their grades should be fairer, because students' true learning will not be masked by their particular disabilities. For example, if a student cannot write well, he might be graded on an oral presentation in which he can demonstrate his understanding of important concepts in a way he could not in writing. If the purpose is to assess the learning of concepts and not written expression, to allow him to improve his potential grade through an assessment accommodation is not to lower standards but to get around his disability.

Who Is Grading?

Another variable in grading students from special populations is the *person* doing the grading. Bursuck et al. (1996) found that when special education students were graded, more often than not the responsibility rested on the general education teacher (60% of the time) rather than on the special education teacher. In the other situations, the general education teachers reported sharing responsibility for grading with special education teachers. In contrast, Polloway et al. (1994) report, "A disappointing finding is that a shared grading system in which input from both special and general education is used, was mentioned in only about 12% of the cases" (p. 166). General education teachers were the ones assigning final grades. Both of these studies sampled a sizable number of teachers (368 teachers in the Bursuck et al. study and 393 teachers in the Polloway et al. study). Both were national surveys, and they were conducted within 2 years of each other. One conclusion is that there is considerable variation in practice, but even if the 40% who shared responsibility were more representative of practice, it would still indicate an undesirably low rate of cooperation between general education and special education teachers around grading.

ELD Concerns

Problems arise when teachers who do not know a student's first language grade or score written performances in particular. Several research studies have shown that non-ELD teachers judge minor errors that do not interfere with meaning more harshly than do ELD teachers (Sweedler-Brown 1993). In the case of younger students or those who are very new to the language, spelling errors may make words unrecognizable to a nonspeaker of the student's language, whereas a speaker of the language can immediately decode the word. An example of this is when a Spanish speaker substitutes *b* for *v* (*bery* for *very*) or uses *ei* to represent the long *a* sound (*leity* for *lady*). In Spanish, *b* and *v* sound almost alike, and the diphthong would be represented by the digraph *ei*. Sometimes a *d* will be heard and written as a *t* (as in the example above), or a *b* heard as a *p*. Such errors do not mean the student has an auditory deficit but that he or she is still learning to distinguish sound categories in English that have somewhat different boundaries in Spanish.

The Grading Study

Background and Purpose of the Study

Because of the relative paucity of research on the grading of special education and ELD students, Henriette Langdon undertook a small-scale study in two districts near San José State University, where she teaches. She wanted to find out firsthand what was currently happening with the grading of special education and ELD students in her own area. She was fortunate enough to have access to teachers through a cooperating relationship that her university has with two local districts.

The intention was to survey as many teachers as possible (general education, special education, and ELD) to find out exactly what their grading practices were and the degree to which practices in grading general education, special education, and ELD students were similar or different. It seemed possible that the adoption of standards-based curriculum, instruction, and assessment (widespread in California) might have led to at least the beginning of an alignment of grading practices with other forms of assessing and reporting. Perhaps the standards movement had provided an opportunity for teachers to engage in dialogue across traditional divisions among general education, special education, and ELD education.

Methodology

Teachers of grades 3 through 6 in four elementary (K–6) schools were surveyed about their grading practices. Principals of all four schools were approached for permission to conduct the survey with their staff. A cover letter explaining the content and purpose of the survey was attached to a three-page questionnaire for the teachers to read prior to completing it. Langdon briefed eight university student teachers, who were doing their student teaching in the schools involved, on the nature of the questionnaires and how to instruct teachers to complete them. Teachers completed the questionnaires during a staff meeting at each school.

The Schools

The schools are in two districts in Santa Clara County, California, in what is usually called the Silicon Valley. Both District A and District B are K–8 schools. District A has an enrollment of 12,500 students distributed among 18 elementary schools and 3 intermediate schools. Twenty per cent of District A's students are classified as limited English proficient (LEP), and one-third of these students are Latinos whose home language is Spanish. Approximately 33% of students in District A are eligible for free or reduced lunch.

District B is smaller than District A, with an enrollment of about 7,500 students. attending nine elementary schools and three intermediate schools. District B has a greater percentage of LEP students (45%), about half of Latino background. Forty-eight per cent of students are eligible for free or reduced lunch.

Three of the schools surveyed are in District A, and one is in District B. Although teachers from grades 3 through 6 were targeted, in a few cases grade 2 was included because of multigrade classrooms.

The Teachers

The teachers were general and special education teachers from four schools in the two districts described, who teach students in grades 3 through 6. All teachers, as is common in many districts in California, have had special training to understand the language acquisition and learning processes of second-language learners and have either an ELD or a CLAD (Cross-Cultural Language and Academic Development) credential.

The Questionnaires

Teachers were asked to complete questionnaires that addressed the following five broad questions:

1. What types of grades and grading systems are used to evaluate students from general compared to special education, and how are those students graded differently, depending on the amount of time spent in the regular education program?
2. What grading procedures are followed with students who are considered LEP?
3. How are final grades awarded to each of the two groups (general and special education)?
4. What accommodations are being implemented in either of these groups to allow them to participate in the regular program and its evaluation?
5. How frequently are grades reported to parents and families?

Teachers were given two sets of questions. The purpose of the first set of questions was to gather some general data from each teacher. Teachers were asked about their number of years of teaching experience, whether or not there were district and school guidelines for grading, and the number of special education and ELD students enrolled in their classrooms. The rest of the questions were more specific to the grading procedures they followed and included eight areas:

1. Form of the students' grades on their report cards, such as letter grades or number grades
2. Grading systems to appraise the students' work such as shared grading, percentage cutoffs, individually referenced or developmental scales
3. Percentage given to various assessment methods such as publishers' unit tests, teacher-made tests, or portfolios
4. Descriptions of procedures used to grade special education students
5. Descriptions of procedures used to grade ELD students
6. Methods of assigning final grades to those students
7. Accommodations made to assist the special education and ELD students
8. Frequency of reporting grades to parents

A final open-ended question solicited suggestions from teachers for improving the grading system used in their school or district.

In the study to be reported on, a sample of the report card used by three of the schools surveyed (all in District A) has a section asking whether the student is included in any of the "resource programs." These programs include adaptive physical education, bilingual education, Title 1, English Language Development, Gifted and Talented Education, Migrant Education, Resource Specialist Program and Speech and Language Therapy. However, there is no indication of how students who are enrolled in any of these programs may be graded differently from their peers attending the general education programs. Therefore, one of the questions in the survey asked how teachers from both general and special education grade those students.

Results of the Study

A total of 27 general education teachers and 5 special education teachers responded to the questionnaire from the four schools surveyed. As mentioned, three of the four schools were in a single district (District A, with 18 general education teachers and 4 special education teachers responding). The fourth school was in another district (District B, with 9 general education and 1 special education teacher responding). Table 7-1 lists the grades represented, the number of teachers by grade level for each district, the teachers' mean number of years of experience at their current grade level, and the mean number of special education and ELD students in each grade. The mean number of years of teaching experience of teachers at each grade level in District A is quite high, ranging from 14 to 24 years. The mean number of years of experience of teachers from District B by grade taught ranges from 4 to 9 years only. Personal reports from one of the teacher supervisors for both districts indicated that District B had recently undergone a widespread rehiring process, because much of the faculty had retired.

The Students

The number of special education students in District A varied from one to three per classroom, a rate that represents approximately 10% of the overall school population. In District B the number of identified students in special education per class at each grade level was lower (0–2), with none reported in the third grade. It could be that in District B stricter criteria are used for eligibility for special education services. The teachers of District A reported that they had a generally low number of ELD students across the grades that were surveyed in this study. Teachers from District B reported a greater number of ELD students in their classes (ranging from 2 to 7 on average per classroom in each grade).[3]

Grading Policies and Methods of Reporting

All of the teachers in both districts responded that there were district guidelines for grading. Only 45% indicated that there were school-based procedures. The rest

---

[3]There is an inexplicable discrepancy between the number of students the districts designate as LEP/ELD and the numbers reported by the teachers.

Table 7-1. *Demographic Information*

General Education Teachers Responding				
District A				
Grade	Total No. of Teachers	Mean No. of TE*	Mean No. of SP**	Mean No. of ELD
3rd	6	20 years	2	4
4th	4	21 years	3	< 1
5th	4	24 years	< 1	< 1
6th	4	14 years	2	< 1
District B				
Grade	Total No. of Teachers	Mean No. of TE*	Mean No. of SP**	Mean No. of ELD
3rd	4	4 years	0	4
4th	3	9 years	< 1	2
5th	2	5 years	2	7
Special Education Teachers Responding				
District A				
Total No.	Mean No. of TE	Mean No. of SP	Mean # of ELD	
4	14 years	27	1	
District B				
Total No.	Mean No. of TE	Mean No. of SP	Mean # of ELD	
1	5 years	26	0	

* TE = years of teaching experience
**SP = special education students

were either unsure about school-based procedures or stated that there were no such procedures.

Table 7-2 lists the methods teachers used to report grades, the kinds of grading systems used, and the percentage of teachers who used each of eight different forms of assessment in calculating grades.

The most frequently used methods of reporting students' grades by general education teachers were a combination of narratives (used by 66.6% of teachers responding), checklists (55.5%), and letter grades (51.8%). It is noteworthy that in District A almost all teachers used letter grades beginning in third grade, whereas in District B letter grades were never used. In District A, for grades 3 and 4 (and

Table 7-2. *Grading Policies*

Methods Used to Report Grades (Districts A and B combined)		
	General Education	Special Education
Narratives	66.6% (18)	20% (1)
Checklists	55.5% (15)	60% (3)
Letter grades	51.8% (14)	80% (4)
(Other methods were used less than 25% of the time by both general and special education teachers.)		
Grading Systems Used		
	General Education	Special Education
Individually referenced	77.7% (21)	80% (4)
Percentage cutoffs	66.6% (18)	60% (3)
Multiple grades	59.3% (16)	60% (3)
Criterion-referenced	29.6% (8)	40% (2)
Normative	25.9% (7)	40%
Shared grading	29.6% (8)	40%
Percentage of Teachers Using Various Assessment Components to Arrive at Grades		
	General Education	Special Education
Teacher-made tests	66.6% (18)	40% (2)
Homework	66.6% (18)	40% (2)
Projects	66.6% (18)	20% (1)
Classroom participation	59.3% (7)	60% (3)
Portfolios	66.6% (18)	40% (2)
Publishers' tests	51.8% (14)	20% (1)
Standardized tests	18.5% (5)	20% (1)
Behavior	37.0% (10)	20% (1)
Methods of Reporting Grades **(General education teachers by district)**		
	District A	District B
Letter grades	84.2% (16)	0%
Narratives	68.4% (13)	88.8% (8)
Checklists	47.4% (9)	66.6% (6)

those second grades combined with a third grade), letter grades were supplemented with checklists that included the categories "areas of strength," "satisfactory progress," and "areas of need." For grades 5 and 6 (and those fourth grades that were combined with a fifth grade), the grades were supplemented with checklists that included categories such as "exceptional achievement," "above average," "satisfactory," or " below average achievement." All but one special education teacher (80%), the one in district B, used letter grades. Three of the five (60%) also used checklists to supplement the final grade.

Grading Systems Used

A large percentage (77.7%) of general education teachers in both districts used individually referenced scores (an "ipsative" process, in which the student is compared to him- or herself) in calculating grades. This kind of scoring or grading is based on student progress rather than on an absolute criterion standard. But there are noticeable differences in practices between teachers in District A and District B. As a matter of fact, all nine general education teachers in District B used an individually referenced system in combination with other systems; whereas only 48% (13) of District A teachers used this method. Percentage cutoffs (setting an A between 93 and 100, a B between 85 and 92, and so on) were used somewhat more often (66.6% across the two districts). Multiple grades—that is, grades based on both performance and effort—were used in 59.2% of cases. Teachers reported using other grading systems—such as criterion-referenced, normative, or shared grading—less frequently (only 30% or less of the time). Apparently, many teachers are using more than one system, and it is not clear how they integrate the different approaches to arrive at their grades. The term "criterion referenced" may have been misinterpreted by teachers, because few acknowledged using such an approach. Yet checklists and percentage cutoffs, for example, are two forms of criterion referencing.

The majority of special education teachers (80%, or four teachers) used individually referenced scores, and fewer used percentage cutoffs or multiple grades (60%). Thus, both general and special education teachers used individually referenced scores most frequently as one basis for determining grades for *all* students.

Use of Various Indexes to Determine a Grade

It was not possible to determine how teachers weighted different components of assessment contributing to students' grades, because so many of the teachers responded by simply checking the item as opposed to assigning a percentage. Once again, however, the responses indicated that teachers base their grading on multiple sources of information. Most often they use a combination of teacher-made tests, homework, and projects (66.6%). Portfolios and publishers' tests are used slightly less frequently (61.5% and 51.8%). Classroom participation is used in grade calculation fairly frequently (by approximately 60% of both general and special education teachers). In contrast, behavior and standardized tests are used much less often (37.7% and 18.5%, respectively) by general education teachers. Only one special education teacher used each of these indicators.

The special education teachers in the study use classroom participation as a more important component in grading (60%), compared to teacher-made tests, homework, and portfolios (40%). More formal measures, such as publishers' tests and standardized tests, are used even less frequently. It is interesting that projects are used in only 20% of instances as a component of grading by special education teachers. Of course, their instruction may not lend itself to such activities. These special education teachers' greater reliance on less formal measures such as teacher-made tests, homework, and portfolios compared to more formal measures like publishers' tests and standardized tests is compatible with an ipsative approach to grading. One of the special education teachers assigns grades based on several of the forms of assessment listed in the questionnaire. Another assigns formal grades only to sixth-grade students; and only one of the five special education teachers responding uses IEPs to determine a grade.

Comments from special education teachers about their grading practices included the following:

"We use narrative descriptions of a student's progress alone when the performance level is significantly below grade level. We may also use narratives with the grades to explain progress with differentiated standards."

"I don't grade. I talk on the phone to my parents on a weekly or monthly basis. We meet at conferences and IEP [sessions]."

"I was giving letter grades and using checklists. I recently just started basing my progress reports on goals and objectives of the students' IEPs."

Accommodations for Special Education and ELD students

The answers to the questions on how special education and ELD students are assessed and graded reveal that teachers have different beliefs about what should be done to make grading equitable for such students. Teachers mentioned a range of strategies for both supporting students' participation in instruction (modification of assignments and teaching methodology) and accommodating assessment and grading to their perceived needs. Teachers were asked, "Do you treat students in special education/ELD differently by making any or combinations of the following accommodations?" This question was followed by a list of possible accommodations along with space to suggest additional strategies. Their answers included the following comments:

"Special education students are scored by ability, IEP and time in class."

"Students are scored by effort and ability."

"Based on their abilities I observe growth. Set my goals before he/she is a part of the class. Working towards achievement skills."

"Differential grading and adjusted assignments."

"Adjusted assignments."

"Differential grading, modified assignments, vary assignments according to ability."

"For ELD language and reading grades are based on different competency in oral and written language."

"Place in a group with strong students, shorten expected work. Provide reading material appropriate to their level. Books on tape. For ELD students, grade more on effort than product."

"Special education students' grades are adjusted to show their performance successfully. I have found students show improvement with adjusted scoring. Same for ELD students."

"These students are graded differently. They are not responsible for assignments we do during their pull-out times. It is not based on a percentage of time. For ELD language is dependent on assignments. Grades are based on content more than on form."

"I assign a buddy to help students who are special education. I read the directions on tests to make sure that the student understands what I am asking. I grade for content. For ELD students, I take their ability into consideration when grading."

"For special education students they might have only half of the assignment to complete depending on the amount of time spent in that class. For ELD students, effort is the key to whether this grade is satisfactory or needs improvement. Actually, that's important for all students."

"I grade Special Ed. students completely differently on their everyday papers. I put a star on all areas that are well done. Same for ELD students."

"For special education students, the material is organized for success. For example, I ask success on fewer spelling words (maybe 3 to 5 out of 16 to start with)."

"If they are learning the skills, that's how I determine their grade. I do not grade ELD students differently."

"Of course, they are graded differently, they are graded on progress. Same for ELD students."

"For special education students, they may do fewer math problems, assign to study fewer vocabulary words. For ELD students, I grade more on effort and working to their abilities."

"I assess my students individually because they are all different whether special ed. or ESL [ELD]."

"I look at their progress from the time they entered my class to the time I write the report. I do not compare them with other students."

"For ELD their grades are based more on effort and progress rather than straight percentage."

"I don't use grades. I look at progress made from individualized students."

The majority of general education teachers indicated that they used several techniques to assist special education and ELD students, which included, in order of highest to lowest frequency: additional time to complete assignments, shortened assignments, more time for tests, and modification of test formats. In only 30% of cases did the respondents say that they were using special space or rooms to accommodate the needs of their students.

Assessing Students in Their Primary Language

It is noteworthy that only 6 of the 27 teachers made a comment regarding assessing the student in the primary language. The rest of the respondents left the item blank or wrote that it was not applicable. One of the teachers mentioned having a parent give classroom tests to the child in his or her primary language. This is a very risky method of assessing a student. One does not know how the parent may be translating the test, whether the parent interprets the teacher's questions (or the questions on a formal test) in the way intended, or whether the parent is interpreting the child's answers adequately. This method cannot be relied upon to assess the student's true learning (see also the discussion of translation in chapter 6.) There are not only validity but also ethical concerns when untrained personnel (including paraprofessional aides) are asked to administer assessments, particularly when decisions are to be made on the basis of such assessments (Langdon, Siegel, Halog, & Sánchez-Boyce, 1994).

Other teachers responded that the testing is done at the district level, or that they assessed their students' language proficiency verbally only. Two of the special education teachers noted that the primary language was used in the initial assessment of the student but that intervention was taking place in English. Another special education teacher who responded indicated that formal testing is supplemented with Spanish formal testing batteries, and informal testing is conducted with the assistance of an interpreter. One mentioned that the primary language was used in assessment but provided no further details. The last one said that this concern did not apply to the current caseload. It is clear that ELD students are not evaluated in any consistent way by either the general or the special education teachers who responded to this survey.

Methods of Determining Final Grades
for Special Education and ELD Students

About 50% of the general education teachers reported that they assign grades to special education and ELD students by themselves, without taking into account the grade that may be assigned by the special education teacher or other service provider. Following are some teacher responses.

"Evaluation of student's work with conferencing."

"Classroom effort and ability."

"Consideration of effort, growth and attitude."

"Sometimes I write a narrative to explain the grade."

"Combination of all aspects of classroom education: participation, effort, assignments, tests, etc . . ."

"Either lower expectations and give letter grade or no letter and use checklist with + or –."

"Completion of daily homework, test scores, and attitude."

"Skills mastered of those taught determine the grade."

"I give the student's grade to the special education teacher."

"By their effort and by turning in some work to show the student was trying."

"Comment about progress."

"Progress and if on grade level."

"According to IEP, but I don't give grade."

"There is no final grade. The special ed. teacher comes to parent-student-teacher conferences and offers input."

"Through discussion."

"I talk to the resource special ed teacher when writing their narrative grades."

Most responses related to what they pay attention to in student performance and behavior in order to arrive at a final grade. It is evident that teachers are conscientiously seeking ways to make the grading system work for their special education and ELD students. Effort and ability are considered, and teachers often seek opportunities to put a grade or narrative in context—either in terms of a student's progress over time or in terms of what can realistically be expected of the student—versus adhering to an absolute standard.

Special education teachers' comments included the following:

"I find out what grade the mainstream teacher would give and raise it at least one letter grade for any special day class student unless the teacher has done a lot of the modification as noted in the section below on accommodations."

"I compile percentage on quizzes, tests, and maybe a project (but we walk through these quizzes and the goal is to learn to read for information)."

"I only get involved in grading if the classroom teacher is unsure about how to grade a lower performing student or if they need my opinion."

Frequency of Reporting Grades to Parents

In 88% of instances (24 out of 27), regular education teachers responded that they reported grades three times a year. About 25% of teachers report progress weekly by phone or through notes in addition to the regular reports associated with marking periods. Similar frequency was reported by the special education teachers. Frequency of grading is of concern, because IEPs have to be updated four times a year. Therefore, some formal assessment and reporting must coincide with the IEP schedule.

Suggestions for Improving the Grading System

Very few teachers answered the question about how they would improve the grading system in their district. Two teachers reported that their district (District A) was working on a new format for the report card that would include more narrative and rubric-based information and less of a traditional grade. This response suggests the district is moving in the direction of a standards-based curriculum and assessment system. One teacher suggested that a computerized system be devised, and another one mentioned that he was satisfied with his own method of reporting grades. One general education teacher answered, "Collaborate more with other teachers. I feel weak in the area of assessment." Only two responses were given by special education teachers, and one was off-topic. The single germane response was, "I really don't believe in grades because they are too subjective."

Discussion

The study was exploratory in nature and limited in size, but it shows in microcosm many of the problems associated with grading special education and ELD students. These are, in large degree, the same problems identified in past literature. In the course of reflecting on the outcomes of the study here, we will emphasize those we think are most important and make some recommendations for resolving them. We will broaden the discussion to consider implications that extend beyond the needs of the schools represented in the study.

Getting General Education and Special Education Teachers on the Same Track

One thing is crystal clear: If grading practices are to be valid and fair for special education and ELD students, their teachers have to come together around a well-defined approach and coordinate the grading of these students. The approach needs to be based on sound educational judgment, not convenience or administrative fiat (Shriner et al., 1994). Grading students who are mainstreamed into general education classrooms should be a shared responsibility, just as their instruction is. The process of "rapprochement" will be far easier in settings where a district is already developing (or adopting existing) standards and attempting to align standards, curriculum, instruction, and assessment. In such cases, the common targets for student achievement and performance criteria are being set. Performance criteria answer questions like, "What is good enough?" "What counts as mastery?" and "At about what age or grade can a student be expected to be competent with regard to a given standard?" In this context, teachers can discuss reasonable performance expectations for special education and ELD students, recognizing that expectations will vary, depending on a student's particular needs. Special educators may have to take the lead and remind their colleagues that addressing "special populations" is something that ideally happens early in a school change process and not as an afterthought. In other words, questions about how the standards will be applied for their students, how assessments can be designed or selected to meet the needs of such students, and how students will be graded should all be posed upfront, *before* a system is in place.

When expectations are clear, parents and students are not left in the dark trying to figure out from teacher to teacher and year to year what grades mean. The same is true of teachers across classes and grade levels. They can be sure what students' grades mean only when grading criteria are explicit.

Deciding on Common Standards

If a district has not established standards for what students should know and be able to do, the question of whether to hold all students to the same standards is moot. In the schools surveyed, it does not appear that uniform standards are guiding teachers' judgments about student achievement. At the same time, districts need to create rubrics or other guidelines that specify the expected kinds and levels of achievement at given grade levels. Although this does not seem to be a common practice, collaboration across districts within a county or metropolitan area to establish content and performance standards would be an excellent way to conserve resources. It would also make sense where student mobility results in students' commonly attending more than one school in a county or area.

Agreeing on Who Assigns the Final Grade

Approximately 50% of the general education teachers stated that they assign grades alone, without taking into account the grade that may be assigned by the special education teacher. This finding is fairly concordant with data reported by Bursuck et al. (1996). Comments offered by the special education teachers about grade adjustment suggest that there is not very much communication regarding this matter with the general education teacher. It is not clear whether parents and students realize this adjustment is taking place. At the very least, the practice should be based on stated school policy. It should not be done just for some students.

Agreeing on the Components of a Grade

It is not just academic content and performance standards on which teachers need to agree, because teachers' grades are rarely based solely on academic performance. We know that effort, growth, and progress toward meeting standards or goals—and sometimes attitude and behavior—are often factored into a grade (rightly or wrongly). The teachers in the current study tend to grade special education and ELD students more on the basis of progress and effort and less on the basis of academic standards. They are not unusual in this regard. Numerous responses mention "participation," "completion of homework," or "turning in work" as factors to consider in deciding on a final grade. (These are often used by teachers as indications of effort.)

Many teachers in the study also claimed to take into account what they perceived to be a student's ability—something they may or may not have adequate grounds for judging. Pencil-and-paper tests, for example, may not reveal a student's true ability or what a student knows. The same student may perform with more or less success, depending on the form of an assessment or the manner in which it is administered. For instance, a student may be more successful in explaining an answer orally than in writing or may be able to illustrate better than write. In fact, several teachers who participated in the study report that they modify assignments or assessments by allowing oral rather than written products or by giving directions orally rather than in writing.

Choosing an Appropriate Form of Grade

Concern about the limitations of single letter or number grades applies to all students, but it is magnified with special education and ELD students. Narratives have often been preferred for younger students and special education students. The special education teachers in the study reported using more narratives in order to convey their student's success. However, narratives may describe what the student has achieved or accomplished, but they do not indicate level of achievement very successfully—something most parents want to know. The general education teachers in this study reported using a variety of methods to record their students' achievement on the report card.

In our opinion, single letter or number grades obscure more than they reveal. The problem is compounded for special education and ELD students, whose developmental profiles may look different from those of the average general education student. For this reason, we believe that multiple grades accompanied by some narrative are far more fair and useful than single grades.

Agreeing on Accommodations and Adjustments

Several teachers in the current study used the word *adjusted* to refer to grades for special education or ELD students. Although their "adjustments" may not be arbitrary, one suspects that the criteria for making these adjustments are not as explicit as they might be. One general education teacher mentions that he or she adjusts special education students' grades by a full grade upward.

Some teachers indicated that they were more concerned about the "content" rather than the "form" of these students' performances. It is encouraging to find out that teachers are using accommodations for special education and ELD students and are trying to move beyond standard formats to evaluate their learning. However, it is important to set criteria for what kind of accommodations can or should be used for assessing students without jeopardizing the validity of the results of their performance.

Using the IEP in Grading

It is interesting that only one of all the general education teachers surveyed indicated that the IEP should be used in evaluating a student's progress. Perhaps if the questionnaire had directly asked general education teachers if they used the IEP, more teachers would have mentioned it. Each IEP has objectives a student is expected to meet, and usually a percentage of mastery is determined for each objective periodically (four times a year, in theory). General and special education teachers need to discuss how the goals and objectives set by the IEP will be monitored and what role they will play in determining grades. One way that special education and general education teachers could use the IEP to determine or contribute to decisions about grades is to decide which objectives are linked to the general education content standards addressed in the curriculum and then weight those objectives in terms of importance. A high level of mastery on the majority of curriculum-linked objectives would lead to a good grade. If IEP objectives were written to be aligned with the standards of the district, judgment of progress vis-à-vis the general education program would be much easier.

Special Concerns About ELD Students

In the districts studied, the primary language of the student was reported to be used in an initial procedure to evaluate an ELD student but not as the language of intervention or ongoing assessment. In some situations, assessments in the primary language seemed to be more the concern of a team in a district rather than teachers at the school level. As noted in chapter 5, there are particular concerns about appropriate assessment of ELD students, whether with regard to grading, for placement purposes, or for accountability purposes. Whenever a student whose English is not fully proficient is assessed in English, it is hard to know whether one is getting a true representation of what the student has learned. Likewise, having untrained personnel or parents translate assessments and/or administer them may lead to spurious data. This practice should be distinguished from legitimate informal ways of gathering information and observations from parents and paraprofessionals about how a child uses his or her first language. Teachers and specialists can interview parents and paraprofessionals and suggest how they may observe children to gather useful language information that can contribute to an understanding of a child's school performance. When formal assessment in the student's first language is not possible, judgments about a student's learning should be based on a range of observations of different types over a period of time.

Promising Approaches

We see considerable promise in portfolio systems for capturing student growth and progress toward standards. Portfolios are not a grading system, of course, but they are an excellent process tool for assessing students. Teacher and student annotations (commentaries on the performances logged in the portfolio and how they were achieved) can put each entry in the portfolio in context. For special education students, a teacher might periodically make note of what kinds of supports resulted in a student's best performance. Alternatively, both teacher and student could include comments with an unsuccessful piece of work to indicate why it caused problems. Portfolios can be used to arrive at a grade, if decisions are made about exactly what will be included, which entries will be graded, which will contribute to a final grade, and how each entry will be weighted.

Curriculum-based assessment is a natural companion to portfolio assessment. The portfolio process, with its expectation for reflection and goal setting, could be used to help special education students develop metacognitive skills, something they are often lacking. However, research suggests that if special education students are to make use of the feedback they get from their performances on curriculum-based assessment, they will likely need specific guidance from teachers. They may not know how to use the information to guide their studying or goal setting (Gersten et al., 1996, citing Fuchs, Fuchs, & Hamlett, 1994). Portfolios could be an excellent vehicle for communication between general education teachers and special education teachers, if they could agree on a common system for selecting and evaluating entries and working with students in the process. Annotations from both general and special education teachers would contribute to an understanding of the student's growth, progress, achievement, and effort (or whatever components of evaluation are decided upon). Teachers would decide in advance exactly how a grade would be derived, and this would be explained to parents as well as students.

Developmental continua (which could be used in conjunction with a portfolio) also seem to hold promise for special education and ELD students. Students could be rated according to which goals they have attained along a subject matter continuum such as the Juneau Primary Reading continuum (Farr & Trumbull, 1997, pp. 290–291). The Juneau continuum rates students on three components: comprehension, skills and strategies, and attitude toward reading. A continuum also allows for comparing the student to him- or herself over time (personal growth) as well as rating the level of his or her achievement with reference to a fixed standard.

Summary

The dilemmas surrounding the grading of special education and ELD students are symbolic of all the usual concerns related to assessment in general. We find ourselves grappling with questions of how to establish appropriate criteria for judgment and how to ensure that teachers adhere to them. We are faced with questions of ethics and fairness as we examine the potential consequences of the ways we assess and grade students for whom the educational system has not historically been adequately responsive. Because most special education students and many English language learners have more than one teacher, confusion arises over who should be grading these students. Another common source of confusion is whether students with special learning needs should be held to exactly the same standards as other students and graded accordingly. It is clear that districts should establish explicit policies about who grades as well as how grades will be derived. Teachers, parents, and students must all be aware of these policies.

The activities in which schools are engaging to align standards, curriculum, instruction, and assessment provide an excellent opportunity to evaluate and improve grading practices for special education and ELD students. Guidelines for establishing fair and useful grading systems associated with standards-based education have been discussed in earlier chapters, and they should apply broadly to decisions about how to grade special education and ELD students.

We have recommended that teachers consider particular reporting tools: portfolios, curriculum-based assessment, and developmental continua. In addition, we encourage teachers to investigate what their colleagues in neighboring districts, counties, and states are doing to address the dilemmas of grading special education and ELD students. If educators can cross traditional boundaries to collaborate and pool their wisdom, teachers can increase their own expertise and power to make the best decisions for children.

The authors wish to acknowledge the assistance of eight students who helped to collect the data—Wendy Cargile, Sue Czapkay, Adele DeAnda, Sheryl Fox, Terry Jacobs, Charity Joy, Marva Lemene, Julie Vissiere—as well as Brenda Fikes and Mary Male. The collaboration of principals and teachers who responded positively to the efforts of this project is also appreciated.

References

Airasian, P. W. (1996). *Assessment in the classroom*. New York: McGraw-Hill.

Austin, S., & McCann, R. (1992). *Here's another arbitrary grade for your collection: A statewide study of grading policies*. Philadelphia, PA: Research for Better Schools.

Blount, P. H. (1997). The keepers of numbers: Teachers' perspectives on grades. *Educational Forum, 61,* 329–334.

Bradley, D. F., & Calvin, M. B. (1998, November–December). Grading modified assignments: Equity or compromise? *Teaching Exceptional Children, 31* (2), 24–29.

Bursuck, W., Polloway, E. A., Plante, L., Epstein, M. H., Jayanthi, M., & McConeghy, J. (1996). Report card grading and adaptations: A national survey of classroom practices. *Exceptional Children, 62* (4), 301–308.

Calhoun, M. L., & Beattie, J. (1984). Assigning grades in the high school mainstream: Perceptions of teachers and students. *Diagnostique, 9,* 218–225.

Christiansen, J., & Vogel, J. R. (1998, November–December). A decision model for grading students with disabilities. *Teaching Exceptional Children, 31* (2), 30–35.

Donahue, K., & Zigmond, N. (1990). Academic grades of ninth-grade urban learning disabled students and low-achieving peers. *Exceptionality, 1,* 17–27.

Education Commission of the States (Ed.). (1997). *So you have standards: Now what?* Denver, CO: Author.

Elbow, P. (1986). *Embracing contraries: Explorations in learning and thinking.* New York: Oxford University Press.

Farr, B., & Trumbull, E. (1997). *Assessment alternatives for diverse classrooms.* Norwood, MA: Christopher Gordon.

Fuchs, L. S., & Fuchs, D. (1997). Use of curriculum-based measurement in identifying students with disabilities. *Focus on Exceptional Children, 30* (2), 1–8.

Fuchs, L. S., Fuchs, D., & Hamlett, C. L. (1994). Strengthening the connection between assessment and instructional planning with expert systems. *Exceptional Children, 61* (2), 137–146.

Geenen, K., & Ysseldyke, J. (1997). Educational standards and students with disabilities. *Educational Forum, 61,* 220–229.

Gellman, E. (1995). *School testing: What parents and educators need to know.* Westport, CT: Praeger.

Gersten, R., Vaughn, S., & Brengelman, S. U. (1996). *Communicating student learning* (ASCD Yearbook, pp. 47–57). Alexandria, VA: Association for Supervision and Curriculum Development.

Langdon, H. W., with Siegel, V., Halog, L., & Sánchez-Boyce, M. (1994). *The interpreter/translator process in the school setting.* Sacramento, CA: RISE.

Mercado, C., & Romero, M. (1993). Assessment of students in bilingual education. In B. Arias and U. Casanova (Eds.), *Bilingual education: Politics, practice, and research.* (pp. 144–170). Chicago: University of Chicago Press.

Owen, W. (1997). Colleges warn of high school grade inflation. *The Bakersfield Californian,* B-1 and B-2. November 18.

Owen, W. (1998, November 18). Grades come into question. *The Bakersfield Californian,* pp. 12–13.

Pennsylvania Department of Education (Ed.). (1997). *Classroom testing and grading practices.* Harrisburg, PA: Central Instructional Support System.

Pollard, R., Rojewski, J., & Pollard, C. (1993). An examination of problems associated with grading students with special needs. *Journal of Instructional Psychology, 20* (2), 154–161.

Polloway, E. A., Epstein, M. H., Bursuck, W. D., Roderique, T. W., McConeghy, J. L., & Jayanthi, M. (1994). Classroom grading: A national survey of policies. *Remedial and Special Education, 15* (3), 162–170.

Regional Educational Laboratories. (1998). *Improving classroom assessments: A toolkit for professional developers.* Portland, OR: Northwest Regional Educational Laboratory.

Seeley, M. M. (1994). The mismatch between assessment and grading. *Educational Leadership, 52* (2), 4–6.

Shriner, J., Ysseldyke, J., Thurlow, M., & Honetschlager, D. (1994). "All means all"—including students with disabilities. *Educational Leadership, 51* (6), 38–42.

Sweedler-Brown, C. O. (1993). ESL essay evaluation: The influence of sentence-level and rhetorical features. *Journal of Second Language Writing, 2,* 3–17.

Valdes, K. A., Williamson, C. L., & Wagner, M. M. (1990). *The national longitudinal transition study of special education students* (Vol. 1). Menlo Park, CA: SRI International. (ERIC Document Reproduction Service No. ED 324 893)

Wiggins, G. (1996). Honesty and fairness: Toward better grading and reporting. In T. K. Guskey (Ed), *Communicating student learning* (pp. 141–177). Alexandria, VA: Association for Supervision and Curriculum Development

Wiggins, G. (1998). *Educative assessment: Designing assessments to inform and improve student performance.* San Francisco: Jossey-Bass.

Wood, P. H., Bennett, T., Wood, J., & Bennett, C. (1990). *Grading and evaluation practices and policies of school teachers.* (ERIC Document Reproduction Service No. ED 319 782)

Reporting to Parents and the Community

8

Tanja Bisesi, Roger Farr,
Beth Greene, and Elizabeth Haydel

> *As parents become more fully involved in schools and assessments,*
> *they become more informed about and more observant of their*
> *children's development. . . . It is the use of communication and*
> *reporting procedures between school and home that enables parents*
> *to talk in productive ways with their children about their [progress].*

> —International Reading Association/
> National Council of Teachers of English, 1994

Reporting systems for communicating educational progress to parents and the community have been around as long as the educational system itself. As indicated in previous chapters, states, school districts, individual schools, and teachers have experimented with a variety of grading and evaluation practices including, but not limited to, numerical or alphabetical grades (chapter 3), narrative descriptions, skill checklists, and portfolios of student work (chapter 4). While the first seven chapters of this book are specifically focused on the educational accountability practices and systems themselves, this chapter explores the ways that data resulting from these systems have been reported.

In this chapter we discuss reporting practices and systems and recommend guidelines for improving them. We begin by briefly outlining the major issues associated with accountability reporting systems that are currently the norm in education. This discussion addresses how and why these systems have evolved and why they have interfered with parental and community understanding of student performance. Second, we discuss the central role of standards in accountability reporting systems. Third, we describe two common mechanisms used for reporting accountability information—report cards and standardized test score reports—and we discuss the problems associated with each reporting practice and some potential solutions. For this, we draw on a range of specific examples with which the authors have experience. We conclude with a brief discussion of the need for everyone to take responsibility for making the assessment process work by getting involved in the development of clear standards that provide a common language and set of expectations for discussing, supporting, and evaluating students' performance.

Issues Associated With Accountability Reporting Systems

Accountability reporting systems are beset by at least three problems that contribute to a lack of parental and community understanding of student performance data. These include: (a) confusion about standards for making sense of and talking about performance, (b) incoherent design and implementation of assessment tools and reporting mechanisms, and (c) failure to reconcile inconsistencies in results reported across different reporting mechanisms.

Confusion About Standards

One problem that contributes to a lack of parental and community understanding of student and educational performance is confusion about standards. Not only is there confusion (and debate) about what standards are, there is confusion about how they should be defined and communicated to parents and the community. For example, Pearson (1993) talks about seven different types of standards that have surfaced since the standards movement gained momentum in the early 1990s. They are as follows:

1. *Content standards*: What should students know and be able to do?
2. *Performance standards:* How good is good enough?
3. *Delivery standards:* What materials and resources are necessary to achieve established performance standards?
4. *Opportunity standards:* What kinds of instruction are necessary to achieve established performance standards?
5. *Instructional standards:* What constitutes exemplary instructional practice?
6. *Assessment standards:* How do we evaluate the quality and validity of our assessment tools?
7. *Process standards:* What guidelines should we follow for developing and implementing standards?

From the preceding list of standards, it should be evident that the range in types of standards currently being discussed by educators is a potential source of confusion, especially to parents and other community members.

Confusion about standards becomes even more evident when we consider the fact that almost every assessment is defined by a different set of content standards. Topics, prompts, and tasks may differ widely from assessment to assessment. In other words, what students are expected to know and be able to do is not the same across assessments, even within subject areas at particular grade levels. District or school standards defined by a report card may specify that students demonstrate different performances (e.g., "appreciates literature," "persists with tasks through to completion") than those required for state-mandated standardized tests (e.g., "recognizes text structures," "identifies vocabulary"). While some overlap may exist, the lack of alignment in the content standards of different assessments no doubt leads to apparent inconsistencies in student performance. Students may perform quite well on one assessment and poorly on another in the same content area. Further, as suggested by Busick in chapter 4, what students are expected to do is not always communicated clearly to parents (and students) and the community (Azwell & Schmar, 1995). Thus, parents and the community are confused about what content standards are and how they are defined, and they fail to understand performance data that are reported.

To complicate matters further, if we are to operate on the assumption that reporting is to let an audience know how well students are accomplishing educational goals, then performance standards need to be defined. Performance standards are benchmarks for understanding and talking about our expectations for the level of student performance on a particular assessment. Like content standards, performance standards may be defined very differently across assessment tools. Performance may be defined and understood in at least three different ways.

1. *Criterion referenced*—in comparisons to suggested levels of accomplishment.

2. *Norm referenced*—in comparisons to other students.

3. *Growth referenced*—in comparisons to previous performances or changes in a student over time.

Performance standards may also be defined differently across different reporting mechanisms. For example, standardized test scores reported to a school administrator may focus on grade-level performance in relationship to specific curricular criteria (i.e., criterion referenced). Information reported to parents, on the other hand, may be limited to their individual child in relationship to the performance of all students at the same grade level in the school district (i.e., norm referenced).

This discussion makes it clear that reporting to parents and the community involves clearly communicating information about student performance in relation to some set (and often several sets) of standards. (Refer to chapter 4 for further discussion of standards-based grading practices). If parents and the community are confused about standards, they will have difficulty understanding student performance data reported to them.

Incoherence of Reporting Systems

A second problem that contributes to a lack of parental and community understanding of student and educational performance data is the incoherence of reporting systems themselves. Most assessment (and reporting) systems are designed and implemented by an agent at one level of the educational system (i.e., classroom, school, district, or state) who has a particular accountability agenda (e.g., state-level educational accountability) and implements a given assessment (e.g., Indiana Statewide Testing for Educational Progress, or ISTEP+) to serve that purpose (Bisesi, 1997). Then that agent decides with which audiences to share the resulting assessment data as well as how it should be reported. Thus, decisions about any single assessment implemented as part of an accountability system typically are made by relatively independent agents who have little knowledge or concern for the other assessments constituting the system or for how and to whom associated information is reported. So, while separate educational agents may carefully think out the design and implementation of any given assessment, a consideration of the entire assessment system is rare. In fact, all the assessment mechanisms taken together may not even be conceptualized as a system.

At the Center for Innovation in Assessment at Indiana University, we are frequently charged with the development of various kinds of assessments. In developing these assessments, we are provided with formatting guidelines and content standards, but we are rarely given insight into just how these assessments will ultimately be used by educators or how associated results will be shared with audiences. While there have been instances when we have been privy to reporting mechanisms for individual assessments, even then we had insight into the reporting practices for only a single assessment. For example, we designed materials for explaining the score report mechanism used to communicate ISTEP+ (CTB/McGraw-Hill, 1997) test scores to parents (discussed in more detail in the second section of this chapter). Yet, despite our knowledge of this important reporting mechanism, we were not in a position to help parents understand the relationship between student performance on this test and other assessments or to reconcile any apparent inconsistencies in student performance. We were not aware of other reporting practices used by teachers, schools, or districts to share assessment information with parents, and we certainly were not cognizant of any reporting system in its entirety.

Table 8-1 illustrates a typical accountability system, including common educational accountability purposes, reporting agents, audiences of assessment information, and mechanisms by which assessment information is most often reported. As Table 8-1 suggests, a typical accountability system is compartmentalized and incoherent. Assessments are implemented for distinct accountability purposes by agents at different levels of the educational system, and they are reported to meet the accountability needs of distinct assessment audiences (Bisesi, 1997; Farr, 1992), with little or no consideration of the system as a whole. For example, standardized tests are frequently implemented by state policy makers for reporting educational accountability data to school personnel, parents, and the community about how well school programs are supporting student achievement. Meanwhile, schools (or districts) independently implement report cards to communicate information to school personnel, parents, and the community about how well classroom instruction is facilitating student performance on school curricula. Teachers may also share student classroom work with parents (and with students and school administrators) to justify marks on report cards or to demonstrate instructional accountability, with little or no knowledge about student performance on standardized achievement tests.

Table 8-1. *Typical Accountability System*

Accountability Purpose	Reporting Agent	Audience	Assessment Information Reporting Mechanism
Educational accountability	State policy makers	• **Community** • Administrators • Teachers • **Parents**	• Standardized test score reports
School curriculum effectiveness	District or school administrators	• Teachers • **Parents**	• Standardized test score reports
Instructional accountability	Classroom teacher	• Administrators • **Parents**	• Report cards • Conferences/ Student work
Student progress	State policy makers	• **Parents** • Students	• Standardized test score reports
	District or school administrators	• **Parents**	• Report cards
	Classroom teacher	• **Parents** • Students	• Report cards • Conferences/ Student work

To complicate matters further, individual assessments and reporting mechanisms often are implemented in an additive manner over time (Bisesi, 1997). Reporting mechanisms and associated standards are not reviewed and modified on an ongoing basis to better meet the changing needs of educational agents and audiences, as social forces and political pressures on the educational system shift and evolve. Reporting systems are incoherent because the design and implementation of accountability systems themselves are incoherent. Different assessments provide information about student performance within different contexts and with respect to different sets of expectations (i.e., standards), making it difficult for parents and the community to make sense of reported data.

Failure to Reconcile Reported Performance Inconsistencies

Fundamental differences in assessments (e.g., purpose, format, and standards) also create apparent inconsistencies in student performance across assessments—the final major problem of accountability reporting systems that we have identified. These apparent inconsistencies in reported student-performance data rarely are explained or reconciled for parents through implemented reporting mechanisms because of the failure to consider reporting systems as a whole.

Inconsistencies arise when parents are told one thing about their child's performance through report cards and student work and something else by district- and state-mandated standardized test scores. For example, a student may receive As and Bs on her report cards in reading. Parents have little difficulty interpreting these grades because they are familiar with this system from their own school experience. The classroom teacher may also report to parents about the quality of specific pieces of student work and how this work supports marks on the report card, positively contributing to the parents' understanding of their child's performance as a coherent whole.

Making sense of performance data may become a problem, however, when parents receive standardized test score reports from the school district or the state. Standardized tests are different from teacher evaluations, providing information about student performance within a different context and set of expectations. For this reason, a student who receives As and Bs on the report card and demonstrates strong classroom work may nevertheless obtain a score on a standardized reading test that indicates performance only slightly above average or even below average. To complicate parental understanding even further, the score report may also imply that the student demonstrates "excellent" reading performance based on a nationwide sample of students her age.

What does all this reported information mean? How should parents and other laypersons in the community make sense of such diverse and apparently conflicting performance data, particularly when no one takes the time to help them understand the relationships between assessments and students' performances on those assessments? It becomes clear from this example that the failure of accountability reporting systems to reconcile inconsistent performance data makes it difficult for parents (and the community) to get a complete and congruous picture of student academic performance or that of the educational system as a whole (Guskey, 1996; Wiggins, 1994).

To this point, we have outlined the major problems associated with accountability reporting systems that interfere with parental and community understanding of student performance. In the remainder of this chapter, we discuss the critical role that standards play in accountability reporting systems and go on to describe two important reporting mechanisms—report cards and standardized test score reports—for communicating with parents and the community.

Standards Play a Key Role in the Reporting Process

As Table 8-1 shows, parents are the most frequently targeted audience for results of assessments, and they may demand that districts make their standards explicit. Since students are graded in comparison to one or more sets of standards, it seems obvious that the standards should be made available for parents, teachers, community leaders, and students. Parents and community leaders need to understand the purpose, use, and implications of standards, and, as suggested by Busick in chapter 4, it is teachers and school administrators who are responsible for promoting this understanding.

Whose Standards Are They, Anyway?

Standards have been around for a long time. When a new driver takes the driving test, the examiner rates the driver according to a set of standards. If the new driver does not meet the standards, he or she fails the test and does not get a driver's license. This example of a set of standards is one to which almost everyone can relate.

In 1990, the U.S. governors formulated a set of National Education Goals. These goals were codified into law in Goals 2000: The Educate America Act (S.846). The purpose of this legislation was to provide a plan for meeting the National Education Goals by establishing a framework for relating federal education programs to education reform and by endorsing the National Education Goals. One of these National Goals is that all children will learn to read by third grade. Whether this and the other goals will have been achieved by the end of year 2000 is not yet known. These goals were formulated and widely distributed; they are, in a sense, a set of standards that every school is expected to reach.

Many states have written their own sets of goals, some of which parallel the National Education Goals. Other states have developed far more specific goals. In fact, many states and large school districts have written detailed goals for all grades and all subjects. These goal statements are often used to develop the tests used in the state-testing program. Sometimes these goals are called "criteria for promotion," "competencies," "proficiencies," or "standards."[1]

Other states have general goal statements, not unlike the National Goals. Sometimes these state goals serve as guides for local school districts to write their own local goals. Local goals tend to be written for specific grade levels and for specific subjects.

In recent years, the media have provided a lot of information about global or international standards. When such reports appear in newspapers and magazines, the point is usually made that international standards are quite different from U.S. standards. These articles also point out that many countries have a national curriculum and that these national curricula are used to formulate the tests. The U.S. does not have a national curriculum. Because these national curricula determine the standards used to develop the international tests, U.S. students sometimes do poorly in comparison to students from other countries.

What Are the Content or Curricular Standards?

"Content" or "curricular" standards refer to what should be learned at a given grade level. Usually standards are developed for individual subjects. For example, the National Council of Teachers of Mathematics developed extensive and detailed standards for school mathematics. These standards include thorough specification of the material to be taught and learned throughout the mathematics curriculum at every grade and in every area of mathematics. In contrast, the International Reading Association produced 11 standards statements for the assessment of reading that do not include any specific content to be taught and learned.

What Is the Point of Standards?

Pearson (1993) categorized several major efforts undertaken to develop standards. In the most general sense, standards are developed to provide goals for teachers and students to use as a guide for what is to be learned. Many people think that the

---

[1]States and districts that receive Goals 2000 or Title I funding are required to develop content and performance standards.

major reason to have standards is to spell out what students should learn. Standards do help to set criteria for what is to be taught and learned. Standards may be used to establish what will be tested on the statewide assessments. Standards may be used to establish content and curriculum at various grade levels for one or more subject matter areas, or they may be used to help teachers decide what to teach. Standards help parents to see what the expectations are for their children. As noted at the beginning of this chapter, most assessment systems are not very coherent; therefore, one important purpose for having standards is to help bring some degree of coherence to any assessment system (see chapter 5 for a discussion of how to design a standards-based accountability system).

What Does a Score Report Tell You?

Parents are used to seeing their children's report cards, most of which use letters or numbers to convey grades. But they may be less comfortable with test score reports. The type of score report most parents see is one produced by the commercial testing company that is contracted to develop the test or tests mandated by the state. This score report is often so complex that many parents are unable to interpret their child's score(s). Parents are still going to ask, "So, how did my child do?" or "How is my child doing?" The next section provides a detailed description of the difficulties encountered when educators try to explain a complex score report to the public. Among the terms that must be explained are the child's score, a passing score, a content standard, a national norm or national standard. Some score reports may include both norms and standards.

What Types of Accountability Information Are Commonly Reported to Parents and the Community?

The educational system shares a range of accountability information with parents and the community. Table 8-1 highlights typical accountability purposes and reporting mechanisms that schools have for parents and the community—that is, an assessment reporting system (Bisesi, 1997; Farr 1992). Table 8-1 indicates that the community is most interested in overall educational accountability, while parents are concerned with a range of accountability purposes, including broad educational progress, school performance, instructional effectiveness, and student achievement. Nevertheless, Table 8-1 also suggests that two kinds of reporting mechanisms are common to the reporting systems used for both parents and the community: score reports for communicating state-, district-, and/or school-mandated standardized test scores, and report cards for sharing numerical or alphabetical grades. Thus, in this section we describe these two common mechanisms for communicating accountability information: (a) standardized test score reports and (b) report cards.

Reporting to Parents

Reporting to parents has a long tradition in education. It has taken many different forms, including parent-teacher conferences (with and without the presence of children), teacher home visits, letters and notes written to parents, and the ubiquitous report card. Other parent reporting processes have included such activities as student demonstrations and work displays that have usually focused on special skills and talents of students. These have been presented as public exhibitions of students' work in art, music, physical education, and other areas.

It is the report card, however, that has been the most common and the longest lasting of these reporting procedures, and we will focus on this tool as a means of communicating student progress in school. We made this choice because we believe that report cards are likely to remain, in most schools for the foreseeable future, the most common means of reporting to parents. Report cards have taken many different forms, depending on the goals for the report, decisions about the kinds of information to include on the report, the means of displaying the information, and the frequency with which they are issued (Azwell & Schmar, 1995; Guskey, 1996; Wiggins, 1994).

The number of different forms of report cards in use today is quite extensive. They range from narrative report cards, which attempt to provide parents with a holistic view of their child's academic progress, to letter grade reports, which resemble very closely those that were in use in schools as far back as the early 19th century. Report cards have used various combinations of letter grades, number grades, and words that represent various levels of progress. They have reported on everything from a few basic skill areas to a long listing of various goals and objectives. They have included attempts to assess attitude, personal characteristics, and the relationship between achievement and aptitude.

We are not going to attempt to deal with the strengths and weaknesses of all of these different approaches to report card development (see chapter 3 for a discussion of these approaches and the technical issues associated with them). Rather, we would like to present a view of what we believe the value of report cards to be in helping parents to better understand their child's progress in school. We would then like to suggest two strategies that we believe could significantly improve report cards.

What Do We Want Report Cards to Do?

Parents are clear about what they want from report cards. Quite simply, they want to know how their child is doing in school. All parents have certain hopes and ambitions for their children, and they want to know how close their children are coming to these expectations. Beyond the basic report as to how their children are doing, parents want to know if there are specific things they can do to help their children do better. Teachers have a similar goal for report cards. They, too, want to report to parents how a child is doing and what the parents can do to help.

Parents and teachers both understand the devastating effect a very negative report can have on a student. Everyone seems to understand that failing grades can cause a child to have a negative self-image and a feeling that he or she cannot achieve. This is the most serious unwanted outcome of grading and reporting, and it must be addressed for a system to be productive.

In brief, if report cards could accomplish the following three objectives, we would have achieved considerable success in helping parents to understand a child's progress and provide a basis for continued efforts to improve.

1. Provide an honest, accurate, and easy-to-understand appraisal of a child's progress in school.
2. Avoid the judgment of failure and emphasize a child's progress.
3. Support the child, the parents, and the teacher in helping the child to make progress by emphasizing success and pointing out areas in need of development.

What follows is a brief description of two approaches that have been developed in schools and which could be combined to meet these objectives. The first involves the development of a report card that relies on specific examples of expected levels of student accomplishment and provides guidelines for evaluating student progress. The second is the use of parent-student conferences (without the teacher being present), which result in a parent-written report card that could be substituted for one teacher report card each year. These two approaches could be used together to provide a viable and effective parent reporting program.

Developing Standards for Report Cards

The following description of a report card plan is based on a report from the Palm Beach public schools (Spinelli, 1996). Some time ago, one of the authors of this chapter spent a number of years working with teachers throughout the system on the teaching of reading and writing. The teachers in several of the schools, already unhappy with their existing report card, believed that the approaches being advocated in teaching reading and writing were not adequately represented by the report card system they were using at the time.

The concerns with the report card ranged from concerns with the arbitrariness of the letter grades teachers assigned to the disregard for individual differences. When some of the teachers and parents heard about the goals for a new report card, they voiced concerns about accountability and expectations. It was clear that the letter grades being used for the report cards gave some parents and teachers a feeling that standards were in place because they felt that everyone knew what an A, a B, or a C meant in terms of student accomplishments. The traditional approach in use in Palm Beach had been to collect weekly student grades and average them for a report card grade. Some of the teachers felt this was the most defensible and honest way to represent a student's accomplishments. Such an approach, however, allowed for great discrepancies between teachers at the same grade level and little understanding of what a student had actually accomplished, since each teacher used different class activities to collect the grades for the 9-week report card period. In short, all of the problems with traditional grading schemes were present in the Palm Beach system.

The group that began working on report cards believed that there was a strong need to communicate across the grade levels first about what students were accomplishing. Teachers began to share samples of writing they thought the average student was able to produce at the beginning, the middle, and the end of the year. This led to a great deal of discussion about what was important in writing. After discussing these examples, the teachers recognized the need to compare these samples with teachers at other grade levels. Before long, the teachers had assembled a collection of papers that represented writing development at three points at each grade level.

One of the interesting and important outcomes of this initial activity was the recognition that the quality of writing produced by a student depended on the situation in which the writing was produced. Teachers recognized that *teacher-led guided writing* would be somewhat different from *student's free writing* or from *on-demand writing* accomplished in response to a teacher-directed writing task.

The value of this review and discussion of writing standards was emphasized by one teacher who commented, "In twenty years of teaching I've never had the opportunity to talk to other teachers at my grade level and to come to consensus about our expectations for students' growth. We need to do this for all subject areas." Eventually this scaling process resulted in a grading matrix. The teachers were able to see the ideal pattern of average student development from kindergarten through fifth grade. The grading document also included a list of descriptors for the type of writing that would be graded.

The teachers were concerned that while the new report card system was unambiguous and specific, the grading of development itself was not appropriate. They knew that parents wanted to know what their children could do, but they did not want to fall into the trap of giving parents—or children—the impression that they could not learn or were somehow failing. They thought it was important to explain that writing development was a process at which every child could be expected to succeed. They explained to parents that while their child was at a specific level at the time of the report, continued reading and writing activities would bring the child to an acceptable level. They likened this process to how a child learns to walk, with some making faster progress than others and some needing special support. The report card system allowed those children to be identified. However, it was reporting on the natural and continuous progress that was the focus of the new report card. (Compare this approach to that of Cabello Elementary School described in chapter 5 and to the Ann Arbor, Michigan, schools described in Sperling, 1994.)

Palm Beach schools have a number of second-language learners and special education students, and report cards for these children presented a special problem. The teachers wanted these children to be evaluated against the same standards and to have the children considered as part of the entire school. After much discussion with the second-language teachers and special education personnel, the decision was made to use the grading matrix with all children. However, it was also decided that the use of word processors, tape recorders, oral reading of stories, and other procedures would be used to provide opportunities for the second-language learners and special education students to enable them to demonstrate clearly their language development. In addition, the special education and second-language teachers retained the freedom to make professional decisions about assessment for the students they served. (Compare this to data reported in chapter 7.)

The district viewed the introduction of the new report card to parents as an important part of the entire process. The teachers planned to develop a multimedia presentation for parents, explaining the stages of writing development and the writing levels at each grade. For those parents who could not attend the meetings or who were unable to understand the presentation, a video in English, Spanish, and Creole was also planned. Copies were to be made for teachers to send home on loan to those parents.

Parent-Student Conferences as the Basis for a Parent Report Card

A second approach to meet the goals for reporting to parents are parent-student conferences that involve parent assessment of a child's reading and writing development. This approach has been tried in the Palm Beach schools and in several schools in Albuquerque, New Mexico. (Note that it is not culturally appropriate for every setting.)

The approach is based on the use of classroom portfolios that each child keeps for the purpose of discussing reading and writing progress with the teacher (Farr & Tone, 1998). The teacher holds conferences regularly throughout the school year with each student to engage the student in a discussion about his or her classroom work. It might include conversations about the kinds of reading and writing being done, ideas for future reading and writing activities, and student ideas about what might make the student's reading and writing more effective. The parent-student conferences are begun as an informal activity that is part of a typical parent day at school. One school holds an annual portfolio party where parents can learn about the school and classroom activities. As part of that session, the parents sit with their child, and the child explains the reading and writing activities for which he or she has been collecting artifacts in the portfolio.

In preparation for this informal activity, each student practices discussing his or her portfolio with another student, who acts as the parent. The students are provided with some very simple guidelines for these practice sessions and for the subsequent sessions with the parents. Prior to the actual student-parent conferences, the parents are also given similar guidelines for the portfolio conference sessions they are to have with their children. These guidelines are listed in Table 8-2.

When the conference is completed, the teacher asks the parents to fill out a questionnaire to help the teacher with planning future parent-child portfolio conferences. These questionnaires can become the basis for a parent report card if the parents find this a valuable means to learn about their child's reading and writing development. When this approach is coupled with the report card approach described above, the parents have a basis for judging their child's reading and writing development by comparing their work with the report card standards.

It is important to note that these conferences do not include the teacher. The teacher can be available to be sure that things go smoothly, to take care of refreshments, and to be sure the parents and children are comfortable. The sessions are held in the classroom, and all of the parents are there at the same time. The room may seem crowded, but with extra chairs and a bit of planning, the day can be a tremendous success.

Table 8-2. *Guidelines for Parents and Students*

Guidelines for Parents	Guidelines for Students
Allow the child to hold the materials. Don't take the materials away from the student unless he or she hands something to you. We want the student to select and discuss with you what he or she feels is important.	Don't let your parents take the materials out of your hand. You need to show the parents what you think is important.
Don't ask a lot of questions about the things the child shows you. Encourage the child to explain.	Explain to your parents the things you show them. Tell them what the story you have written is about, why you liked it, and when it was done.
Whenever possible, encourage your child by remarking about a similar (or the same story) you have read. If you can recall, tell about the types of stories you liked to write and read when you were in school.	Be sure to tell your parents why you like some stories. Tell them what you think makes a story fun to read—and the kinds of stories you like to write.
Try to sit in one of our chairs so your eyes are on the same level as your child. It is easier for a child to talk to an adult who is at eye level.	Invite your parents to sit at the table with you.
Try to talk less than your child does. That is sometimes difficult to do, but when a child talks, he or she develops language skills, and you learn more from listening.	Be sure to explain all that you can about the stories we have been reading and writing. Your parents want to know what we have been doing.

Some teachers have been concerned that not all the parents can come to the sessions. In these cases, a note to the parents asking if a grandmother, grandfather, aunt, uncle, or family friend could substitute is often successful. In other cases, when parents have not been able to attend, the child picks someone from the school staff such as a bus driver, a kitchen or office worker, or even the school principal to substitute for the parents. In these cases, the teacher completes the parent report card. Each class and school situation will need to be handled differently so that special circumstances can be addressed. The effectiveness of the parent-student conferences, and the insights parents gain about their child's reading and writing development, can be seen in the following examples of parent report card comments from a Palm Beach first-grade classroom.

"Michael's reading has improved dramatically! He reads and writes about things important to him!"

"Erin is surer of herself when she reads and writes. She writes a lot about her family."

"Blake is certain he will become a microbiologist. He will read and write about anything that has to do with ocean life and strange fish."

"Tienelong's fascination with aliens is spurring him to read and write. He needs to do more!"

"Kelsey has many great story ideas! She loves to write about animals and then illustrate them. Her reading and writing have improved 200% this semester!"

"Melanie loves discovering new words and ideas when reading, and they show up in her writing!"

"Tara's writing has really taken off! She writes with lots more details that often come from her reading!"

It easy to see from these comments that the parents have learned about their children's reading and writing. As the parents become comfortable with this process, it will be possible to move to having the parent-child conference in the middle of the year result in a parent report card, rather than simply being an informal process. In fact, some of the parents in classes where the informal conferences have been held have commented on how much more valuable the conference is than the report card in revealing their children's progress. If a formal report card process is established, it is important that parents not be asked to put letter grades on a report. Rather, the goal is to help parents understand their children's progress as readers and writers. The formal parent report card might look something like what is shown in Table 8-3.

Table 8-3. *Sample Report Card*

Anyplace Elementary School **Parent Evaluation of a Child's Progress as a Reader and Writer**	
Student's Name:_____ Grade: _____ Date: _____ Parent's Name: _____	
1. What new thing did you learn about your child from the portfolio?	
2. What did you learn about your child's reading and writing?	
3. What topics does your child enjoy reading and writing about?	
4. Could your child retell the stories with ease? Was he or she able to explain the work?	
5. What piece of work was your child most proud of and why?	
6. What kind of reading and writing does your child do at home?	
7. What kinds of changes and growth do you notice in your child's reading and writing?	
8. How well did this time for open communication go for you and your child?	
9. How does the portfolio compare with the report card in revealing your child's progress?	

The value of the parent report card is that it accomplishes the intended goals very directly. It provides an honest, accurate, and easy-to-understand appraisal of a child's progress. It avoids a focus on failure, emphasizes a child's progress, and supports the child, the parents, and the teacher in continuing to make progress by highlighting successes and pointing to areas in need of development. Parents in one elementary school, where this process has been in effect for several years, commented on its value and importance to them:

"A simple report card cannot explain her interests, her strengths and weaknesses."

"Until I saw the portfolio, I didn't realize how she is growing scholastically."

"The portfolio allows us to see hands-on how our daughter is doing."

"We're impressed that Daniel is so proud of his work and that he's not afraid to use big words."

"The portfolio, and our interest in it, have helped improve his self-esteem."

"She really enjoys writing and seems to be finding it easier to express herself."

"I can see the improvement just since summer."

"She has confidence that she can write what she's thinking. What improvement!"

"A report card couldn't begin to show the progress."

A teacher in the Albuquerque public schools has included in the portfolio conference process a request to parents that they write a note to their child after the conference. These notes are then kept in the portfolios. A few examples of notes written by parents will show how valuable this process can be:

Briscoe,

Congratulations on putting together a well-organized portfolio. You learned a lot of interesting things in many areas. I appreciated the way you answered questions and took time to explain what you have learned. Bravo!

Dad

Madison,

It was apparent from your portfolio that you have done a lot and learned a lot in fourth grade. Your work in all subjects was wonderful!

Thanks for sharing it with us.

Mom and Dad

Kailey,

What a wonderful demonstration of the work you have done this year and all the things you have learned. What an impressive collection. I am so proud of you.

> Love,
> Mom

Some of the parents of students in this classroom wrote notes to this teacher commenting on the value of the portfolio process:

Mrs. Debbie,

It was a lot of fun seeing what she has been working on all year. She seems to have a clear understanding of her strengths and weaknesses.

> Thanks,
> Madison's parents

Mrs. Debbie,

This was very nice. A lifetime keeper. It is amazing. Kailey did a lot of hard work and it shows! I love it. Now we are fighting about who gets to keep it! Kailey or me.

> Great work,
> Kailey's mom

Mrs. Debbie,

You requested feedback from our family regarding your teaching efforts for the 1996–97 school year.

We have been very pleased with the progress of Anthony both academically and [in] his personal growth. One of your greatest strengths is the way you lead the kids through the process of self-evaluation. In addition to the feedback you provide them, they are also learning the importance of assessing their own strengths in areas that need more attention.

We as parents would hope for our children that they become lifelong learners. By providing our children with a foundation for continual self-evaluation, they are gaining a skill that allows them to gauge themselves and critically evaluate their own progress. The student portfolio is a wonderful vehicle to help the students to discover their growth and achievement this school year. They can also use their portfolios to determine areas they see as their greatest challenges.

> Thank you again,
> Tom, Janet, and Anthony

These examples demonstrate that it is possible to develop more honest and more effective reporting systems. All of the teachers who have engaged in the preceding projects will attest to the value of getting improved information to parents. They all confirm how effective and rewarding these processes have been. Specific processes need to be tailored to specific contexts, however cultural and linguistic differences may mean different approaches will work better.

Reporting to the Community: Standardized Test Score Reporting

One of the most common means for conveying accountability information to parents and the community is the standardized test score report. Standardized testing represents one way to generalize across a population and to obtain both an overall and individual view of how students are progressing in an academic area and how one group of students (or one individual student) compares to another group of students tested. Because of the high-stakes nature of many standardized testing situations (which may affect a student's graduation or college admission), reporting to parents and to the community is imperative. This reporting cannot be considered complete simply through the distribution of score reports, however. It is important that reporting be seen in a larger context that includes communicating information before and after administration. Reporting before test administration needs to include information about the content standards being tested ("What should students know and be able to do to complete the assessment?") and the performance standards expected ("How good is good enough?"). When parents understand the meaning and importance of testing, they can also become partners with schools in ensuring that students are prepared mentally and physically. After administration, reporting must communicate individual student performance ("Are students demonstrating mastery of the standards?") and overall performance ("Is the community or state performing adequately compared to other communities or states?").

Standardized test reporting differs from individual classroom teacher reporting in that we cannot easily show parents and the community examples of each child's work. Thus, we have to rely on some coding system that becomes a stand-in for actual individual student products. For performance assessments, model papers and rubrics can be shown; but for multiple-choice instruments, scores become more important. It is essential, therefore, to understand what those scores mean in terms of actual student work.

In this section, we discuss the reporting of standardized test scores to parents and the community, using our experiences communicating information about the Indiana statewide assessment program as an example. Indiana's statewide assessment program has components that are similar to those of many other statewide assessment programs and standardized test programs in use. Consequently, it is our hope that the reader will gain insight from this example for use in his or her specific state context.

Background on the Indiana Statewide Assessment Program

Indiana, like many other states, has recently made changes in its statewide assessment program. The previous Indiana statewide assessment, ISTEP, was a norm-referenced test, which placed student performance in relation to other students' performance taking the same test under standard administration procedures. It consisted of multiple-choice questions only. ISTEP was revised in 1995, and renamed ISTEP+, to also include a criterion-referenced component. This criterion-referenced section evaluated student performance compared to the Indiana Proficiency Content Standards in English/language arts and mathematics, rather than to the performance of other students. The revision also brought about the following changes:

- *Inclusion of short-answer and essay questions:* Constructed response items (i.e., items that required students to supply an answer rather than select from a list) were included so that the assessment would better represent tasks that students will encounter in the real world.

- *Determination of performance standards:* Performance standards were set at each grade tested. At the 10th-grade level, the standard must be met, starting with the high school graduating class of 2000, in order for students to qualify for high school graduation.

- *Remediation of students who do not meet the state standards:* Remedial instruction was mandated for students who do not meet state performance standards to ensure that these students get the help they need immediately.

ISTEP+, like any statewide standardized assessment program, serves a number of different accountability purposes for parents and the community:

- The assessment program lays out academic expectations to parents and the community.

- At each of the grade levels tested (3, 6, 8, and 10), ISTEP+ results help to measure student progress and preparation for future coursework as well as student mastery of the Indiana Proficiency Content Standards in English/language arts and mathematics.

- Score results allow parents to better understand their child's progress in school.

- ISTEP+ scores allow people in the community to gauge student achievement statewide and the effectiveness of specific education programs.

With the implementation of this new statewide assessment system came the need to communicate the changes mentioned above to parents and the community. The Indiana Commission for Higher Education and the Indiana Department of Education looked to our Center for Innovation in Assessment for assistance in communicating information about the assessment program to these audiences. We developed two separate documents: (a) a detailed document tailored to the information needs of Indiana educators and school administrators, who would respond to many inquiries from parents and community members about the assessment; and (b) a concise document tailored to the needs of parents. The eight questions we found most important to answer for parents and the community are listed in Table 8-4 and will be elaborated on throughout this section. They ask in more detail, "Who is being assessed?", "Why are they being assessed?", and "What are they being assessed on?"

Table 8-4. *Questions Asked by Parents and the Community*

Who is being assessed and how?

1. What grade levels are being assessed, and are all students being tested?

2. What is the purpose of the assessment?

3. What are the content standards being assessed and the performance standards expected on the assessment?

4. What is the nature of the assessment instrument being used? What are the differences between norm-referenced and criterion-referenced assessments?

5. What are the linkages among specific assessment items, content standards, and the curriculum guidelines?

How is student performance reported?

1. How should information provided on the score reports be interpreted?

2. What are the distinctions and relationships among report card grades, students' mastery of the proficiency standards, and their scores on the norm-referenced and criterion-referenced components of the statewide test?

Who has responsibility for student success?

1. Who is responsible for making the assessment process work?

The Challenges of Reporting Standardized Assessment Information

In preparing these documents, we faced a series of reporting challenges that are no doubt familiar to many teachers and administrators who are asked by parents and the community to explain their statewide testing program (State of Indiana, 1997). The challenges we faced are as follows:

- *Covering the volume and complexity of information:* As the description above clearly demonstrates, we faced a challenge in that we had to report a large volume of highly complex information.

- *Reaching different audiences:* This challenge was compounded by the fact that we had to convey the basic information in a way that would be clearly understood by all parents and members of the general population.

- *Conveying politically sensitive information:* The implementation and reporting of a new statewide assessment system can be politically sensitive, especially with regard to how the assessment program will assist those students who do not meet the standards and how it will include special needs students. It is important to take care in the language used to address these areas.

What We Learned

Through our development of these documents and our subsequent interactions with parents and members of the community, we learned much about the public knowledge of standardized test reporting. What follows is our less-than-exhaustive list of the areas in which educator understanding and reporting to parents and the community is most essential. The lessons learned reinforced our beliefs that everyone involved in the assessment system, including district administrators, school administrators, counselors, and individual teachers, needs to be knowledgeable about who and what is being assessed on the assessment. Similarly, they need to know why the assessment program is in place, how student performance is reported, and whose responsibility student success is.

Reporting begins before the assessment has been administered, for parents and the community should have answers to the questions in Table 8-4 by that time. Communication about these issues can be done in a number of ways. For example, the Indiana Department of Education communicated information to the public through TV and radio advertisements, billboards, and direct mailings to parents. However it is done, clear communication plans, goals, and a timeline must be part of the original discussions about implementing the new assessment system. A lack of planned communication can cause numerous misunderstandings within the educational and general community.

Who Is Being Assessed and How?

There will be many questions from parents and community members about who is being tested. These questions will include, but not be limited to, the following: What grades are being tested? Are students new to the state or district being tested? Are students for whom English is not a first language being tested? Are special needs students being tested? Are any accommodations being made for special populations?

What Is the Purpose of the Assessment?

Many community members may believe that this is just "one more test" that students have to take. It is useful to communicate the purposes for the assessment so that parents and community members can see the benefits of a strong assessment program. The more parents and the community understand the value of the assessment, the more supportive they will be. For example, in Indiana, the revisions to the assessment were in part a response to community concerns that Indiana students graduate from high school with the tools they need to achieve in postsecondary education and in the workforce. With the new High School Graduation Qualifying Exam component of the assessment, parents and the community can be assured that students who graduate from Indiana high schools do so by having reached or surpassed a set performance standard.

What Are the Content Standards Being Tested and the Performance Standards Expected?

Parents and the community need to understand what is being assessed and what level of achievement is expected. It is not enough to communicate the standards—either content standards or performance standards—by themselves. This information will not be meaningful to the general population unless samples are given and the general standards elaborated. It is important to communicate in language that is appropriate for a wide audience. In addition, rather than communicating the performance standard only through a number (e.g., 450 out of 800), performance standards can be better communicated through anchor papers or through elaboration of the descriptions on rubrics that correspond with a passing score.

In Indiana, for example, while educators may have no trouble interpreting what was intended by the Indiana Proficiency Content Standards, parents may find it difficult to understand the description of certain proficiency standards and how those standards might be represented on the assessment. Consequently, we found that, whenever possible, sample items should be included so that members of the lay community can actually see what is tested and how it is tested. If supplying actual items from the assessment is not possible because of test security issues, then at the very least we recommend providing sample items that reflect item types and formats. If these items are not available from the state Department of Education or testing department, then educators can work together themselves to create sample items that reflect the standardized test types.

For example, in our informational documents on ISTEP+, we provided the Indiana Proficiency Content Standards for English/language arts and mathematics with a general description of "what it means" (in less jargon-laden terms), how it is tested on ISTEP+, and how the standard appears on the ISTEP+ student report. For example, one of the content standards assessed on the 10th grade ISTEP+ is: "Use meaning (semantic), structural (syntactic), and sound (phonetic) clues to construct meaning." While the language here may make this content standard confusing to the general public, everyone can understand that reading skills are important in life and that one reading skill is being able to determine the meaning of a word from the content that is read. A sample item testing this content standard might be to ask students, after they have read a short passage, whether they can understand a given word from the context of the passage. The item might be phrased, for example, "When the author writes that 'The world of work has undergone a *sea change* with the advent of new technologies, the expression *sea change* means . . .'"

What Is the Nature of the Assessment Instrument Being Used?

It is important that parents and the community understand the process of developing the assessment instrument, what the assessment instrument looks like, and how performance will be measured through that instrument. In Indiana, some members of the community—unfamiliar with constructed response items on an assessment like this—expressed concern that the open-ended items on the assessments would ask students personal questions that could not be scored objectively. Once sample items were released, and a discussion of the process of developing and scoring these types of items was started, these community members' concerns were allayed; and they felt comfortable with the assessment instrument. Other questions arose from confusion about the two components of the assessment—the norm-referenced component and the criterion-referenced component. This issue will be discussed later in the score report section.

What Are the Linkages Among Specific Assessment Items, Content Standards, and the Curriculum Guidelines?

It is important that parents and the community understand the alignment between what is being taught and what is being tested. If there is not alignment in some areas, parents and the community need to understand why some standards may be taught but not tested, or vice versa.

In the case of Indiana's new assessment system, many were concerned about whether it was fair for the state to assume that students had been adequately prepared by their teachers in earlier grades for the "new" assessment. In fact, the standards being tested had been in place for some time, and so it was reasonable to assume that students had had an opportunity to gain proficiency in the content standards being assessed. In addition, the standards being assessed on the 10th-grade Graduation Qualifying Exam represented 9th-grade standards—the assessment truly being a *qualifying* exam, not an exit exam. Once this information had been adequately communicated to those interested, these concerns were alleviated.

How Is Student Performance Reported?

Because parents and the community will be placed in the position of interpreting the results of the assessment and understanding how they relate to other kinds of results reported (including grades and other assessment scores), they need to know (a) how information provided on the score reports should be interpreted, and (b) the distinctions and relationships among report card grades, students' mastery of the proficiency standards, and their scores on the norm-referenced and criterion-referenced components of the statewide test.

How Should Information Provided on the Score Reports Be Interpreted?

As teachers and school administrators will often be the first people to whom parents, students, and community members turn for assistance in score interpretation, they need to understand the different components and terms that appear in a typical score report. This includes terms such as "norm-referenced scores," "criterion-referenced scores," "national percentile ranks," and "scaled scores," The information provided in score reports can be useful to educators for planning curriculum and student remediation and to teachers for determining whether certain areas of the curriculum require increased emphasis or particular students need more individual attention.

Score report interpretation provided one of the biggest challenges, both to us in developing the informational and explanatory ISTEP+ documents and to parents and students in trying to interpret the results. With due respect to the work of the Indiana Department of Education, the Indiana Commission for Higher Education, and CTB/McGraw-Hill (the test development company), we must acknowledge that the format of the score report distributed after the fall 1997 administration of ISTEP+ was an improvement over prior statewide assessment score reports. However, as with many standardized reports, there were still several areas that were difficult for the general population to understand.

A sample score report that includes some of the information included on the Indiana score report used after the 1997 administration of ISTEP+ is provided in Figure 8-1. There were four main areas of the score report about which parents had questions. These are described below.

Student Performance

Parents often asked teachers questions about student performance. Most often, these questions could be grouped into two general categories: (a) questions about apparent mismatches between student test performance and demonstrated classroom performance, and (b) questions when the student had not met the established Indiana Academic Standard. The questions asked in both of these cases are ones to which teachers need to have planned, careful responses: "What can we do to make sure that my child does better on the assessment next time?" "Why is my child passing your class but not passing the assessment?" "Why didn't you better prepare my child for the assessment?"

In order to respond to these types of questions, teachers need to be familiar with the content of the standardized score report and to have considered carefully how they will deal with student "failure" on the assessment. These questions may be easier to respond to if the student had an isolated physical or emotional problem on the test day, or if the student simply suffers from test anxiety. In the latter case, building student confidence through daily activities similar to those on the assessment should take care of the problem. If the teacher believes that there are discrepancies between local curriculum and state proficiencies, then the assessment offers a good opportunity for teachers to determine areas of mismatch and refine instructional and classroom assessment strategies as needed. In addition, there may not be a discrepancy between what is taught and what is tested as much as a discrepancy between local and state performance expectations. Teachers gaining familiarity with the items and scoring procedures employed on the assessments can help to resolve apparently conflicting outcomes. In addition, teachers can use the same rubrics that were used to score constructed-response writing on the assessments in their own classrooms to show how students would have fared based on criteria by which they were used to being judged.

Figure 8-1. *Excerpt from the ISTEP+ Report Form*

Section I (upper left corner of the score report) shows the student performance on the criterion-referenced component of the assessment. This section shows how the student performed in each of the Indiana Essential Skill areas. This breakdown by skill area makes it easier for students and teachers to work together to determine students' areas of strength and help students improve in their areas of weakness.	Section II (upper right corner of the score report) shows the student performance on the criterion-referenced component of the assessment presented as a scaled score compared to the Indiana Academic Standards in English/language arts and mathematics. This is the section of the report that shows whether the student passed or failed the Graduation Qualifying Exam.

Section III (bottom half of the score report) shows the student performance on the norm-referenced component of the assessment. This section shows how the student performed in reading/language arts and mathematics compared to the performance of a sample of students tested on the same measurement under similar conditions. This score is presented as a national percentile score.

INDIANA STATEWIDE TESTING FOR EDUCATIONAL PROGRESS

Student Report
For
TOM   STUDENT   GRADE: 10

Indiana Essential Skills

English/language arts	Points Obtained	Points Possible	Percent of Points Possible	Mathematics	Points Obtained	Points Possible	Percent of Points Possible	Indiana Academic Standards
Construct Meaning (mc only)	2	4	50	Problem Solving (mc & oe)	9	14	64	Indiana Academic Standards define student achievement based on the Essential Skills and are expressed as scale scores. The standard for English/language arts is 469 and the standard for mathematics is 478. Your scores are 431 in English/language arts and 498 in mathematics, indicating that you are BELOW the English/language arts standard and ABOVE the mathematics standard.
Compare/Predict (mc only)	0	1	0	Communicate/Reason (mc & oe)	8	15	53	
Textual Clues (mc only)	2	4	50	Algebra (mc & oe)	4	6	67	
Writing Development (writing)	7	10	70	Functions (mc & oe)	5	8	63	
Language-in-Use (writing)	5	8	63	Geometry (mc & oe)	3	7	43	
Punct./Capitalize (mc only)	2	4	50	Statistics (mc & oe)	5	8	63	
Usage (mc only)	2	4	50	Probability (mc & oe)	4	6	67	
Spelling (mc only)	2	4	50	Computation (mc only)	6	10	60	
Revise Written Text (mc only)	2	4	50					
Make Inferences (mc & oe)	11	14	79					
Cause/Effect (mc & oe)	2	4	50					English Standard: 469
Purpose/Perspective (mc & oe)	7	10	70					Your Score: 431
Compare/Contrast (mc only)	1	3	33					Math Standard: 478
Influence/Persuade (mc only)	3	5	60					Your Score: 498
Fact/Opinion (mc & oe)	4	7	57					
Literal Meaning (mc only)	3	5	60	mc: Multiple-choice items				There is no relationship between these scores and the norm-referenced scores reported below.
Genres/Conventions (mc & oe)	4	7	57	oe: Open-ended items				

National Percentiles

(1996 Norms)

	NP		National Score Comparisons
Reading/language arts			
			Your test performance may be compared with that of the National Norm Group by referring to the National Percentile. For example, you achieved a National Percentile of 41 in Reading. This means you scored higher than approximately 41 percent of the students in the 1996 norming study.
Reading Comprehension	35		
Reading Vocabulary	49		
Total Reading	41		
Language Expression	37		
Language Mechanics	19		
Total Language	25		
Mathematics			
Math Concepts & Applications	35		
Math Computation	49		
Total Math	39		
Total Battery	35		

Norm-Referenced Versus Criterion-Referenced Scores

As mentioned earlier, the revision of ISTEP to ISTEP+ mandated the inclusion of the criterion-referenced portion of the assessment. However, largely in an attempt to keep a familiar anchor for those not used to the new criterion-referenced testing and reporting, the norm-referenced component of the assessment was maintained. This led to some problems in score report interpretation, as it was difficult for students and parents to understand that the results reported for the norm-referenced and for the criterion-referenced components of the exam represented two separate testing components that would not necessarily lead to similar student results. For example, in the sample score report shown in Figure 8-1, you can see that this fictional student achieved a passing score on the criterion-referenced mathematics section of the report, but received only a 35 national percentile score in "Math Concepts and Applications."

Passing Score

Another issue in the analysis of the ISTEP+ score reports had to do with the notification of the passing or failing mark. Clearly, the creators of the document did not want to notify students that they had "failed" the assessment for fear that this would lead to students' feeling insecure or unable to achieve. As a result, the score report does not clearly indicate passing or failing. Instead it indicates, in the upper left corner, the student's criterion-referenced scores, and in the upper right corner, the Indiana Academic Standards, which must be reached in 10th grade to qualify for graduation. Parents approached teachers with questions about whether their child had passed the Graduation Qualifying Exam, and teachers needed to have prepared a way of informing parents of their child's "failure."

Scaled Scores

A final issue, related to the previous one, is that the criterion-referenced scores and the level of the Indiana Academic Standard were represented as scaled scores. Therefore, students, parents, or teachers trying to take the score point totals provided in the first section (upper left) and translate them into the scaled scores in the second section (upper right) found that there did not seem to be any clear relationship between the two. This led to questions about how the scaled scores were determined. Although most people are familiar with some examples of scaled scores (the 800 scale of the SATs is the most familiar), most are not familiar with the statistical process used to determine the scaled scores. This confusion suggested that whatever purposes scaled scores provide to test developers and data analyzers, for parents and students, a simple numerical score would provide more satisfaction. Or, if the score is reported as a scaled score, it would be useful if it were reported along with the average scaled score received or the total points possible on the scale and a sentence explaining the relationship between the simple (raw) score and the scaled score. If this strategy is not possible, it is important that teachers understand the scale and can communicate what they know to parents and students.

What are the distinctions and relationships among report card grades, students' mastery of the proficiency standards, and their scores on the norm-referenced and criterion-referenced components of the statewide test? As noted above, it is important that there be an alignment between what is taught in class and the performance expected in class and what is tested and expected on the assessment. It is important that educators think through the alignment of curricular content standards, report card grades, content assessment scores, and assessment performance standards and can communicate this to parents and community members who may perceive mismatches.

Who Has Responsibility for Student Success?

The answer to the last question in Table 8-4, "Who is responsible for making the assessment process work?" is "We all are." Preparing for assessment at all levels must be a team effort made by educators, parents, students, and the community. All involved must understand that they have a personal responsibility for making the assessment work.

Who Is Responsible for Making the Assessment Process Work?

Educators have a tremendous responsibility for developing a solid assessment program. It is a long process to go from standard setting, to implementation of standards as part of the curriculum, to testing the standards as part of a high-stakes accountability system. The alignment among standards, curriculum, instruction, and assessment at all grade levels is crucial. Teachers at all levels need to communicate with each other on matters of curriculum and standards implementation to ensure that there is clear articulation from grade level to grade level. But parents and community members can share in this hard and rewarding work. Student success at each grade level can be the shared responsibility of parents, students and educators at all grade levels, and community members. If reporting of standards and assessment information is done thoroughly, parents and the community can better understand where their help is needed and what they can do to create a stronger educational foundation for the community's children.

Summary

In this chapter, we have discussed mechanisms and systems for reporting assessment information to parents and the community, including report cards and standardized test reports. We have suggested ways in which reporting practices can be greatly improved.

Current systems for reporting accountability information to various assessment audiences—including school administrators, teachers, students, parents, and the community—have evolved through a complex history. Districts, schools, and teachers have struggled to communicate different kinds of student performance information (e.g., test scores, classroom performance) to different assessment audiences who often possess different assessment information needs. Rather than being useful, these often incoherent assessment reporting systems have come to interfere with parental and community understanding of student performance.

Standards have a central role in accountability reporting systems. Parents and the community, in particular, may be confused about what the different kinds of standards represent. It is important for educators to help these stakeholders understand the standards, because clear standards provide the link between classroom instruction, performance expectations, and the report of student achievement to parents and the community. Without clear standards any reporting mechanism will create as many questions about student performance for parents and the community as it answers.

We have described two common mechanisms used for reporting accountability information—report cards and standardized test score reports. These two mechanisms create different problems for parents and the community as they try to make sense of student academic performance. We have provided some potential ways of making these reporting mechanisms easier to use and more informative for the assessment audiences they target, based on specific examples drawn from real experiences.

Teachers around the country have designed report cards that work for their particular settings. One report card we described is a developmental scale for writing that allows a teacher to help parents see where their child fits along that scale. A second type of report card we discussed is a "parent report card." Following a conference at which a child presents his or her reading and writing samples, the parent writes comments on a prepared form or writes a note to the child or the teacher commenting on the child's work.

To help parents and the community understand standardized test score reports, it is essential to share important information with them. First, a description of the test itself is needed *before* the test is administered. Second, written materials given to parents or community should have a specific audience focus, since a single document cannot meet the information needs of all audiences. Finally, we suggest that clear, understandable standards be provided so that the child's score on a test can be matched to a stated goal.

Everyone who has a stake in the educational process needs to take responsibility for making assessment and reporting systems work. School administrators, teachers, students, parents, and the public need to come together to discuss expectations for students' performance, establish clear standards, and encourage student performance and achievement. Again, the key to a successful system is the establishment of clear standards, which will provide a common language and set of expectations for discussing, supporting, and evaluating students' performances.

References

Azwell, T., & Schmar, E. (Eds.). (1995). *Report card on report cards*. Portsmouth, NH: Heinemann.

Bisesi, T. (1997). *Examining the value of a performance-based assessment: A social validity study*. Unpublished doctoral dissertation, Michigan State University, East Lansing, MI.

CTB/McGraw-Hill (1997). *Indiana Statewide Testing for Educational Progress (ISTEP+)*. Monterey, CA: Author.

Farr, R. (1992). Putting it all together: Solving the reading assessment puzzle. *The Reading Teacher, 46* (1), 26–37.

Farr, R., & Tone, B. (1998). *Portfolio and performance assessment: Helping students evaluate their progress as readers and writers* (2nd ed.). Fort Worth, TX: Harcourt Brace.

Guskey, T. R. (Ed.). (1996). *Communicating student learning* (ASCD Yearbook). Alexandria, VA: Association for Supervision and Curriculum Development.

International Reading Association/National Council of Teachers of English. (1994). *Standards for the Assessment of Reading and Writing* (pp. 34, 38). Newark, DE, and Urbana, IL: Author.

Pearson, P. D. (1993). Standards for the English language arts: A policy perspective. *Journal of Reading Behavior, 25* (4), 457–475.

Sperling, D. H. (1994). Assessment and reporting: A natural pair. *Educational Leadership, 52* (2), 10–13.

Spinelli, K. (1996). *Writing assessment: A common sense approach to change.* Unpublished mimeo. Palm Beach, FL: Palm Beach County, Area 3 Schools.

State of Indiana (1997). *ISTEP+ informational guide (grade 10).* Indianapolis, IN: Indiana State Board of Education and the Indiana Commission for Higher Education.

Trumbull, E., Greenfield, P. M., Rothstein-Fisch, & Quiroz, B. (in press). *Bridging cultutes between home and school: A guide for teachers.* Mahwah, NJ: Lawrence Erlbaum.

Wiggins, G. (1994). Toward better report cards. *Educational Leadership, 52* (2), 28–37.

Taking Steps Toward Standards-Based Report Cards

9

John Carr and Beverly Farr

A journey of a thousand miles begins with one step.

—Confucius

Ready, Set, Go?

In the chapters leading up to this one, the authors provided explanations of the various purposes of grading and compared various approaches to grading practices, traditional and innovative. They discussed issues related to those approaches—technical considerations, bias in grading students with particular needs, and reporting to parents and the community. In several of the chapters, authors suggested models and strategies for moving in the direction of a standards-based reporting system. Three broad themes run through the chapters:

- Grades should reflect academic achievement of content standards that were taught.
- Quality of instruction and assessment must be fair for all students, especially for subgroups such as English language learners and special education students.
- Reporting to parents must be accurate and informative about what the student has learned over time.

School districts must address these three themes as they negotiate a path toward a standards-based approach to instruction and assessment for all students.

We hope that you are now reading this chapter because you are interested in learning how to take serious steps toward building such a system. The intent of this chapter is to provide guidance for schools and districts that want to move from a traditional report card to a system of standards-based reporting. We cannot provide a fully articulated set of clearly defined steps to guide the transition because such a transition must, of necessity, be a function of the district or school context. We do provide some general guidelines, a few anecdotes from districts that have tried to make the transition (and are succeeding), and some tools to help you move down the road.

Why Change to Standards-Based Grading?

Standards-based grading is a natural part of a comprehensive, standards-based accountability system (Figure 9-1). Switching from a traditional report card to a standards-based reporting system is no simple feat, however, and it is not simply a technical exercise. There are, undeniably, technical issues involved in deriving a

---

Legislation as a Catalyst for Change

State and federal legislation and policy are propelling school districts throughout the nation toward the development and implementation of a system of standards-based accountability. The major elements of such a system are the following:

- District content and performance standards clearly describe what all students at all grade levels should know and be able to do and their expected level of achievement, at least in language arts and mathematics.

- Curriculum, instruction, and assessments are integrated and aligned to the standards.

- There is a plan for implementation: content standards taught and assessed in every classroom (what the teacher does when the door closes), and a procedure for teams of teachers to use student results to make informed decisions about the instructional program (what the teacher does when the door opens).

Standards-based assessments are an essential part of this system—assessments that directly measure the content standards and produce scores tied to the performance standards. Assessments must be reliable; they must accurately measure a student's true achievement level and do so consistently. No one assessment can serve all purposes nor is the fairest measure of true achievement for all students, so multiple assessments over time and by different means are necessary to confidently and accurately compare students to the performance standards. Students and their parents have a right to know the student's performance compared to district standards. The community has a right to know what the school district expects, how well the student population measures up to those expectations, and when there is a gap what the district will do to improve teaching to improve student performance. Report cards are the tool of communication in the district.

Figure 9-1

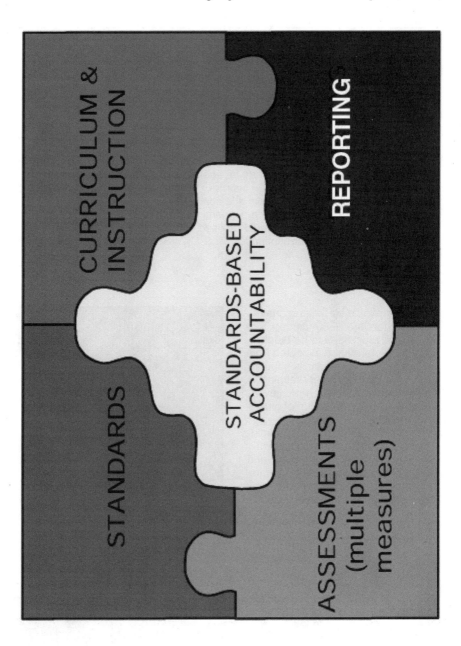

Standards-Based Accountability System

A comprehensive accountability system that is based on standards is well integrated, with each of its components linked to the other. These linkages must be clear and strong to forge a system that is valid, reliable, and transparent to those who are interested in the results and want to use them to make important decisions. These decisions may be about student placement, or they may be instructional or programmatic. The system should provide detailed information on the academic performance of students that should be used by schools and districts for continuous improvement of the instructional program.

Standards

A system should be built on challenging standards—the content, skills, and processes to be taught and the performance expected from students. These standards should result from a process of teaching consensus about student achievement among all major stakeholders of the educational community—students, teachers, parents, administrators, school boards, business and legislative representatives, and the public. Content standards state explicitly what students are to learn by subject and grade level. Public

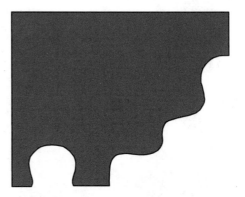

agreement about how students will demonstrate their learning in relation to *clearly specified levels of achievement* drives the teaching-learning process and ties standards to assessments and assessments to curriculum.

Curriculum and Instruction

Curriculum committees should plan articulated alignment of the curriculum with the standards by grade level and subject. Materials should be reviewed and aligned through staff development, coaching, and monitoring. Teachers teach according to the vision presented in the content and performance standards. Alignment and articulation can be enhanced through teacher discussions and application of information gained from observations.

Assessments

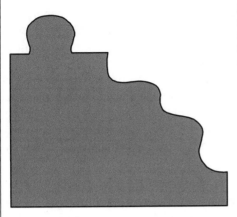

A comprehensive assessment system must: 1) include a description of assessment purposes (to report; to sort, grade, rank; to make instructional decisions); 2) demonstrate alignment with standards; and 3) show how these are matched to a selection of appropriate assessment tools. Select or develop measures for standards. Evaluate the depth and breadth of standards coverage as well as the instructional usefulness of each measure. Identify the set of measures that will be used to identify proficiency levels in each subject area. Each measure in a set in one area should be weighted and then combined to specify the proficiency level. Teachers should participate in professional development sessions and receive coaching and support that enables them to examine and evaluate student work in relation to standards. They should discuss how to analyze all student achievement data and adopt a format for reporting that makes the data meaningful and supports decision making.

Reporting

1. Teachers need detailed information at the individual student level in order to evaluate the effectiveness of instructional materials and strategies.

2. Reports on student achievement are necessary for a variety of purposes, including, but not limited to, planning, continuous improvement, and generating local support and involvement in schools.

3. Reports should be tailored for the information needs of each specific audience. For example, parents need information on their own children's performance and how to help them as well as on other students' general performance.

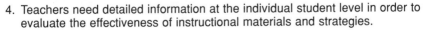

4. Teachers need detailed information at the individual student level in order to evaluate the effectiveness of instructional materials and strategies.

5. Consider various reporting needs and audiences, determine the report content, and design the report format at the same time as developing the plan for collecting and analyzing student data (not as an afterthought).

6. All reporting should have as its ultimate goal the improvement of the educational and developmental experiences of all children.

valid and reliable grade based on valid and reliable assessment data, but a great deal of time and attention needs to be directed toward development strategies that build understanding and support among stakeholders—especially teachers and parents. School district personnel need to see the big picture and all the interrelated pieces of a system of standards-based accountability.

It might be best, however, to map out the development process as a series of steps over several years, working on a standards-based reporting system as content standards and standards-based assessments become established and accepted. A long-range, step-by-step work plan might start with developing and implementing content standards in all classrooms, then standards-based assessments, and finally a system for public reporting as part of a comprehensive system of accountability.

All Aboard?

A school or a district may develop a strong standards-based reporting system that is backed by technically sound measurement methodology, but it may be resisted or rejected by teachers or parents for a variety of reasons, including merely any deviation from the status quo. This chapter presents ideas and perspectives to help teachers, principals, and district administrators think through many interdependent issues and carefully plan the steps to establish a standards achievement report. Each school district must find its own way, but success will be difficult to attain if an educative approach is not taken—one that involves all stakeholders in learning and talking about new ideas, includes them in decisions, and achieves mutual support.

The development process can be more important than the actual product that is developed. An understanding of the *why* and *how* is accomplished through a thoughtful process that involves those who are key to implementation. Failure to address issues having to do with teacher time and capacity or with parents' need for a clear understanding of how their children are doing can spell failure at the outset. A common mistake is to have a small group of persons develop a process or product quickly in response to a state or federal mandate. Such quick fixes are typically not sustained and often lead to greater problems (Senge, 1990). The literature about educational reform is replete with admonitions to use meaningful participation of a representative group of stakeholders, with regular communication to constituencies, making it possible to weigh different perspectives and move toward consensus on an initiative. A standards achievement report that looks fantastic, and is backed by technically sound measurement methodology, may be summarily rejected by teachers or parents for various reasons, including those barriers generic to any impending change. An administrator in a small school district said they are going to try to implement a standards achievement report for the third time; twice before the change was rejected by parents.

What Is a Standards-Based Report Card?

The word *grade* is defined in Webster's Third International Dictionary as "a mark indicating a particular position or level." A report card grade uses a discrete scale; it could be a traditional letter grade (A, B, C, D, F), a numerical score, or another marking used by a teacher to provide feedback to students and parents about the student's *overall classification or level of achievement*. A traditional report card grading practice conflicts with reporting achievement in a system of standards-based accountability. In the traditional report card, letter grades are given for subject areas, or courses at the secondary level. In the new system, grades apply to content standards and performance standards. Principals and teachers are quick to admit that there has been little consistency across teachers in how traditional report card grades are derived and what they represent (e.g., academic achievement, progress, effort, or some combination). In the new system, grades must be valid and reliable, accurately measuring the content standards and being comparable across students because of consistency across teachers in linking each student's achievement to district performance standards.

In a school district's *system of standards-based accountability*, student assessment results are based on the district's content standards and reported in terms of *performance levels* (e.g., advanced, proficient, partial, minimal). There is alignment among content standards, assessment, and instruction. Teachers, students, and their parents use this information to make a variety of educational decisions. Students and parents receive feedback through some sort of reporting system, commonly a "report card" with a parent-teacher conference for selected or all students at selected or all grading periods.

A "standards-based report card" reports student performance for at least the school district's language arts and mathematics content standards in terms of the district's performance standards. Reeves (1998) uses "Standards Achievement Report" instead of "report card" to refer to such a report, which shows achievement levels on the district's academic content standards (and/or parts within standards). "Marks" are scores that represent the levels of the district's performance standards (e.g., 4 = Advanced, 3 = Proficient, 2 = Partial, 1 = Minimal). Each standard's score is a composite of various assessments during the grading period, covering at least key benchmarks within the standard. The performance level for each content standard ideally reflects a combination of multiple measures. There is a procedure established for determining which assessments are to be included in the grading process and how scores from these assessments are to be combined so that there is consistency across all teachers.

Rules or guidelines structure how teachers combine scores and derive the composite report card score. The method for combining scores may be tightly or loosely rule-bound by the district. The district might have a fairly rigid model that defines a specific set of assessments and a formula for combining scores, with little room for a teacher's discretion or personal judgment regarding what goes into a grade or what grade to give when the composite score is between two performance levels. On the other hand, a district might have stipulated a core set of assessments for each standard and allowed teachers discretion to include other projects, quizzes, performance observations, and perhaps certain homework assignments. (Such a model was proposed by Marzano & Kendall, 1996). The key point is to include assessments of what students learned—not what they are in the process of learning. Other information about the student, such as effort, progress, citizenship, and study behaviors, may appear in a separate section of the report card, perhaps using traditional types of markings (e.g., O = Outstanding, S = Satisfactory, N = Needs Improvement).

An important assumption in standards-based grading is that all teachers teach to the standards and make the curriculum accessible to all students. Thus, every student has equal opportunity to learn the key concepts and skills at that grade level. Assessment methods offer alternatives and accommodations so that every student is motivated and has equal opportunity to show accurately what he or she knows and can do. Equity in the instructional setting means that grades truly represent a student's learning achievements, not other student factors or inequitable learning opportunities.

Ready or Not...

Generally speaking, a school district is ready to implement a standards-based grading system if certain conditions have been met. The district must have the following:

- Content standards at each grade level, at least for language arts and mathematics
- General performance standards—descriptions of each performance level that apply to all grade levels and all content standards
- Assessments that measure the content standards to some extent (at least key benchmarks within a standard) and yield scores aligned to the general performance standards
- Curriculum and instruction that are aligned with the content standards and that address a diverse student population

Content standards are broad statements about what a student is expected to know and be able to do by the end of a grade level. Districts should identify key parts of standards when they find it impossible to effectively teach content standards in their entirety. Often a single assessment is able to measure parts of, but not the entire, content standard. To say that "a content standard has been assessed," the assessment(s) should at least measure the key parts that are taught. Teaching and assessing all content standards in their entirety is an ideal that may take years of work to achieve. Schmoker and Marzano (1999) looked at the scope of many districts' content standards and cautioned practitioners to focus on teaching and assessing what is manageable and most important.

The first two conditions (content and general performance standards) must be met before initiating a standards-based report card system. The second two conditions are, by nature, usually considered works in progress. Under these four conditions, a school district can embark on developing a standards-based report card or Standards Achievement Report (SAR), in Reeves' term, as a tool for feedback to parents and students. Figure 9-2 gives a quick look at the steps involved in moving to a standards-based reporting system.

Figure 9-2. *Steps in Moving to a Standards-Based Reporting System*

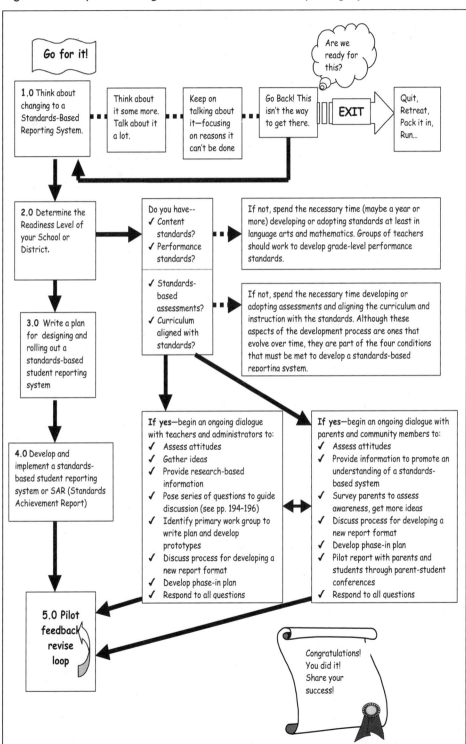

Using Questions to Frame Solutions

The movement to standards-based report cards is new and evolving, so it seems premature to offer a model process and product that have been proven to work. Schools and districts must assess their own context and progress at appropriate rates, often on somewhat different avenues. (See district vignettes in next section.) In this context, we offer a series of questions that school and district educators may find useful as they consider and then begin taking the steps toward standards-based report cards as part of an integrated system of accountability and decision making. We suggest that planning sessions be framed around some or all of these questions as a way to lay the groundwork and to support the development of a consensus about new approaches to grading based on standards.

Questions About Purpose

1. What is the purpose in our district for report card grades? Is it to reward or punish students? To inform parents? To make decisions about student placement, retention, interventions, or promotion? To reflect on our teaching practices and programs?

2. Why should we change from traditional letter-grade report cards with high teacher discretion to a standards-based report card with less teacher discretion? Does our teacher's union support a change from the traditional to standards-based grading practices, as well as monitoring to ensure consistent implementation? How might this change benefit students, parents, and teachers? Is it a worthwhile endeavor? How might this change support improvement in the instructional program?

3. Will report card grades be included in district decisions about student proficiency to fulfill mandates of the Title I legislation and/or other state legislation (such as retention and promotion)? Does our current grading system have validity and reliability? Does it reflect academic achievement or some composite with other factors, such as effort and progress? Is there grade inflation in our district, and, if yes, why?

4. What part could a standards-based report card play in an integrated system of standards-based assessment and accountability? How might an integrated system of teaching and learning, assessment, reporting, and databased decision making lead to greater parsimony and effectiveness?

Questions About Process

Development

1. What rules or guidelines are needed to ensure that teachers are consistent in their grading practice(s) so that grades reflect what the student knows and can do, not who the teacher was?

2. Who should be involved in developing the rules and guidelines for a Student Achievement Report, and on what level (e.g., decisions, advice, or

dialogue)? Which stakeholders should be involved—committee members representing which stakeholder groups?

3. How much time do we have, and how much work is there to do to develop a well-thought-out plan and to build understanding and support among stakeholders to initiate it with minimal conflicts, difficulties, or apprehension? What time is needed to discover what others have learned from their pioneering efforts? What time is needed for adequate communication among stakeholders, and for surfacing problems that need solutions?

Implementation

4. How will we train all teachers to use the new system consistently? How are we training teachers to provide all students equitable opportunities to learn and show what they have learned on assessments? What scoring guide will ensure that report card marks reflect, as purely as possible, student academic achievement and not other factors or unequal opportunities to learn? How will training become an ongoing process for current teachers to grow in their expertise and to initiate new teachers each year to the system?

5. How will we know if the new system is working well? How can we monitor to catch problems early and make adjustments? Are teachers scoring each assessment consistently—is there consistency by a teacher and across teachers? Are teachers following the district's scoring guide consistently? Are students and parents satisfied with the information about student performance, its fairness and accuracy? What impact does this new system have on teachers in terms of their instruction, knowing the child, and peer collaboration and coaching?

6. How and when will we use the report card grades to make student and program decisions? What data collection process and tools are needed to efficiently update a database for various reporting purposes? Will we use first-period grades as part of an early identification of "at-risk" students, and do we have time at the end of the school year to use last-period grades and still make decisions in time for retention or summer school intervention?

7. Is the amount of time for standards-based scoring feasible and reasonable for teachers at the elementary and secondary levels? Does the time for administering and scoring assessments and determining composite scores for report card grading for each standard support effective instruction or hinder it?

Questions About the Scoring System

1. What number of performance levels is best for our district? How many levels are on scoring guides currently in use? Will they need to be changed or can they be converted to district performance standards and levels? How useful are the performance levels? Do our levels directly relate to

decisions about types of programs and subgroups of students? Does the "Minimally Proficient" level help to identify students who are at risk of failing?

2. Will we continue to use grades or switch to numeric scores or some other symbols and for what reason? Will "subscores" such as + and – be included on individual assessment scores and/or the grades appearing on the standards-based report card?

3. Will there be a separate area to provide a grade for a student's effort, progress, citizenship, etc.?

4. What level of specificity should we provide in the scoring guide in terms of what assessments to include, their weights, and the method to combine scores? Should some form of teacher observation, assessment options, or other types of informal assessments be part of the composite grade? Should we use an algorithm to combine scores with no teacher discretion, or set guidelines with some level of teacher judgment, especially for students with a composite between performance levels?

5. We are moving from indicators of achievement for a few domains (e.g., reading, writing, mathematics) to a larger set of content standards and could go deeper to parts within standards. Multiple assessments can provide different information about student achievement for a particular standard. How many assessments and in what depth are right for our district? What system of assessment is valid and adequately reliable, while supporting, rather than hindering, a focus on instruction?

6. How do we align grade-level assessments and specific expectations with grade-span content standards? What is the right balance of specificity and generalization to report that our assessments are valid measures of our content standards? How do we address advanced placement courses when they do not conform to our content standards?

7. The final report card grades should reflect achievement of year-end grade level expectations. What should grades for prior reporting periods reflect— current grading period expectations, year-end expectations, or some notion of progress toward year-end expectations?

Glimpses Into the Process: Three Vignettes

Step-by-Step in a Small, One-School District

Pleasant Grove School District, a rural K–8 school in Sutter County, California, has been part of the state's consortium of "Challenge Districts" for several years. For two years, the superintendent/principal has worked mainly through the School Site Council (a Title I–mandated committee composed of staff and parents) and with school staff (including nonteaching staff members) to develop challenging content standards. Last year, teachers began formally teaching to the standards in their classrooms. Meetings were held and letters were sent home to inform parents about the content standards and their purpose in setting common, high expectations of all students. This year, the staff has been working on developing assessments that measure the standards and, at parent-teacher conferences, discussing student performance with parents. Thus, teachers and parents were introduced to, and accepted, successive steps in the system of standards-based accountability. Parents now want to see assessment results for their children reported as performance levels and measuring the content standards being taught. The school is not quite "there" yet in the design of multiple, standards-based assessments at each grade level. All along the way, the school board has been supportive by providing necessary resources for development and capacity building and making standards-based accountability a high priority.

Teachers and parents are beginning to talk about the conflict between their traditional report card and standards-based reporting. At the same time, the principal has been collecting models of standards-based reporting systems from other districts and keeping abreast of the literature in anticipation of the change in their grading system. He and his staff are exploring devising a form for each report period that contains only the benchmarks (parts of content standards) that were the focus on instruction during that period, and reporting standards-referenced scores (see a description of standards-based scores below). This novel approach deserves consideration. Because staff and parents have experienced a step-by-step developmental process toward a system of standards-based accountability, they understand and support each step and see the natural linkage to the next step.

Leaping Several Steps at a Single Bound

San Juan is a large, suburban K–12 school district in Sacramento County, California. San Juan is also a "Challenge District" and a pioneer in the standards-based accountability movement in the state. This district has a history of ongoing, integrated staff development coupled with an evolving, cutting-edge system of assessment and use of results for program decision-making. Central office administrators guide schools through a proactive plan, developed by key administrators with approval by a committee of stakeholder representatives, and systematically seek and use feedback to refine the plan. A history of good management and capacity building for many initiatives enabled this large district to jump right into standards-based instruction, assessment, and a system of reporting and using results.

The report form for kindergarten through sixth grade has numeric academic grades for language arts and mathematics standards with four performance levels—"Advanced," "Proficient," "Approaching," and "Below." For each standard, a grade (score) and benchmarks or components are shown but not separately graded. Traditional letter grades ("Outstanding," "Satisfactory," and "Needs Improvement") are given for effort and progress for traditional subject areas, as well as for social skills and work habits. The second side of the form gives descriptors of the standards-based and traditional grades and refers parents to "Student Standards" brochures for more explanation. (Table 9-1 presents the descriptors for the standard levels.)

It has taken the integrated efforts of key district administrators, and knowledgeable principals working with their staff and parents, to make this quick transi-

Table 9-1. *Standard Levels (adapted from the San Juan Unified School District)*

Advanced (4)	The student consistently meets and often exceeds the standard as it is described by the grade-level *key indicators*. The student, with relative ease, grasps, applies, and extends the key concepts, processes, and skills for the grade level. The student's work is comparable to the student models and rubrics that are labeled **advanced (4)**.
Proficient (3)	The student regularly meets the standard as it is described by the grade level *key indicators*. The student demonstrates proficiency in the vast majority of the grade-level *key indicators*. The student, with limited errors, grasps and applies the key concepts, processes, and skills for the grade level. The student's work is comparable to the student models and rubrics that are labeled **proficient (3)**.
Approaching (2)	The student is beginning to, and occasionally does, meet the standard as it is described by the grade-level *key indicators*. The student is beginning to grasp and apply the key concepts, processes, and skills for the grade level but produces work that contains many errors. The student's work is comparable to the student models and rubrics that are labeled **approaching (2)**.
Below (1)	The student is not meeting the standard as it is described by the *key indicators* for this grade level. The student is working on *key indicators* that are one or more years below grade level. The student's work is comparable to the student models and rubrics that are labeled **below (1)**.

tion successful. The switch to a standards-based report card was started as a pilot in 1998–1999 in the elementary schools that were ready for the change, with the expectation to expand to the secondary schools the next year. Some preliminary work actually began with teachers at the primary grades. The leap "in all directions"—implementing all parts of the accountability system virtually at the same time—has had the positive effect of creating a coherent system with each part acting in concert with the other parts, rather than creating a disconnected system.

But rapid change has taken a toll in some ways. Key central office administrators as well as school principals have worked long hours to make it all happen and now must keep up the pace to implement their plan and patch up the rough spots. Additionally, as pioneers, they feel obligated to respond to requests from other districts for guidance in the process and products. Teachers are feeling a bit overwhelmed by the increase in assessments and by having to quickly learn the new, formal grading system. Bugs in the system are popping up—to be expected in any new initiative, but especially one developing rapidly. Not all parents are welcoming the rapid change, so attention to communication is still a priority to sustain parental support.

Growing pains come with rapid progress in the standards-based accountability movement. San Juan has produced high-quality products and, more important, has been successfully implementing a comprehensive system of accountability and living to tell about it.

Elementary Changes

Buckeye is a small rural K–8 school district with four elementary and two middle schools, serving about 3,800 students in El Dorado County, California. Buckeye also has been a state "Challenge" district. Four years ago, teacher committees, with the leadership of a principal, developed content standards in language arts and mathematics. At the same time, the report card at the elementary grades (K–5) was changed to reflect achievement of their content standards. The report card has three possible grades for "above," "at," and "below" grade-level performance. There are guidelines for how to derive grades, but teachers have discretion both in terms of what data is included and how it is combined.

Committees continue to refine a set of assessments, and the school staff uses student results to inform instructional decisions. Parents were not represented on the committees but have been kept informed throughout the process and informally give feedback. Teacher-parent conferences about report card grades include review of student work and progress.

While the elementary schools have made a successful transition to standards-based assessment and reporting during the past 4 years, the two middle schools have not participated in this initiative. For a variety of reasons, this seems to be a common pattern in school districts.

Things to Think About

What Makes a Grade Valid and Reliable?

A valid and reliable grade for a content standard indicates a student's level of learning of the content taught by the teacher. It indicates a student's achievement level, not extraneous things such as effort, attendance, or completion of homework assignments. As stated before, a grade should not be based on the results from one assessment; it should be a composite measure of multiple assessments. So to determine if a grade is valid and reliable, we must begin with the score for an individual assessment and work up to the composite represented by the grade.

Each assessment must yield a score related to an absolute scale, such as performance levels related to the district's general performance standards. The score should not be related to a relative scale, such as a comparison to other students in the class, school, or district. When the assessment fairly and accurately measures the content taught for all students, then it is a valid assessment. When a teacher is consistent in scoring all students, then the assessment is reliable within the context of that teacher's classroom. When all teachers in the district are consistent in their scoring, then scores are reliable throughout the district.

Should Effort, Attendance, and Homework Be Part of an Academic Grade?

Effort is not a measure of achievement. If a teacher feels compelled to reward or punish a student for showing much or little effort, then the report card should have a separate area for a judgment about effort. In this case, effort should be rated

according to as objective a set of criteria as possible, and certainly not in comparison to other students or to the teacher's notion of a student's "potential" or "ability."

Attendance is not a measure of achievement. If a student is able to come late
or never attend a class and still score 100% on the test, then so be it. Perhaps this
student was making much better use of his or her learning time. Attendance in a
challenging course with powerful teaching should normally be necessary for a
student to learn the content standard and perform well on a test. Attendance can be
shown in another area of the report card in terms of tardiness and absenteeism.
Low attendance might be one reason why the student was unable to perform well
on all the assessments and received a failing grade, but it should not be "factored
into the grade."

Most of the time, homework should not be part of the grade. It is (or should
be) an activity to support the learning process. It is not usually an assessment of
what was learned. There are other ways to reward or punish a student for completing or not completing homework. Homework should be a risk-free chance to experiment with new skills. Homework should require students to apply what they
have learned so they find out what they really do understand and can return to class
to ask questions about what was not understood. A good teacher incorporates the
homework assignment into the next day's lesson to motivate students to complete
the homework, and targets teaching to what students misunderstood. Homework
may be used to teach work habits and responsibility as well as to give parents a
way to know what the student is learning (Heathman, personal communication 1999).

Only when homework is truly an assessment instrument to measure what has
been learned should it be included in an academic grade. To be an assessment
instrument, it needs to be formally scored, to have a scoring guide tied to the district's
content and performance standards. An example of such a homework activity would
be a long-term research project completed in and out of school.

How Will We Grade at Each Reporting Period?

This is, perhaps, the most difficult decision to make when making a shift from a
traditional report card to one that is based on standards. Content and performance
standards target year-end, grade-level expectancies. Discussions in the literature
about standards-based report cards tend to focus on grades at the final reporting
period. But what should the standards-based report card grades for the periods
prior to the final period reflect? Should grades at all reporting periods reference
year-end standards, or reference something particular to each point during the school
year? How will the students and parents react to whatever method is used? How
will the teacher use a particular type of grade at each reporting period to make
instructional decisions?

Three options for what grades at each reporting period might reflect are considered. Grades can reflect performance compared to (a) proficiency at this point
in time, (b) adequate progress toward grade-level proficiency, or (c) year-end grade-
level proficiency.

With the first type, *period-referenced scores*, the focus is on expected learning for a specific period. Performance-level scores refer to performance up to a

certain period during the school year, not year-end expectations. For validity and reliability, standards and scoring guides are established for each reporting period during the year for each content standard. The underlying assumption is that learning is a cumulative process over time. Period-referenced scores are particularly appropriate when the content standard is tied to cumulative learning, such as reading at the lower grade levels. Period-referenced scores are not appropriate when learning is not cumulative, as with procedural knowledge. Expanding from a few subject areas to many content standards is often complex enough without a further subdivision into time periods—all of which may lead to more confusion and divert the focus away from year-end expectancies.

With *progress-referenced scores*, teachers somehow judge whether students are progressing toward year-end expectations at a "good" rate. As with the period-referenced grading method, there is the assumption that learning is cumulative. It is difficult, however, to get consistency across teachers on a slippery notion of expected progress at 2- or 3-month intervals. New labels and descriptors must be invented for scores in periods prior to the final period where grades suddenly switch from referencing progress to referencing achievement.

Standards-referenced scores are based on scoring guides referenced to the district's year-end, grade-level content and performance standards. Scores at the first grading period might be 2 for standards that tend to reflect cumulative knowledge and 3 or 4 when the knowledge is discrete and the standard was taught and mastered within that period. This method gives teachers feedback about the gaps between "what is now" and "what is expected at the end of the year" in order to implement interventions early for students needing special support to accelerate their learning. The problem with this scoring method is helping parents and students to understand and accept the change (e.g., from getting As each report period to some 2s in the first period, 3s in the second period, and finally 4s in the last period). District communication and dialogue prior to the implementation is critical.

The assessment system that supports best instructional practices needs to be simple and focused on performance in relation to standards. Teachers need time to reflect on results, ponder new strategies, and keep improving instruction to support all students to achieve the standards. A simple process with simple probing questions should be devised for collecting, reviewing, and discussing student results. What is the standard? How much more does a student need to accomplish to reach the standard? What instruction and interventions are needed for the student to achieve proficiency? These three simple questions are the basis for discussions and solutions in San Juan Unified School District. When a school or district is moving towards a standards-based system, those involved must arrive at a decision about what approach and format to use for grading at each reporting period. In some cases, it may be best to phase in some aspects of the new report to ease the transition.

What About Teacher Autonomy?

In traditional grading systems, teachers have been able to determine how they will grade students. Teacher's discretionary power in grading has been used to leverage good behavior and punish students who did not "work to their potential" or misbehaved and yet had high scores on all exams. Some teachers have tried to use what are supposed to be academic grades to get students to turn in homework and attend class. But academic grades should reflect only academic achievement. A standards-based grading system does take away much of the teacher's autonomy. A shift to uniformity, to standards, must be seen as good for students, but it will only be accepted after long discussions among teachers to let go of old practices and reach new, fundamental agreements.

Idiosyncratic grading practices is a symptom of the traditional culture of teacher isolationism (Reeves, 1998). Uniformity of grading practices is not an issue in schools where teachers feel they are part of a team with responsibility for all students in the school, a team of professionals who consult and collaborate with each other.

What Are the Important Characteristics of the District and School Culture?

Do all teachers believe that all students can achieve district standards? Are poor test results used to blame students or their parents for students' failure, or to look at how the instructional program might be improved to the point where no student fails? Do staff and principals eagerly await assessment results and plan meetings to discuss and use the results, or do they avoid data like the plague? Do staff celebrate just on holidays, or also when assessment results have improved? When trust, professionalism, and high expectations for all students characterize the culture of the school district, and there is a focus on continual school improvement, the concept of a standards-based report card can become a reality. In such a "learning organization," change is not only welcomed, it is sought. In this culture, continual dialogue and inquiry bring all stakeholders to a common commitment to try an innovation, with critics helpfully pointing out potential pitfalls and then working within the team to find solutions. The school district with this kind of culture will be able to weather the storms of changing to a standards-based report card.

Guides for Development of Standards-Based Report Systems

This section contains three different rubrics that a school district might use to assess its current status in developing a standards-based report card or Standards Achievement Report (SAR), and use as guides as the district moves away from a traditional report card. States that require school districts to submit Title I reports that give evidence of the validity and consistency of their multiple measures might consider using these guides to help communicate expectations of future reporting and then to judge the quality of the reports. Consistency can be viewed as (a) the degree to which a teacher consistently scores or grades all students and (b) the degree to which scoring or grading is consistent across all teachers in a grade level.

The first rubric (Table 9-2) focuses on validity and consistency of any assessment or grading system, with the highest level specifying a standards-based system. The second rubric (Table 9-3) focuses on the process of developing a standards-based report card. The third (Table 9-4) focuses on the development of a standards-based report card, blending descriptors of process, validity, and consistency. The rubric might be used like a profile by highlighting statements that are most like the district. A score would be the level that most closely fits the district, giving equal weight to each dimension ("validity" and "consistency") or perhaps more weight to the "consistency" dimension, especially the first part, which targets consistent implementation.

Rubrics

The first scoring guide (Table 9-2) may be particularly useful to determine the degree to which report card grades meet an acceptable level of validity and consistency regardless of whether they target the traditional academic domains (e.g., reading, writing) or content standards. This rubric might be useful at the state level when reviewing Title I reports of student results to judge the quality of grades as one of the multiple measures.

The rubric has five levels. It is highly unlikely that the district uses standards-based grades at the lower levels (1 or 2) and subject areas or content standards at higher levels (3 or 4). A district must be using a standards-based report card at the highest level (5). Validity and consistency increase across the levels as the district provides evidence through a description of its guidelines, implementation, and monitoring system.

Table 9-3 presents a rubric that identifies stages in the development of a standards-based system of grading. It focuses on the process of moving from a traditional report card to a valid and consistent standards-based report. The rubric has three dimensions: (a) the guidelines and report format, (b) the planning process, and (c) the implementation process.

Table 9-4 is another developmental rubric covering six stages. It blends descriptors for the process a district uses to establish a standards-based report card, both through the work of a panel representing various stakeholders and ongoing staff development and teacher collaboration. The panel creates the system of scoring assessments and combining assessment data into the grading process. This panel designs the assessment scoring guides and standards-based report card grading guides to be used by teachers. While the panel is working, teachers are discussing and collaborating on their teaching and assessment practices to build effectiveness and consistency. As teachers pilot the draft work of the panel, they suggest revisions to the panel.

It may be difficult in the beginning stages to achieve districtwide implementation of a relatively small set of standards-based assessments. But those involved should not lose sight of the fact that, just as true equity in learning requires that teachers use a variety of teaching strategies to meet the needs of diverse students, so too must there be a variety of assessment alternatives so that all students have the opportunity to show what they have learned. Equity in learning and assessment are *especially* important for English language learners (i.e., limited English proficient) and special education students.

Table 9-2. *Validity-Consistency Scoring Guide for a Report Card System*

	1 Unguided	2 Minimal	3 Partial	4 Satisfactory	5 Standards-Based
Validity	District grading policy and guidelines give very general directions about how grades are determined by teachers. Academic grades may be influenced by non-achievement data (e.g., effort, attendance) Validity is doubtful.	Guidelines restrict academic grades to reflect only academic achievement (excludes nonachievement data). Validity is doubtful.	Besides the restrictive guidelines, grades are based on a "core" set of assessments. Teachers may add other assessments. Weighting of the core assessments may be specified. Fair validity.	Guidelines specify the core set of assessments and a uniform procedure for combining scores to derive grades. Each assessment is assigned a weight, and a scoring guide or formula is used to combine the data into a grade. Teachers may not alter the procedure. Satisfactory validity.	District guidelines specify the core set of *standards-based assessments*, and there is a uniform scoring guide or formula for combining scores to derive grades for content standards. Satisfactory validity.
Consistency	Teachers have great or full autonomy in how they determine grades. New teachers are informed of district policy and guidelines. Veteran teachers might be reminded. There is no review of grading practices. Consistency is doubtful.	Teachers are informed of the guidelines. There is no review of grading practices. Consistency is doubtful.	Principals discuss the guidelines with teachers to ensure understanding and foster compliance. Teachers score their own students' assessments. There is no review of actual grading practices. Consistency may be weak.	There is adequate staff development in the grading system (test administration, scoring, combining scores) to foster consistency. An adequate assessment scoring method is used to ensure consistency; percentage agreement is adequate. Principals review teachers' grade books and forms to ensure grading procedures were followed. Consistency is satisfactory.	There is adequate staff development in the grading system to foster consistency. An adequate assessment scoring method is used to ensure consistency; percentage agreement is adequate. Principals review teachers' grade books or forms to ensure grading procedures were followed. Consistency is satisfactory.

Table 9-3. *Developmental Scoring Guide for a Standards-Based Report Card*

	1	2	3	4
Report Design	Traditional grades for subject areas; great teacher autonomy; grades may reflect academic achievement plus nonachievement data (e.g., attendance, effort, progress).	Grades for subject areas; guidelines base academic grades on academic achievement; an area exists for other information (e.g., attendance, effort, progress); teachers have some autonomy to add assessments and determine grades.	Standards-based grades as performance levels, at least in language arts and mathematics; guidelines base academic grades on academic achievement; there are core assessments, but teachers may have some autonomy to add assessments and determine grades.	Standards-based grades as performance levels, at least in language arts and mathematics; guidelines specify assessments, with scoring guides for each assessment and combining scores into final grades.
Planning	Planning committee may be exploring a change.	Committee is working on a plan to change to a standards-based format to begin next year.	Committee work and staff development are ongoing to improve the process and expand to all schools and grades.	Continuing to refine the process.
Implementation	Board policy or guidelines, but no formal monitoring.	Board policy or guidelines, but no formal monitoring.	Standards-based report card is being piloted this year; there is a plan for full implementation next year.	Full districtwide implementation of standards-based report card; monitoring of grading practices to ensure consistency.

Table 9-4. *Developmental Scoring Guide for a Standards-Based Report Card*

	0 No Progress	1 Starting	2 Partial
Standards-based Process	• Content standards adopted by board • Grading policy, general guidelines exist • No grading or accountability panel, representing all stakeholders; little or no discussion about changing report card	• Some staff development • Teachers beginning to teach to content standards • Representative panel starting work on SAR • One or more districtwide assessments yielding performance levels; panel exploring inclusion in SAR	• Adequate, ongoing staff development • More teachers teaching to the content standards • Panel adopts some Standards-Based Assessments (SBAs) at some grade levels in reading, writing, and/or mathematics; working on plan to expand • SBA results are part of parent reporting and conferences
Standards-based Product — Validity	• Dubious validity • Grades reflect subject areas; teachers use idiosyncratic grading; may include nonachievement factors (e.g., effort, homework)	• Dubious validity • Grades reflect subject areas; idiosyncratic grading; may include nonachievement factors • Piloting changes at some schools may occur	• Dubious validity • One or more grade levels districtwide piloting a standards-based report card in language arts and/or mathematics
Standards-based Product — Consistency	• Dubious consistency • Teachers do not collaborate on scoring assessments or grading • No monitoring of scoring or grading	• Dubious consistency • Teachers collaborate on scoring some assessments at some schools • No monitoring of scoring or grading	• Dubious consistency • Districtwide, one or more grade levels collaborate on scoring SBAs and at least discuss performance standards and student work • No monitoring of scoring or grading

		3 Approaching	4 Proficient	5 Advanced
Standards-based Process		• Adequate, ongoing staff development • All teachers at some schools and/or districtwide at some grade levels teaching to content standards, use SBAs • Panel drafts standards-based report card; grades reflect at least key language arts and mathematics content standards • Standards-based report card results reported to parents; part of conference	• Ongoing staff development targets key revisions • All teachers at elementary and/or secondary grade levels teaching to content standards, use SBAs • Panel revising standards-based report card based on experiences and new ideas, with focus on equity for all students and expansion to all grade levels • Standards-based report card results reported to parents; part of conference • Standards-based report card results used in student and program decision-making processes	• Ongoing staff development targets refinements; alternatives for equity for diverse students • All teachers collaborate on teaching content standards and using SBAs; students self-assess as part of process • Panel continues to refine and monitor the process • Standards-based report card results reported to parents; combined with portfolios for student-led conferences • Standards-based report card has high utility in results-driven district
Standards-based Product	**Validity**	• Probable validity for those using standards-based report card • Specific set of SBAs for elementary or secondary grade levels; specific (assessment) scoring guide and (standards-based report card) grading guide	• Validity is satisfactory; grades reflect achievement of content standards according to performance standards • Standards-based report card grading guide is based on SBAs with scoring guides	• Validity continues to be strengthened, especially for diverse students • Standards-based report card grading guide is based on SBAs with scoring guides, with alternative assessments for diverse students
	Consistency	• Probable consistency • Most teachers collaborate on scoring SBAs; most teachers who use standards-based report card discuss their use of grading guide • Piloting system for monitoring scoring and grading practices	• Consistency is satisfactory; there is ample evidence of teacher consistency • All teachers discuss teaching, and collaborate on scoring and grading practices • Systematic monitoring of SBA scoring and standards-based report card grading; use formal scoring process	• Consistency continues to be strengthened, especially for diverse students • All teachers collaborate on teaching, scoring, and grading practices • Systematic monitoring of SBA scoring and standards-based report card grading; use formal, high-quality scoring process

Summary

This chapter begins by defining a standards-based system and presenting reasons for moving to such a system. We provide some guiding principles and describe some conditions that should be in place if a school or district decides to embark on the journey toward a standards-based grading and reporting system. In order to assist with the process, we supply some questions that can frame planning discussions and give impetus to the development of a standards-based system. Additional aids that are included are brief vignettes of three districts that have initiated the development of new systems of grading, suggestions about important issues to think about, and a set of rubrics to use to assess progress toward standards-based systems.

References

Marzano, R. J., & Kendall, J. S. (1996). *A comprehensive guide to standards-based districts, schools, and classrooms.* Alexandria, VA: Association for Supervision and Curriculum Development.

Reeves, D. (1998). *Making standards work.* Denver, CO: Center for Performance Assessment.

Schmoker, M., & Marzano, R. J. (1999). Realizing the promise of standards-based education. *Educational Leadership, 56* (6), 17–21.

Senge, P. (1990). *The fifth discipline: The art and practice of the learning organization.* New York: Doubleday/Currency.

Afterword

Ursula Casanova

I am going to begin with a story that illustrates the timeliness of this book. One of my current projects is assisting in the restructuring of a secondary school where student performance on standardized tests has been consistently well below the state's (Arizona's) median. In separate surveys administered recently, most students claimed to be achieving at A, B, or C levels while their teachers said that most students were working below average. However, a subsequent examination of the grades awarded to students by their teachers showed they were receiving mostly As, Bs, or Cs, thus supporting the students' perceptions. And yet, the teachers do not believe these grades reflect their students' performance.

As of the year 2000 students in this state are required to pass a test to measure their competence against the recently developed state standards. Graduation from high school will depend on their success in passing that test. Current levels of performance suggest that many of the students at this high school are likely to fail the state test and therefore to be denied a high school diploma. How will their teachers explain the discrepancy between the favorable grades reported to parents and their children's failure on the state test? Who will be held responsible for student failure? These questions are among those that will need to be answered by many schools in the next few years.

I do not remember spending much time on grading policies during my many years as a teacher and later as an elementary school principal. I remember discussing the format and our attempts to distinguish between effort and achievement and also about communicating effectively with parents, but those were simpler times for teachers.

During the 1970s, although standardized tests were the major measure of school accountability, the results were neither published in the newspapers nor shared with parents. We did not have to contend with the hasty imposition of standards at various levels, or with the high stakes consequences now associated with many of those tests. It was enough to have an easily understood report card that successfully communicated student progress to parents.

Grading was a simpler, if not necessarily a more accurate or equitable, process during the 1970s and early 1980s. Today, the complexity of the emergent assessment systems and the public nature of results are combining to place much greater demands on educators. What was mostly a private ritual among teacher, student, and parents is now a public performance with real consequences for all involved.

In spite of their training and experience, few teachers or administrators are well prepared to respond effectively to the new landscape of assessment. The overlapping characteristics of all the instruments and processes used to assess students today require a clear understanding of the purposes each is intending to serve. In addition they need to fit together as different but compatible pieces of a puzzle. In order to make sense, the various sources of data now provided to parents must be in accord with each other. Large discrepancies between a student's teacher-assigned grades and the student's performance against the state standards will require explanations.

It is unfortunate that political interests promoting an adversarial relationship between policy makers and educators have most often guided the current movement to performance standards. Had it followed instead a collaborative model similar to the example offered by Waters (chapter 5) of the Cabello–New Haven School District, it would have been more warmly welcomed. It will be difficult, in the current climate of mistrust, to become a positive architect of a new and rational system of assessment. However, whether they want to or not, teachers and administrators must now engage in just such a process in order to respond to the demands posed by the new requirements. This book should be of immense help to educators at all levels who are trying to carry out that task.

Among the recurrent themes within this volume you will find the assertion that a teacher's own philosophy of learning should be a point of departure for the development of a grading system. Through the creation of two fictional teachers, YAC and MAC, representative of two extreme philosophical positions, Carr (chapter 3) successfully illustrates the ways in which a teacher's own beliefs and values can influence his or her grading policies.

While several of these authors discuss this aspect of grading (see chapters 2, 3, 6), the influence of a teacher's beliefs and values on grading is not often mentioned in the schools, although it is especially relevant today. There was a time when teachers taught in settings close to their own communities, but today most teachers are unfamiliar with the communities within which they teach. Their students often speak a different language and bring to their classrooms a set of experiences widely different from those of their mostly middle-class teachers.

Most of the teachers in today's urban classrooms know little more than what is displayed in the media about their students' lives. And the media promote a distorted view of poor urban neighborhoods. Many teachers face their students convinced of the impossibility of their instructional task and thus fail to expect their students to achieve at levels much higher than average, if that. On the other hand, they may also feel a great deal of sympathy for what they perceive to be their students' plight, and thus emphasize "effort" as a substitute for achievement. This appears to be the tension that prevails in the secondary school described above, a current example of what Trumbull calls the tension between being a judge or an advocate for the students.

For students who are English language learners (ELLs), problems of differences in ethnicity, color, and class are compounded by their temporary limitations in English. Few of their teachers have reached even a modicum of competency in a language other than English, or have any understanding of the process of second-language learning.

As Trumbull points out in chapter 6, English learners are doubly punished. On the one hand, as they become adept in the use of routine conversational forms that mask their academic limitations, their competence in English is overestimated. On the other hand, the difficulties they may have in speaking English lead educators to underestimate their cognitive abilities and sometimes place them in special classes.

Children who lack full competence in English are sometimes also judged by standards that are beyond them as developing second-language learners. The problem with the correct placement of articles, noted by Trumbull (chapter 6), is one of those. Similarly, some Spanish speakers may appear to be poor readers of English because they drop off ending consonants in English as they are accustomed to doing in Spanish. To avoid misjudgment, teachers need to be made aware of the likelihood of certain errors when appraising the work of students who are second-language learners.

Another theme that permeates this book and should be heeded by all educators is the need to use multiple assessments. All of us can name the forms of assessment we would prefer because we are aware that our performance will vary accordingly. And yet, schools may limit the opportunities students have to demonstrate their competence in a variety of ways.

Kessler and Quinn (1987) showed the potential of alternative strategies in a study. These researchers wanted to compare the performance of bilingual (Spanish-English), low-achieving, "barrio" students against that of monolingual (English), high-achieving, middle-class students. After using filmstrips to teach science concepts through experiments to both fourth-grade groups, the researchers asked them to watch another set of filmstrips and explain what was happening and why. Within this format the low-achieving, bilingual students exceeded the performance of the high-achieving, monolingual, middle-class students in all measures, including language complexity. It is unlikely that a paper-and-pencil test would have yielded similar results.

The availability of different opportunities for students to demonstrate what they have learned is especially important for students with special needs. As recommended by Langdon and Trumbull (chapter 7), the assessment of those with serious developmental problems will best be achieved ipsatively—that is, on the basis of their own growth.

A similar approach should guide the assessment of English language learners through the developmental stages. Newly issued standards developed by several organizations concerned with second-language learners (Teachers of English to Speakers of Other Languages [TESOL], The Center for Applied Linguistics [CAL], and the National Association for Bilingual Education [NABE]) provide an excellent form of alternative assessment. These organizations can be reached through the World Wide Web at www.tesol.org, www.cal.org, and www.nabe.org, respectively. Appropriate expectations for every level of English development, at every level of schooling, are illustrated with rubrics accompanied by interpretations and suggestions for further development. These materials provide linguistically appropriate standards against which a student's growth can be assessed. Through periodic audio-recordings of these informal assessments, teachers, parents, and students can gauge the adequacy of a student's progress in English through the years so as to plan for appropriate instruction.

Fairness is a concept that underlies every attempt at judging others. It becomes critical when those judgments are likely to affect the life chances of students. It is a theme that underlies every chapter in this book. The need to be fair in the assessment of special populations becomes much more important in light of the demand that every student achieve at the same high standards, and that they all be tested. While those are worthwhile goals, directed at ensuring accountability for every student, they have to be applied judiciously. It is unreasonable, as well as unethical, to expect a recent immigrant to submit to a test in an unknown or barely understood language. This would be akin to insisting that a blind student take a written language test without a Braille translation, or that a deaf student take an oral examination. Thus, there are limitations, some of which are more important than others.

The solution policy makers propose to this conundrum is the use of accommodations. In chapter 7 Langdon and Trumbull review many of these and point out the advantages and difficulties associated with them. The problem is that we know very little about how these accommodations are decided upon, by whom, and how they affect the validity of a test. Recent research (Shepard, Taylor, & Bettebenner, 1998) suggests there is little agreement about who should be accommodated and how. These researchers found wide variety across schools and teachers regarding those important decisions. The results of this research also suggest serious validity problems associated with accommodations.

Accommodations seem to be designed to draw attention away from the most important cause of variability in student achievement: the opportunity to learn. It is a simple notion: A person is not likely to learn what is not taught. Wide differences in the availability of resources, such as teachers well-trained in their subject matter (including bilingual competence), well-equipped schools with science and technology laboratories, and adequate amounts of challenging instruction, are all critical variables in student achievement. The inequity implicit in holding students to similar outcomes while their opportunity to learn is limited is not only obvious, it also sabotages the legitimacy of standards.

Educators in low socioeconomic areas face a daunting task in their attempts to respond to the demands being placed upon them within inequitable systems. But they must place the welfare of their students above all else. While some things lie beyond their sphere of influence, others can be addressed within schools and classrooms. A challenging curriculum aligned with the new standards, thoughtful and clearly defined grading practices, and coherent grading systems that include various ways to measure student learning, will go a long way toward maximizing students' opportunity to demonstrate their potential. Many of the ideas within this book can help caring educators to accomplish those tasks.

References

Kessler, C., & Quinn, M.E. (1987). Language minority children's linguistic and cognitive creativity. *Journal of Multilingual and Multicultural Development, 8* (1 & 2), 173–186.

Shepard, L., Taylor, G., & Bettebenner, D. (1998, September). *Inclusion of limited-English proficient students in Rhode Island's grade 4 mathematics performance assessment* (Technical Report 486). Los Angeles, CA:CSE.

Dr. Ursula Casanova is at Arizona State University. You can reach her by e-mail at casanova@asu.edu.

Author Index

Subject Index

217

Editors' and Contributors' Biographies

Elise Trumbull, Ed.D., is a senior research associate with the Language and Cultural Diversity Program at WestEd, the Regional Educational Laboratory based in San Francisco. She is an applied psycholinguist specializing in research and development on language, culture, literacy, and schooling and has been active in efforts to ensure equity in the assessment of English language learners and students from nondominant cultural and linguistic communities. Recently she and a colleague worked with staff in a school district to develop an alternative literacy assessment for students transitioning from bilingual to English-only instruction. Trumbull currently directs Bridging Cultures, a teacher research and professional development project focused on interpreting anthropological theory for the classroom.

A former special education teacher and school assessment team chairperson, Dr. Trumbull completed her doctorate at Boston University and is the author of numerous articles and several book chapters. She is coauthor with (Beverly Farr) of *Assessment Alternatives for Diverse Classrooms* (1997).

Beverly Farr, Ph.D., recently joined the American Institutes for Research in Palo Alto, California as a Principal Research Scientist. In this role, she is involved with the development of the National Assessment of Educational Progress, conducts program evaluations, and works on a number of projects associated with assessment and accountability. Farr spent 15 years of her professional career providing technical assistance to Title I and other federal programs. She has worked with the United States Department of Education, State Departments of Education, schools, and districts in 20 states and the District of Columbia on issues ranging from the development of assessment systems to school improvement and the design and use of effective instructional strategies.

Farr received her Ph.D. in Reading Education from Indiana University. Farr has taught elementary and high school language arts and undergraduate and graduate courses in reading and language arts at several universities and served as a consultant to Educational Testing Service as a member of the Reading Specialist Committee. Most recently, she coauthored a set of integrated reading/writing performance tasks in English and Spanish for The Psychological Corporation and is author with Elise Trumbull of *Assessment Alternatives for Diverse Classrooms* (1997) for Christopher-Gordon Publishers.

Tanja L. Bisesi, Ph.D., is coordinator of Literacy Assessment Research and Development at Indiana University's Center for Innovation in Assessment in Bloomington, Indiana. She received her doctorate in Educational Psychology from Michigan State University in East Lansing, Michigan. She currently works with state agencies and other organizations to develop literacy assessments and establish evaluation policy. Her research focuses on delineating assessment-curriculum alignment processes, and the uses that assessment consumers and clients, including policy makers, school administrators, teachers, parents, and students, make of assessment information. She has published several chapters and articles on literacy assessment methodology and policy. She has also taught undergraduate and graduate courses in various aspects of educational psychology and has conducted workshops on literature-based reading instruction and classroom literacy assessment. She formerly taught as a public school speech-language pathologist.

Kathleen Busick, Ph.D., received her doctorate from the University of New Orleans in curriculum and instruction. She has been a program specialist at Pacific Resources for Education and Learning (PREL) since 1987, working with Pacific island educators to provide professional development in the area of classroom assessment, school renewal, and standards-based learning. In her consultations in Hawaii and Micronesia, Busick studies the impact of language and culture on judgments of student learning. She has worked with teachers, principals, parents, specialists, and students to expand knowledge and understanding of exemplary classroom assessment. Through a national collaborative among 10 regional educational laboratories, she has co-authored *Improving Classroom Assessment: A Toolkit for Professional Developers* (Regional Educational Laboratories, 1998). She is also author, with Richard J. Stiggins, of *Making Connections: Case Studies for Student-Centered Classroom Assessment,* second edition (1997).

John Carr, Ph.D., is a senior research associate with both the Assessment and Standards Development Services Program and the Comprehensive Assistance Center at WestEd, a regional educational laboratory based in San Francisco. He completed his doctorate in educational research and evaluation methodology at the University of California, Berkeley and worked for 13 years in the research and evaluation offices of two school districts in California. His interests center around developing and implementing standards-based accountability systems, particularly those that use classroom performance assessments and ongoing program evaluation to improve teaching and learning.

Ursula Casanova, Ph.D., is associate professor in the Division of Educational Leadership and Policy Studies, College of Education, Arizona State University. She has also been an elementary teacher and principal. She is an expert on issues relating to language, culture, and schooling and the coeditor (with B. Arias) of *Bilingual Education: Politics, Practice, Research,* Part II.

Roger Farr, Ph.D., is a Chancellor's Professor and director of the Center for Innovation in Assessment. He also serves as the associate director of the ERIC Clearinghouse in Language Arts and as associate dean for Research and Graduate Development. He served as International Reading Association president in 1979–80, and he was a member of the Board of Directors from 1974–77. He served as coeditor of the *Reading Research Quarterly* for 12 years. Farr is the author of the Metropolitan Achievement Test: Reading and the coordinating editor for the Iowa Silent Reading Tests. He recently coauthored the Language Arts Performance Assessments, a series of integrated language arts performance assessments for grades 1 to 8 published by *The Psychological Corporation*. He has written over 200 articles and monographs on reading, writing, and assessment. His most recent book is *Portfolio and Performance Assessment: Helping Students to Evaluate Their Progress as Readers and Writers,* which he coauthored with Bruce Tone. Farr is a senior author in the area of measurement and evaluation for the language arts programs published by Harcourt Brace, and is the senior author of *Treasuries of Literature* published by Harcourt Brace and Company.

Beth G. Greene, Ph.D., is associate director of the Center for Innovation in Assessment at Indiana University in Bloomington, Indiana. She received her doctorate in Educational Psychology from New York University. She conducts research on literacy assessment, reading and writing development, and speech perception and spoken language understanding. Her current research and development projects are concerned with language arts performance assessment (elementary and secondary), assessment of language arts and mathematics (secondary), and general education (postsecondary). She teaches courses in reading and language arts in the Language Education Department at Indiana University. She also serves as development editor and manager for journal columns for the ERIC Clearinghouse on Reading, English, and Communication.

Elizabeth Haydel is the project manager for Indiana University's Center for Innovation in Assessment in Bloomington, Indiana. She holds a B.A. in American Studies from Stanford University, with a concentration in American literature. She is particularly interested in literacy assessment and has worked on a number of projects developing assessments for elementary- through college-age students. Most recently, she developed informational materials for the state of Indiana to inform educators and parents about the new Indiana statewide assessment program, ISTEP+.

Henriette W. Langdon, Ed.D., is associate professor in Special Education at San Jose State University in San Jose, California, where she teaches courses in language development, assessment of language-learning disabilities, and instruction. She has 25 years of experience in working with bilingual students with language disabilities. She completed her doctorate at Boston University in Applied Psycholinguistics. Langdon is a frequently invited speaker at national and international conferences. She has lectured widely on issues pertaining to bilingualism and assessment and intervention. A certified speech and language therapist, Langdon has published two books and numerous journal articles pertaining to assessment of second-language learners, with an emphasis on distinguishing problems of normal language development from actual learning disabilities. She is fluent in Spanish, French, Polish, and English.

Rick Stiggins, Ph.D., is founder of the Assessment Training Institute, which provides educators with professional development in assessment. He received his doctorate in educational measurement from Michigan State University and has served as a school district assessment director, director of test development for the American College Testing Program, and director of the Centers for Classroom Assessment and Performance Assessment at the Northwest Regional Educational Laboratory in Portland, Oregon. He is the author of *In Teachers' Hands: Investigating the Practice of Classroom Assessment* (1992), and *Student-Centered Classroom Assessment* (1997) and has developed more than 20 assessment training videos.

Louise Bay Waters, Ph.D., is the principal of Cabello Elementary School in the New Haven Unified School District in Union City, California. Prior to this administrative position she was an associate professor of Teacher Education at the California State University, Hayward, where she directed a number of award-winning inner-city school reform and teacher preparation programs. In both positions she has focused on standards and assessment in schools with highly diverse student populations. Her developmental approach to standards-based assessment has been recognized as both a state and national model, and she currently serves as a consultant on this topic to the U.S. Department of Education.